THE ART OF
JUDGMENT

 Advances
in Public
Administration

Sponsored by
the **Public Administration Theory Network**
and **Lewis and Clark College**

Advances in Public Administration is a series of books designed both to encourage and to contribute to the vital processes of rethinking public administration and reconceptualizing various aspects of the field in an insightful manner that goes well beyond traditional approaches.

SIR GEOFFREY VICKERS
Centenary Edition

THE ART OF JUDGMENT
A Study of
Policy Making

 Advances in Public Administration

Sponsored by the **Public Administration Theory Network**
and supported by **Lewis and Clark College**

SAGE Publications
International Educational and Professional Publisher
Thousand Oaks   London   New Delhi

For information address:

SAGE Publications, Inc.
2455 Teller Road
Thousand Oaks, California 91320
E-mail: order@sagepub.com

SAGE Publications Ltd.
6 Bonhill Street
London EC2A 4PU
United Kingdom

SAGE Publications India Pvt. Ltd.
M-32 Market
Greater Kailash I
New Delhi 110 048 India

Printed in the United States of America

Library of Congress Cataloging-in-Publication Data

Vickers, Geoffrey, Sir, 1894-1982
    The art of judgment: A study of policy making / Sir Geoffrey
Vickers.—Centenary ed.
      p. cm.—(Advances in public administration)
    Includes bibliographical references and index.
    ISBN 0-8039-7362-4 (cloth: alk. paper).—ISBN 0-8039-7363-2 (pbk. :
alk. paper)
    1. Decision-making. 2. Public administration. 3. Executives.
I. Title. II. Series.
HD 38.2.V53 1995
350.007′25—dc20   95-17018

This book is printed on acid-free paper.

95 96 97 98 99 10 9 8 7 6 5 4 3 2 1

Sage Production Editor: Diana Axelsen
Sage Typesetter: Danielle Dillahunt

Contents

Series Editor's Introduction

THE RATIONALE for this series lies in the ongoing need to reexamine and enrich thinking in the field of public administration. It can be argued that few fields need efforts of this sort more urgently. Twenty years ago, Vincent Ostrom declared that an "intellectual crisis" existed in public administration. Significantly, that crisis has continued unabated into the 1990s. Meanwhile, the public's faith in the administrative state has declined precipitously, and, in the words of Herbert Kaufman, bureaucrat bashing has become "pandemic."

Intellectually, this crisis lies in the discrepancy between the field's 19th-century roots and the postmodern realities we must face at the turn of the 20th century. Despite 20 years of intellectual foment by academics, most practitioners still adhere to a model of public administration shaped in a world that no longer exists. The Progressive era that gave birth to modern American public administration was an age that believed in universal technical/rational solutions to political, social, and even moral problems. It was a time in which strong Western nation-states and their empires were commonly viewed as the anointed agents of progress and civilization. Most of all, it was a period in which government was beginning to be seen as part of the answer, rather than part of the problem.

Virtually none of these views holds in the contemporary world, yet public administration and its literature have been indelibly marked by these roots. As a result, it remains grounded in the classic model of the centralized nation-state at a time when a global economy is a reality, Western empires disintegrate, and a new feudalism based upon warring ethnic and racial communities seems emergent. Its literature still takes a largely technical/rational view of the world, though the practice of public administration increasingly requires decidedly *nontechnical* ethical and political decisions. Even more troubling, although a thorough reevaluation of first principles and assumptions is in order, the literature, like the field itself, too often retreats into bureaucratic defensiveness or formulaic "solutions" to problems.

It can be argued, then, that public administration badly needs new literature that reexamines its basic premises. There is little question that the materials for this reexamination are present. Certainly they exist in disciplines such as history, philosophy, the humanities, and the social sciences. They range backward and forward in time. Some present a vision of existence in a disordered, fragmented, but exciting postmodern world. Some reach backward to apply traditional philosophic thought to current issues. Others suggest radically new ways to view human thought and action. Still others depict an environmentally centered world in which people are no longer masters but stewards of the world in which they live.

Because public administration often is referred to as an inter-disciplinary study, it seems reasonable to expect it to break out of its traditional paradigm and use this body of knowledge to advantage. Two factors seem to prevent this, however. First, to the degree public administration has drawn on other disciplines, it has chosen to rely upon those that fit most easily into its universalistic and rational tradition. Thus, modern economics, analytic philosophy, systems analysis, and behavioral science all have had far more impact on the field than history, contemporary social philosophy, humanities, or qualitative social science research.

Second, to the degree that scholars have developed alternative conceptual rather than technical approaches to public administration, they are more frequently the subject of debate among academics than grist for the professional mill. Academic movements in public administration calling attention to constitutional history, critical theory, Jungian psychology, and postmodern thought have had surprisingly little impact outside scholarly journals. The reasons for this are severalfold. Until recently, the intellectual crisis in the field has not been clearly tied to what might be called the operational crisis in public administration. The traditional paradigms of public administration might be questioned intellectually, but at the level of practice, the general philosophy was "If it's not broken, don't fix it."

In addition, it can be extremely difficult to relate philosophic and social theory to practice in a manner that is readily accessible to students and practitioners. It is inherently difficult to frame much of this thought clearly and cogently enough to speak to individuals who have little background in fields such as history or philosophy. It is even more of a challenge to show how such theories relate to practice in concrete ways, and, conversely, to criticize the applicability of these theories in terms of the experience gained from using them in practice. Yet, unless these two tasks can be accomplished, a firm linkage between theory and practice rarely is achieved.

However, it can be argued that public administration has reached the point at which this situation is ripe for change. In this country, political gridlock, fiscal deficit, administrative scandal, and the sheer inability of government to deal with human needs ranging from health care to disaster relief have caused people to question the viability of the American administrative state as never before. In short, it is harder and harder for thoughtful practitioners and students to dismiss the crisis in public administration as merely "intellectual."

Advances in Public Administration is an occasional, open-ended series designed both to encourage and to contribute to the vital process of rethinking public administration in the light of the issues just discussed. To this end, the editorial board has sought works that meet the following set of criteria as far as possible. Each volume will seek to reconceptualize some aspects of the field in an insightful manner that goes well beyond traditional approaches to the subject. Specific goals will be to accomplish the following:

- Stimulate students and practitioners to reflect critically on the practice of public administration
- Utilize cutting-edge conceptual materials drawn from a variety of disciplines, especially those that have had less impact on the study and practice of public administration
- Apply theory to practice and conversely use practice to evaluate theory
- Set forth complex theoretical concepts in an understandable manner without unduly sacrificing their meaning or content
- Provide adequate background material for those readers unfamiliar with the disciplines upon which the work draws
- Be of potential use as classroom material in graduate and/or upper division courses in public administration

The series will consist of monographs, texts, closely edited collections and an occasional reissue of a valuable out of print work. Although the works will vary in topic, they will be unified by the editorial selection criteria just outlined.

As Coordinating Editor of **Advances in Public Administration,** I wish to take this opportunity to thank the members of the series Editorial Board, the Public Administration Theory Network, and Lewis and Clark College for their generous sponsorship of this project. Finally, I would be extremely remiss if I did not recognize the efforts of my Associate Editors Camilla Stivers and Guy Adams and those of Carrie Mullen of Sage Publications and my colleague Dr. Douglas Morgan for the unfailing support and encouragement they have given me in launching the series.

Henry D. Kass
Coordinating Editor
Lake Oswego, Oregon

Foreword to the Centenary Edition
of The Art of Judgment

GUY B. ADAMS
BAYARD L. CATRON
SCOTT D. N. COOK

The sanest like the maddest of us cling like spiders to a
self-spun web, obscurely moored in vacancy and fiercely
shaken by the winds of change. Yet this frail web,
through which many see only the void, is the one
enduring artifact, the one authentic signature of
humankind, and its weaving is our prime responsibility.

—Sir Geoffrey Vickers (1964b, p. 477)

TO ANYONE FAMILIAR WITH THE WORK of Sir Geoffrey
Vickers (1894-1982), the broad conceptual shifts in the
social sciences, social theory, and philosophy that have occurred
in the thirty years since *The Art of Judgment* first appeared might
well confirm the sense that Vickers was ahead of his time and make
the reissue of this, his most widely referenced book, a welcome
and timely event. For those new to Vickers's thought, it may be
especially exciting to find a study crafted in the mid-twentieth
century that is so keenly applicable to understanding and dealing
with the complex issues of public affairs that face us at the dawn

of the twenty-first—a century Vickers foresaw as one of unparalleled opportunities and dangers.

In recent years, the traditional understanding of concepts central to the study of organized human activity (such as fact and value, theory and practice) have been irrevocably questioned. Efforts to give them new meaning are among the most crucial intellectual tasks at hand. In this context, it is particularly telling that the work of Sir Geoffrey Vickers, who was classically educated in the humanities and enjoyed several successful careers in both the public and private spheres, should gain new relevance. Indeed, both those who study and those who carry out the work of public policy making and administration are perhaps now in a better position to find value in Vickers's work than was the case in 1965, when this book was first published.

The Art of Judgment, as a classic study of management and decision making, establishes Vickers as one of the twentieth century's premier theorists in the field, along with such figures as Chester Barnard and Herbert Simon. *The Art of Judgment,* however, is not only a classic, but to our minds, there is to date no better treatise on the nature of judgment in policy making and none better suited to the emerging demands of the twenty-first century. This is a bold claim. Yet in Vickers's work, and in *The Art of Judgment* in particular, one finds insights into the making of judgments that remain far richer than the bulk of contemporary treatments of management and decision making, which have typically shared a narrow focus on cognition and analytic techniques.

In this introduction, we wish to convey a sense of how *The Art of Judgment* fits into public administration and management thought and into Sir Geoffrey's broader work. At the same time, we want to note the profound degree to which Vickers the thinker was fully and richly informed by Vickers the person (as Margaret Blunden's biographical essay in this volume communicates so wonderfully). As doctoral students, each of us was fortunate to know and interact with Sir Geoffrey during his numerous visits to the United States in the 1970s. We came to admire the clear and immediate ways his ideas were drawn from and manifested in his own life. We were struck by his conscientious and gentle manner, his tough-minded acuity, and his limitless curiosity. He was unfailingly open to the breadth and diversity of human experience and invested an intensity of thought and feeling in all he did. His wisdom was apparent in his capacity to make powerful, incisive reflections on human affairs without losing a feeling for their grounding in practical experience or for the position of his inter-locutors. For us, this personal connection was a moving exposure to a person of marvelous integrity and intellect, and it remains a source of insight and joy for each of us.

This edition of *The Art of Judgment,* conceived during the centenary anniversary of his birth, reflects our hope that Sir Geoffrey's work will continue to reach a widening audience of those concerned with understanding that essential art of judgment that informs and gives direction to our public lives and work.

Management and Policy Making

When he published *The Functions of the Executive* (1938), Chester Barnard, like Vickers, had had a long and successful career as a practicing manager. Barnard was highly influenced by work then being done by prominent social scientists, in particular Talcott Parsons, and saw great promise in the structural-functionalist school of social theory. However, Barnard has not been described as a "scientific" thinker, since *The Functions of the Executive* bears little resemblance to the more rigorous and objective style associ-ated with the social sciences—especially as they developed over the next quarter century. The social scientists who studied various aspects of management throughout the 1950s and 1960s rarely, for example, addressed the moral or the aesthetic dimensions of management. But Barnard did so eagerly and with great eloquence. He stated his challenge in describing managerial behavior as one of communicating "the sense of an organization, the dramatic and aesthetic feeling." And he lamented those efforts that take a nar-rowly scientific view, "because they are oblivious to the arts of organizing. . . . They miss the structure of the symphony, the art of its composition, and skill of its execution, because they cannot hear its tones" (Barnard, 1938, p. xiv).

A decade later, when Herbert Simon (1947) published *Administrative Behavior*, he critiqued the prevailing notion of the "principles" of management, which he debunked as "proverbs," masquerading as science. A truly scientific explanation of human action, Simon argued, ought to be able to account for the fact that organized human behavior consistently appears less rational and less self-maximizing than existing perspectives suggested ought to be the case. To address this conundrum, Simon introduced the useful and evocative concepts of "bounded rationality" and "satisficing." Ironically, instead of exploring further the human motivations and value judgments that some might see as informing these concepts (as Vickers did), Simon (1960) went on—in *The New Science of Management Decision*, especially—to cast them into a surprisingly narrow technical rationality. Simon finally came to extol the prospects of computerized models of decision making and the potential for artificial intelligence applications to management with such *unbounded* enthusiasm as to suggest the near removal of human beings from these practices altogether.

In taking the path he did, Simon was both leader and follower. Many of the twentieth century's efforts to understand the nature and regulate the practices of social, political, and economic affairs have been dominated by technical rationality, specialization, behaviorism, and bureaucratization. This approach grew, in no small part, from the dominance of the scientific worldview that arose out of the Enlightenment and the parallel succession of socially influential technologies and techniques. By the beginning of this century, the physical sciences were so widely regarded as triumphant that many scholars in the social disciplines quite understandably wanted to apply the same methods, the same science-like precision and objectivity, to our investigation and understanding of the social world. This tendency left no foothold for meaningful engagement with the larger ethical and political concerns of the social world.

With the practical sensitivities of Barnard and the conceptual depth of Simon, Vickers's *The Art of Judgment* has remained one of the few notable and rigorous exceptions to this tendency. For Vickers, as we outline below, the making of judgments is a necessary element of all human action, including professional practice. To practice management entails the assessment of the situation at hand against generalized standards and thus requires knowledge of both abstract theories and the specifics of one's context. Also, the making of judgment, to Vickers's mind, is never confined to the determination of facts only; it also always entails the evaluation of those facts, our placing a relative weight on such matters as their ethical and political implications.

Systems Thinking

Following World War II, writers such as Norbert Wiener, Ludwig von Bertallanfy, Ross Ashby, and later, Gregory Bateson, introduced the broader intellectual community to a set of ideas about systems and their control that had its origins in various technical areas. This broader discussion quickly developed its own specialized applications and conceptual tangles. The idea of a system itself, however, was generally understood to refer to a whole of interrelated parts, greater than and different from their sum and dependent on a "steering" mechanism to maintain the stability of the relationships between the parts, both over time and in interaction with the environment. Vickers, like many, was deeply influenced by the early work on systems and came to make a particularly valuable contribution to this work, largely through his concept of the "appreciative system."

Around the time of his retirement in 1955, Sir Geoffrey began to see in the systems metaphor a promising way to address some questions about organizations and societies that had been nagging him throughout the years of his work in public and private institutions. In particular, he was concerned with the role played by the making of judgments in collective human activity. For Vickers, such activity is constituted not around information but around meaning, and the regulation of that activity is much less a product of "goal seeking" than of "goal setting." Each he saw as entailing a distinct type of judgment—the first epistemological and the second evaluative. A third type of judgment—instrumental—he saw as concerned with picking the best means for acting on what is determined by the other two. Vickers saw these different types of judgment as inseparable parts of a single human activity he called "appreciation," which, in turn, he saw as a key element in the organization and regulation of human systems.

Many of the early systems theorists quickly became focused on the notion of a general systems theory, which could apply equally to all forms of systems—natural, mechanical, and human. In keeping with the modern epistemological dominance of technical rationality, such theories were usually cast in terms of those systems that could be most fully described and executed technically. The concomitant developments in computers and artificial intelligence, along with the emergence of sophisticated management information systems, further intensified this bent in systems thinking. In many quarters, theorizing was reduced to technical modeling and thus became increasingly inimical to the examination of processes such as human judgment, which, due to their tacit elements, unfailingly resisted capture in wholly explicit and analytic schemes.

Beginning with *The Art of Judgment* and culminating in 1983 with *Human Systems Are Different*, Vickers was concerned to avoid the narrowing of scope that had become a remarkably powerful force in both the theoretical and empirical study of organized human activity. His concept of appreciation was a pivotal element of this effort. Gregory Bateson (1972) also wished to keep the sense of "system" more open than was the norm. Yet while Vickers and Bateson admired one another's work, they parted intellectual company on the origin and role of ethics. For Bateson, since all systems are identical, morality enters, if at all, in systemic processes that would be found in all systems. Vickers, by contrast, saw a moral character within human systems that distinguished them from both natural and man-made systems. Vickers argued that appreciation is an inherent and essential part of human activity from the level of individual consciousness to that of human cultures. It was for him a way to achieve the broadening of scope that he felt to be essential both to a practical understanding of the world of action and to responsible action within that world.

Appreciation

The exercise of appreciative judgment, the central theme in this book, has three components. The first is the making of reality judgments: those judgments concerning what is or is not the case—ranging from basic cause-and-effect beliefs to more subtle and complex "facts." The second facet is the making of value judgments: those concerning what ought or ought not be the case—including imperatives, wants and desires, prudential or self-interested considerations, and individual and collective goals and norms. The third is the making of instrumental judgments: those concerning the best means available to reduce the mismatch between is and ought—including the personal resources of time, attention, intellect, passion, money, and power, along with those social resources that can be marshaled and applied (by influence or command) through communication, coalition, and access to social institutions.

Along with being a single activity composed of three interrelated but distinct forms of judgment, appreciation, Vickers argued, is always partly tacit. Human judgment, he insisted, cannot be fully described in explicit or analytic terms. But to hold that something is tacit, he maintained, is not to relinquish hope of describing or understanding it, nor does it relegate it to the realm of the mystical. The analytic and the appreciative, he maintained, are not conflicting but complementary, not dichotomous but dialectical. Vickers saw it as a regrettable prejudice of our times that those things that can be described explicitly are honored with the terms *scientific* and *rational*, while those that are not are often correspondingly deemed unscientific or irrational. In his interest in understanding the tacit and his insistence on treating it in its own right, Vickers clearly reflects his long personal and intellectual friendship with the philosopher Michael Polanyi (1958).

The incorporation of the epistemological and ethical along with the instrumental in the single activity of appreciation is a central feature of Vickers's thought. The more economic and analytic treatments of judgment and decision making common in the social sciences provide a means of assessing only the instrumental (epistemological and ethical judgments are typically treated merely as "givens"). For Vickers, human action (as distinct from reaction, instinct, or reflex) inextricably entails all three forms of judgment; it is a product of judging what is, what ought to be, and what can be done to reduce the difference by selecting specific means from the set of possible actions at hand.

Kenneth Boulding, in his foreword to the 1983 edition of *The Art of Judgment,* concluded that Vickers's concept of appreciation remained a more robust way to account for the exercise of human judgment and decision making than the "facile models of maximizing behavior in economics or rat and pigeon behaviorism in psychology" that were then still dominant. Now, in this centenary edition, we come to the same assessment yet again.

The Appreciative System

Through appreciation, Vickers maintained, human beings locate themselves, find meaning, and seek to maintain stability within that "self-spun web" of our social worlds that constitute our only distinctly human home. It was one of Vickers's central contentions that this enterprise lies at the heart of human experience from the level of individual consciousness to the level of culture. And this undertaking and its artifacts are what he called "the appreciative system."

To be conscious is to locate oneself within the natural and human worlds by finding meaning in them. Cultures, meanwhile, are constituted by the manifold relations of individuals who share sets of meaning attached to those worlds and who act on them through self- and mutual expectations. Linking us to the world and to each other, such expectations are built up through accretion within our experience and compose the standards against which we individually and collectively determine what ought to be and by which we recognize what is deviant. They thus constitute the basic regulators of society, yet they are constantly on the move, adapting and modifying under the influence of the very activities they mediate. This interrelated scheme of expectations and appreciative judgments constitutes an appreciative system, whether in the mind of an individual, in the ethos of an organization, or in the norms of a culture.

Appreciative systems are essential to a variety of activities and capacities, including the ability to discriminate figure from ground and signal from noise, the ability to create and alter organized patterns with subtlety, the interaction of theme and variation, and the ability to harmonize disparate ideas and mute dissonance through selective inattention. These are not simply subjective processes that occur only within an individual's head; they are relational, intersubjective processes that involve communicative interaction with other people.

Other features of appreciative systems explored in *The Art of Judgment* include the following:

1. *The ability to find pattern in complexity and to shift our choice of pattern according to varying criteria and interests.* Coupled with this is our ability to suspend the tendency to lock onto a single pattern as the only possible one, a tendency that can close off a search prematurely. This openness to search enables us to consider different interpretations of a situation and assess a broader repertoire of responses.

2. *An artful selectivity in deciding what features of a situation are most important, in keeping with shifting interests, values, and concerns.* In making and drawing on mental images of such situations, we are more like a painter than a photographer: What is highlighted or omitted is wholly a product of our appreciative judgments. In management, executive attention is always among the scarcest of resources—deciding what to pay attention to and what to ignore or set aside is, or ought to be, therefore, the product of careful consideration and judgment. No management information system, however responsive and sophisticated, can substitute for the skillful exercise of this kind of judgment. Put baldly, formal systems cannot make exceptions to themselves; the only way to determine whether a case at hand is an exception to a system's rules, or not, is by a judgment call.

3. *The ability to "read the situation," which is particularly pronounced in first-rate management.* This includes judgments about how much to simplify the complexity of the environment

and in what ways. Indeed, appreciation works more by analogy than by logic. It entails recognizing the fit or misfit of ideas, values, experiences, and the like in a way akin to aesthetic judgments—both in the sense of a sudden realization and as the exercise of a taste that can be developed, sharpened, and changed over time.

4. *The investment of the self in the situation at hand.* Unlike the objective detachment emphasized by "scientific" methods, the self may be viewed as the medium through which appreciation works in giving shape or direction to a situation. Similarly, the making of appreciative judgments depends on the presence of a caring bond between the self and others, subject and object. The bond may be between two people (as in a conversation or a dance); between a person and object (as between a sculptor and clay or a scientist and a telescope); or between members of a group, organization, or society (as in the skillful performance of a group task or the response to a national crisis).

From Management to Culture

Vickers's interests evolved and broadened over the course of his last career as a traveling academic and prolific author. He moved in successive stages from the sociology of management, to issues of governance, to a broad concern with the stability of Western culture.

One of his favorite images (drawn from the nineteenth-century biologist and Darwinist T. H. Huxley) was the metaphor of the jungle and the garden. For Vickers, nature, as represented by the jungle, has its own regulators: It crowds as much as possible into a given space through the push and pull of adaptation and survival. Natural selection occurs in the constant, daily test of the fit and misfit between the organism and its environment. The gardener, meanwhile, prunes and weeds, sows and thins, using as the criteria of selection the uniquely human standards of value judgments.

In human culture, as in agriculture, the selection of the normative criteria by which we govern ourselves (that set of standards and regulators that constitute our moral and political systems) is wholly and singularly up to us, delimited only by the constraints of nature that define the domain but not the content of morality and politics. Our first and inescapable task as culture-bound creatures is to appreciate what it means to live and grow within a culture and to understand the responsibilities that our dependency on it entails. Vickers was deeply concerned that we in the West show too little understanding of the scope of our community membership and are woefully disinclined to acknowledge our dependence upon it (J. Vickers, 1991). His last book, *Human Systems Are Different* (1983), was perhaps his most eloquent expression of this concern.

From Vickers's perspective, our notion of the autonomous individual has become foolish and dangerous. It is foolish because we see in it a kind of rugged and total independence, yet autonomy itself can be constituted only within a system of relations. It is dangerous because it implies that we can neglect community with impunity, yet the untended garden quickly becomes jungle again. The regulators of nature by themselves can give rise to neither garden nor culture, and only culture can give rise to individual autonomy. No system of relations capable of sustaining and enriching us as individuals, whether garden, nation, or culture, can emerge from the independent actions of an aggregation of singularly self-maximizing gardeners, consumers, or citizens. Because of this, culture is not, from Vickers's perspective, something remote and abstract; it is close by, personal, and terribly important for our human future.

Our social institutions, including organizations both public and private—which are now the most ubiquitous embodiments of our culture—require our most tender and tenacious ministrations. For our culture to survive in any form that we are likely to wish for ourselves, these ministrations, Vickers maintained, must include our acquiescence to greater institutional limitations to our individual autonomy, submission to the broader exercise of authority beyond ourselves (even though it will doubtless be abused), and the offering up of even greater effort in sustaining our institutions in opposition to the forces that threaten to disintegrate them. Given this, if we are to avoid the tyranny of instrumental rule, we must include in the design and control of our social institutions the making of judgments of value, which are the sole source of moral and political standards. To fail to do so is to shirk our prime responsibility.

We hope this centenary edition of *The Art of Judgment* will add to the renewal of appreciation of Vickers's work. Such a renewal of appreciation is, we believe, richly deserved and seems to be building. Within the last year, a centenary dinner in honor of Vickers was held at the University of Westminster in London (Adams, 1994). And an entire issue of the *American Behavioral Scientist*, including eleven original essays, was devoted to ideas and themes developed or inspired by Sir Geoffrey (Blunden & Dando, 1994). The *American Behavioral Scientist* issue was entitled "Rethinking Public Policy-Making: Questioning Assumptions, Challenging Beliefs." The wellspring for this line of inquiry is in *The Art of Judgment*.

Exercise in the Creation of Form

The Life of Sir Geoffrey Vickers

MARGARET BLUNDEN

My message . . . is what my experience has fitted me to see and say.
> —Letter to Adolph Lowe, December 15, 1968
> (J. Vickers, 1991, p. 56)

GEOFFREY VICKERS'S MAJOR WORKS were published in the twenty-seven years between 1955 and 1982, the period between his retirement from the British National Coal Board and his death. Vickers's abiding concerns—the meaning of stability and the nature of regulation in human societies—cut directly across the prevailing academic disciplines and science-based culture of the United Kingdom and the United States, the countries he knew best. The unrealized potential of his powerful concept, the appreciative system, remains enormous.

Vickers's writings drew on a long and distinguished career spanning the army, the law, the civil service, and the management of a major national industry. His penetrating interpretation of his times—and in particular, his sense that "to be human *now*, in the last third of the twentieth century, is to share a common threat . . . and a common responsibility" (J. Vickers, 1991, p. 50)—came from a particular set of readinesses to notice and to value, formed during a long life of exceptional range and variety.

Geoffrey Vickers was born October 13, 1894, in Victorian England, the most powerful country in the world, with a culture at the height of its confidence, pride, and optimism. His father, Charles Vickers, ran the family lace manufacturing business in Nottingham and since these were difficult times, the family lived simply in a small house. Charles Vickers was a man of great vitality and intellectual curiosity. In particular, he loved poetry, science, and philosophy. Geoffrey, the youngest of three children, was a child of unusual sensitivity and intellectual awareness. His family life was both happy and cultivated. His parents, who were Baptists, created an atmosphere that encouraged confidence, curiosity, and originality.

At the age of twelve, he was sent away, first to preparatory school and then to Oundle, a Church of England public school in the tradition established by Thomas Arnold at Rugby. The school aspired to provide an initiation into the moral and intellectual achievements of European civilization, an entry into the partnership between past and present. The development of attitudes, belief, and character was paramount. At Oundle, the academic curriculum, centered on the humanities, was part of a total educational experience embracing the school chapel, the Officers' Training Corps, and organized team games. Boarding school life was designed to imprint a sense of membership and its associated loyalties, commitments, and responsibilities—to the school, the church, and the country. Looking back on his school as a man in his forties, Vickers marveled at its effectiveness:

> At the turn of the century the public schools offered something which was supposed to be "pure" education but which was in fact a subtle blend of vocational and cultural training, well suited to the ruling class of that particular place and time. It was a preparation for the Government services and the professions; and at that time it developed in the individual a set of attitudes, towards himself, his fellows and authority so constant and so pronounced as to constitute one of the most recognisable human types in the world. The most determined experiments of the totalitarian states in

standardising human attitudes by education still look amateurish when compared with the effortless and unconscious achievement of the Thring-Arnold tradition. (G. Vickers, 1940b, p. 5)

Although greatly influenced by the experience, Vickers was not suited to public school life. He was not good at team games. He felt anxious in the company of unfamiliar adults. He spoke later of the anguish reserved for nonconformists who long to conform and for the awkward who long to excel in dexterity. But there was no question of complaint or protest. He did not speak of his unhappiness in letters home.

Early in 1913, in an interlude between school and university, Vickers spent a few months in Germany. The memory of Europe in 1913—a world where national and international order could be taken for granted—was something he was long to remember and to value:

When I first visited the continent, no frontier asked to see my passport, and a golden sovereign (there were no pound notes) was exchangeable at a fixed rate for any currency from Antwerp to Athens. My standards of stability were set in a world which still looked and felt far more stable than it was or ever has been since that glorious sunset. (G. Vickers, 1982a, p. 6)

The young man of seventeen who, in October 1913, went up to Merton College, Oxford, to read "Greats"—classical languages and civilization—had a secure sense of continuity and identity:

To be English was to belong to a community and a culture deeply rooted in time and locality, to be the heir and transmitter of an ancient heritage of enormous value, to share its past shames and defeats as well as its glories and achievements, to be an inseparable part of it. (G. Vickers, 1980, p. 41)

He assumed that the calm he had always known would continue indefinitely. "Freedom and order, security and stability, progress and unity seemed to my young eyes to be operative standards, enjoyable realities, even natural assumptions" (J. Vickers, 1991, p. 4). He and his contemporaries were unaware of the dangerous developments in Europe, with particular implications for their generation:

Most of my coequals even at Oxford were as unpolitical and naive
as I. The negative memory constantly reawakens in my mind an
uneasy awareness of what may be the greatest of human limitations—the distinction between what they believe to be real and that
tiny part of it which to us individually is actual, able to awake
sympathy or indignation as a fact, not a generalisation, to become
a matter of personal concern. (G. Vickers, 1982a, p. 6)

When in August 1914 Britain entered the war against Germany,
Vickers immediately enlisted, along with two thousand other volunteers from the university. This was not so much a decision as a
reflex. War was the normal instrument of last resort in international politics, not the occasion for crisis of conscience or political
doubts. There was a strong tacit consensus.

We conformed spontaneously in the old days, not to save our lives
but to avoid damaging a sense of solidarity which we valued.
Empire, security and the rest had helped to build up a sense of
something worth belonging to. *Civis Britannicus* had the same
overtones as *Civis Romanus*. (J. Vickers, 1991, pp. 168-169)

Much was expected of a young man of his background and the
Army immediately assigned him onerous responsibilities:

At Oundle and Oxford I had been in what was then called the
Officers' Training Corps, so I was deemed fit, without further
screening, to command in battle men of whom many were much
older than I. I was given a commission in our local territorial
battalion, the 7th (Robin Hood) Battalion of the Sherwood Foresters
without even a medical examination. I was with them before the
end of 1914 and in France in February of the next year. (Sutton,
1983, p. viii)

In the spring of 1915 Vickers's battalion was involved in heavy
fighting in Flanders. To some men, life in the trenches was barely
endurable; Vickers, however, seemed to thrive: "A fight is a re-
freshingly simple and supportive situation; in few other circumstances do we have so many comrades and so few doubts" (G.
Vickers, 1964a). On October 13, 1915, his twenty-first birthday,
Vickers showed exceptional gallantry in defending, wounded and

almost single-handed, a barrier against enemy attack, and he was awarded the Victoria Cross.

It took him twelve months to recover from his wounds, and during his convalescence, his brother, Burnell, was killed at Ypres. In October 1916, he returned to France to command a company in his old regiment. He knew hardly anyone in the battalion, since those he had left the previous year had nearly all been killed or wounded on the Somme. At the age of twenty-two, he commanded four subalterns, three even younger than himself and one twenty years older. The bonds formed in these circumstances were among the most powerful he ever knew, and maintaining these relationships soon became more important than any question of personal survival:

> One day, just before we were due for a week out of the line, I received a chit from Battalion H.Q. It said simply—"You will proceed to London on the—[the next day] and report to the War Office room so-and-so. You will be struck off the strength of the battalion." No explanation. Some home job presumably. Utter darkness fell. I passed it round the dugout in silence. It was read in silence. We came out of the line that night. Next morning after a silent breakfast the mess cart came round (horse drawn, two wheeled, with a tilt and one cross seat). My things were stowed in. I shook hands with the other four, I couldn't speak but otherwise I kept up appearances until we drove away. Then sitting with my back to the horse to hide my face from the driver, I wept all the way to railhead. Never, in a life full of many partings, have I felt so diminished and lost from the ending of a relationship (except once by death). (G. Vickers, n.d., p. 7)

Vickers was assigned to training activities on the home front for almost a year. During this time, he met Helen Newton, whom he married early in 1918. He returned to France in March 1918, saw more action, and received the Croix de Guerre. After discharge at the end of the war, he held the rank of major.

When the war was over, Vickers went back to Oxford. Many of the class of 1913 did not return. Some of his contemporaries now believed the war to have been senseless slaughter, a tragic waste that nothing could justify. Vickers, however, emerged from the war with his beliefs intact, and in a paper on "Poetry and War," which he read to the Bodley Club at his college (G. Vickers, 1919), he approvingly quoted lines from Siegfried Sassoon:

> The anguish of the earth absolves our eyes
> Till beauty shines in all that we can see
> War is our scourge, yet war has made us wise
> And fighting for our freedom we are free. (p. 8)

Vickers took a degree in classics in 1921, qualified as a solicitor in 1923, and became in 1926 a partner in the City of London firm of Slaughter and May. He was already reputed to be an almost dangerously brilliant lawyer. To grow into a profession was different from contracting to an employer (G. Vickers, 1980, p. 40). To belong to a great profession was to adopt a traditional standard of behavior, to play a particular set of roles, to be loyal to a professional ethic—in short to *have membership* of a body of practicing professionals. Vickers, whose work involved him in the legal aspects of large financial operations, often with an international dimension, became an outstandingly successful and high-earning City of London lawyer.

He was not much interested in politics at this stage of his life, and he paid little attention to the growth of the Nazi movement in Germany. The selectivity of human consciousness in general and his own astonishing lack of political awareness until middle age in particular, much exercised his mind in later life. He was to define the *appreciative setting* as a readiness to notice some aspects of reality and not others. His appreciation of the situation was influenced by his respect for fellow German professionals with whom he occasionally worked and by what he later called the "comfortable, even pampered, life of the self-employed professional, who need not talk to anyone not willing to pay for the privilege" (G. Vickers, 1974, p. 185).

When British Prime Minister Neville Chamberlain capitulated to Hitler's demands at Munich in September 1938, Vickers woke up with a shock. What alarmed him was not the possibility of foreign domination but the prevailing confusion in Britain. There was no coherence or sense of national purpose. He grasped intuitively what he would later express in systems terms: that the effectiveness of a state in the international system depends on its internal coherence (G. Vickers, 1980, p. 41). He felt he must *do* something and proceeded to set up in the City of London a group he called "The Association for Service and Reconstruction," committed to thinking through what was needed in the face of current confusion.

The association received widespread support, and through it Vickers met J. H. Oldham, secretary of the International Missionary Council, and joined a discussion group called "The Moot." The distinguished membership of the Moot included Karl Mannheim, sociologist and epistemologist; Reinhold Niebuhr, professor of ethics and technology; the poet T. S. Eliot; Michael Polanyi, then a professor of physical chemistry and subsequently an epistemologist; and Adolph Lowe, economist, émigré from Nazi Germany, and recent author of a pamphlet, *The Price of Liberty* (Lowe, 1937), which Vickers much admired. He blossomed in this heady intellectual environment. At the time, he was particularly impressed by Mannheim; Polanyi and Lowe were to be both influential intellectually and lifelong friends. Vickers and Lowe were to correspond for most of the rest of their lives, a correspondence rooted in their common concern about the appropriate balance between freedom and order in complex modern societies.

Vickers began to clarify his political views. He detested the "hateful gangster rule" of Hitler in revolutionary Germany and vehemently rejected pacifism; he did, however, now believe that the classical liberalism in which he had grown up had its weaknesses. Britain could learn something from the "state-socialising elements" of National Socialism. A typescript written in 1940 makes clear how far he was now questioning the liberal assumptions of his class and milieu and demonstrates his emerging intellectual quality:

> "Freedom" is . . . ambiguous. . . . To some it means "freedom from interference"; to others "opportunity." The negative concept of freedom which expresses itself by "let me alone" is characteristic of the comfortably situated. The others express their demand for

freedom by "give me a chance." The comfortable take opportunity for granted, but their illusion only reflects their good fortune. Between these conceptions of freedom there is a great gulf. (G. Vickers, 1940a, p. 14)

By spring 1940, Vickers had moved away from classical liberalism, with its emphatic individualism, toward something more like social democracy. In eighteen months of heightened political awareness, he had come to reject the appropriateness in all circumstances of the "free" market as a distributive mechanism and to support a more active role by the state. He believed that a shared national purpose, a national consensus about what to want, was essential if order and stability were to be preserved. His conviction, expressed so often in later writings, that "no human society can cohere and survive unless [its] standards are sufficiently comprehensive, sufficiently cogent and sufficiently shared" (G. Vickers, 1980, p. 9), was now explicit. Social coherence could not be assumed.

In 1940, at the age of 46, Vickers reenlisted as an infantry lieutenant in his old regiment. Initially, he was sent on an intelligence mission to South America; he found it hard to accept a safe posting abroad while his second wife, Ellen, and their baby son were left to face the threat of bombs in England. He spent the rest of the war, not on active service as he had expected but as a civil servant. He was assigned to the Ministry of Economic Warfare, where he rose to become director and member of the Joint Intelligence Committee of the chief of staff. By the closing states of the war, when he was involved in discussions about the postwar settlement in Europe, he was not confident that international order could be restored:

> By 1944 all my early assumptions were shaken, if not destroyed. Stability could not be taken for granted, could not even necessarily be assured by even the greatest conscious effort . . . neither automatic regulation nor human design could be trusted to achieve "betterment" by any of the diverse criteria that had emerged. (G. Vickers, 1987, p. vii)

He was, however, impressed by the quality of his colleagues in the public service:

> In my experience public servants, whether in central or local
> government, are far more dedicated to the responsible performance
> of their job, less greedy for power, and more widely informed and
> concerned about the circumstances in which they are acting than
> the general run of those for whom they are providing service. The
> bureaucracy may be faceless but bureaucrats have faces, and usu-
> ally more trust-inspiring faces than non-bureaucrats. (G. Vickers,
> 1980, p. 46)

He was heartened by wartime solidarity on the home front and
by public support for government control—rationing of food, some
control of prices, wages, land use, and private wealth—all coexist-
ing with much self-help and mutual help at the grassroots (J.
Vickers, 1991, p. 68). The physical and psychological disparities
of private capitalism were much abated. The widely shared understanding of the situation and trust in the institutions of the state
allowed the country to contain potential conflict. He was encouraged that centralized control, where necessary, could work effectively without undermining individual self-reliance, if supported
by a strong consensus.

The lessons that Vickers drew from the war and postwar periods were quite different from those of Margaret Thatcher, some
thirty years his junior, who referred in her memoirs to the "atmosphere of envy and tittle-tattle . . . the petty jealousies, minor
tyrannies, ill-neighbourliness and sheer sourness of those years"
(Thatcher, 1993, p. 12). In such ways did different appreciations
of the same historical period go to shape Geoffrey Vickers, believ-
ing to the end of his days that the gigantic machine of modern
government operated more efficiently and less corruptly than far
smaller organizations in the past (G. Vickers, 1983, p. 75), and Mrs.
Thatcher, convinced of the "overwhelming evidence for the lam-
entable performance of the state in running any business—or
indeed administering any service" (Thatcher, 1993, p. 677).

In 1945, Vickers was knighted for his services in the Ministry
of Economic Warfare. When at the end of the war, he returned to
legal practice at Slaughter and May, he was proud of what had been
achieved. "It meant something to belong to the country which had
played Britain's role in the war and had entered the peace with
such a declaration of social solidarity" (G. Vickers, 1980, p. 41).

He was confident that the Labour party, unexpectedly arrived in power, and its Conservative opposition shared those underlying values that he believed essential for the success of two-party politics. The Beveridge legislation, which laid the foundations of the welfare state, became law with abundant general support, and national pride was high. He was later to contrast these years favorably with the dismal aftermath of World War I and saw no sign that the British were not as united and self-confident as during the Battle of Britain (J. Vickers, 1991, p. 222).

In 1947, Sir Geoffrey received out of the blue an invitation to become legal adviser of the National Coal Board. The newly created Coal Board was one of the biggest industrial enterprises in the world, taking into public ownership the assets of some 600 undertakings, consisting of 900 collieries and employing 750,000 men. Vickers accepted without hesitation, to the astonishment of colleagues and friends in the city. It meant a big drop in income and status. The public sector was, in his view, bound to become so important that large public monopolies of this kind had to be made to work (G. Vickers, 1979). It was characteristic of Vickers to throw himself with confidence and enthusiasm into whatever came his way and to relinquish it totally and unthinkingly when the next call came.

The following year, he became board member in charge of manpower, training, education, health, and welfare, a seat he was to hold until 1955. Vickers, like his father, had little class consciousness and easily shared a frame of reference with "trade unionists who came to consciousness in the 1930s." He later told Lowe that he had felt more at home with the national executive of the Miners' Union than with his fellow board members (J. Vickers, 1991, p. 222).

Life as a functionary was less comfortable than that as a self-employed professional. Vickers found what he described as his "graduation" from private practice to public service a strange experience, and it encouraged him to write a paper on the intellectual issues raised by the implementation of socialist ideas. How could personal incentive and public service, self-fulfillment and national needs, be harmonized (G. Vickers, 1956a)?

During his time at the Coal Board, Vickers encountered systems thinking. In the decade after the war, a set of concepts about systems and their control that had been maturing in technological contexts during the previous decade was developed and circulated in the general intellectual community by such writers as Norbert Wiener, Ludwig von Bertallanfy, and Ross Ashby. Vickers was highly excited: He believed that the study of information regulated by advanced forms of communication had set rolling a revolution in scientific thinking. "The effect on me was not so much revelation as liberation. The ideas did not seem surprising or even new, but they provided a new language in which to talk about the perplexing experience of my lifetime and a new point of view from which to regard it" (G. Vickers, 1987, p. viii).

Vickers immediately saw the relevance of systems thinking to government and administration, and it seemed to him "that these ideas were ideas that everybody, governors and administrators, should be excited about" (G. Vickers, 1982c). It surprised him to find that this was not the case. Technologists, on the other hand, embraced the ideas with enthusiasm. Vickers was to spend some twenty years resisting the brash incursions of technologists into social systems (J. Vickers, 1991, p. 135) and the tendency for systems concepts to acquire an exclusively technological flavor. He deplored attempts to assimilate politics to engineering, what his contemporary Michael Oakeshott (1991), the distinguished political philosopher, described as "the myth of rationalist politics" (p. 9).

During his time at the Coal Board, Ellen's poor health increasingly brought Vickers into contact with psychiatrists, opening up a whole new dimension of experience. He became, in 1951, a founding member and chairman of the Research Committee of the Mental Health Research Fund, a voluntary position that he held for sixteen years. He acted as lay chair to a body of about twenty scientists, including psychiatrists of different persuasions, representatives of the preclinical sciences, anthropologists, sociologists, psychologists, social psychiatrists, animal ethologists, and specialists in mental retardation. Probably, the research committee brought together a more comprehensive gathering of medical and social scientists than met regularly round any other table. The valuable and unusual procedure that members could speak on subjects outside their own specialism was entirely characteristic of the large-minded approach of the chairman, whose personal authority was impressive.

The exchange of ideas and associated wide range of reading gave Vickers a whole new education. He now added to his experience in the humanities, law, management, and government, a new competence—in psychology—and a new interest, the organization and promotion of health from the individual to the national level. His chairmanship of the research committee was followed quickly by appointment to the Medical Research Council (1952-1954). During the next ten years, he became a frequent contributor to the British medical journal *The Lancet* and to professional debate in the fields of occupational and cognitive psychology and psychiatry. Psychology, combined with the systems concept of information, was to be a key component in his great conceptual advance, the appreciative system.

In March 1955, Geoffrey Vickers, now just past 60, gave up his membership of the National Coal Board, left London, and moved with his wife to a cottage at the foot of the chalk downs in Berkshire. He did not see the move as a retirement:

> I wanted to keep in touch with public and private affairs sufficiently to remain in circulation (and hopefully to sustain solvency at a not too acute level of austerity). But what I most wanted was to contribute to what I believed to be a revolution in human thinking which had been reaching and exciting me for the previous ten years. (G. Vickers, 1981, p. 3)

At this timely moment, Charles Hendry, director of the School of Social Work at the University of Toronto, invited Vickers to spend three consecutive terms there. This put him into an academic environment for a sustained period—the first since his undergraduate days thirty years before—and required him to formulate and structure his ideas at a time when his intellectual powers were approaching their peak. Hendry was, Vickers later wrote, "one of the many to whom I shall always be grateful for opening unexpected doors which opened into fascinating places and led on into yet others" (G. Vickers, 1981, p. 22).

In Toronto, Vickers began to apply concepts drawn from systems control theory and psychology to the questions of social stability that had long concerned him. Control theory directed attention to goal setting rather than goal seeking, the normal focus of interest. In his address at the School of Social Work on "values and decision-making," he began to formulate the idea that goals, at both the individual and the social levels, were set by a circular causal process, operating over time (G. Vickers, 1956c).

In November 1957, he took advantage of an invitation to address the School of Public Health at Harvard to apply the concept of goal setting to public health policy. Speaking on "What sets the goals of public health?" he developed the idea of goal setting as a historical process, consisting of both the manipulation of the environment and the redesigning of human expectations. His perception of change over time as the progressive redefinition of the unacceptable, gave him a unique understanding of the difficulties inherent in the future of health provision. The prophetic insight of his Harvard address of 1957 makes astonishing reading nearly forty years later:

> At one point it was widely, if half-consciously, held that a health service was a self-limiting service. When the demands of health were fully met, there would be nothing more to do. Indeed, better preventive services might in time reduce the total resources needed to provide optimum health for all. It is clear, I think, that health services are not self-limiting in this sense. The amount of effort which can plausibly be devoted to the health of the individual and the community increases with every scientific development and will, I think, increase indefinitely. Thus the services which might be provided may well continue to exceed, perhaps by an ever-increasing margin, the services which can in fact be provided, since the total will be limited by the amount of resources available, having regard to conflicting demands. . . . These decisions will grow harder, not easier, with the passage of time. (G. Vickers, 1958b, p. 599)

Vickers was by now fruitfully applying his understanding of systemic behavior in a wide range of fields—medicine, public

health, engineering, social work, and management. Every paper
was a synthesis of unusual methodological and interdisciplinary
insights. Although much of the work was addressed to academics,
Vickers's approach was entirely distinctive from theirs. He defined
himself not as an academic—drawing boundaries in whatever way
seemed convenient for the pursuit of ever more specialized knowledge—but as a professional, with a different and inbuilt standard
of relevance by which to define the academic knowledge he needed.
The professional, he believed, seeks knowledge where he or she
can find it and generates it himself or herself if no academic
discipline is interested or able to meet the need (G. Vickers, 1983,
p. 153).

Those interested in his work were nearly all American. American academics were less locked into a disciplinary mind-set than
was customary in Britain and were more willing to address big
questions. By the 1960s, Vickers had established correspondence and
collaboration with American scholars who shared his concerns
and whose intellectual fellowship meant much to him. He shared
with them the excitement of a search for meaning (G. Vickers,
1984, p. 136).

During the 1960s, Vickers brought to fruition his great concept
of the appreciative system, with explanatory power of behavior
and change at the individual and societal levels. The quantity and
the quality of his output had never been better. He was, however,
becoming painfully aware of resistance to his ideas, just at the time
when social changes—the emergence of the permissive society—
were beginning to alarm him.

The concept of the appreciative system was first outlined in
1963 in a paper titled "Appreciative Behaviour," written for *Acta
Psychologica* (G. Vickers, 1963a), the European journal of psychology, one of the few articles to appear in a purely scientific journal
and the first written with the full knowledge that what he was
saying was not orthodox. The concept was developed and elaborated in *The Art of Judgment* (G. Vickers, 1965a). The appreciative
system brought together concepts of information, communication,
and control and applied them in the provinces of psychology and
the social sciences. Vickers set out to understand motivation, not
in terms of goal seeking, a concept derived from energy systems,

but in terms of norm holding, a concept derived from information systems. The goal-seeking paradigm, while adequate to explain the behavior of rats in mazes, was totally inadequate to explain what went on in boardrooms, committees, and everyday life. He was replacing both the goal-seeking and the cybernetic (goal-seeking-with-feedback) models by one in which personal, institutional, or cultural activity consisted in maintaining relationships over time (Checkland, 1981, pp. 262-263). The process is a cyclical one: The appreciative setting—a set of readinesses to notice and to value—both conditions new experience and is modified by it.

The implications of this shift in understanding were potentially enormous, and Vickers hoped that psychologists and historians would help to develop his model, which was still rough and speculative. He found, however, little willingness to address these ideas. Psychologists continued to concentrate on the study of observable and measurable behavior, observable in the sense that rats and stars are observable, and to hold to the concept of goal seeking as the paradigm of rational behavior. Increasingly, Vickers came to understand the problem as a cultural one, reflecting a science-based epistemology that focused on linear causal chains.

The publication of *The Art of Judgment* marked the culmination of ten years of intellectual advance, the most creative and fruitful of his life. William Robson, professor of government at the London School of Economics and editor of the *Political Quarterly* described it as subtle, original, and profound and called it "the most important contribution to administrative theory which has been made by a British thinker in the past twenty-five years" (Robson, 1965, p. 477).

Vickers was exhilarated by Robson's review, but the diffusion and development of his concepts for which he had hoped was not in practice forthcoming. As he wrote sixteen years later to the young American scholar Guy Adams,

> Ever since I published *The Art of Judgment* in 1965 I have not read a practical book about administration which took seriously the primacy of human motivation, still less one which questioned the rational model of action which insisted that no action at human level was possible unless it was explicable as the pursuit of a

purpose. The attack on rationality and purpose or rather the effort
to place these in relation to more subtle forms of human regulation
is a mammoth task. (G. Vickers, 1982b, p. 29)

The cultural changes of the 1960s, with their explosive assertion of individual autonomy and emancipation and rejection of
commitments, restraints, and role-playing, reinforced a growing
sense of intellectual isolation. He was horrified by what he saw as
"the almost total withdrawal of trust from every centre of power
and authority and from every power holder—even from all its
traditional foci of loyalty: country, service, *metier*, class and family" (J. Vickers, 1991, p. 18).

The emphasis on the autonomous individual, rather than the
responsible person, was, he believed, peculiarly inappropriate for
the highly interdependent technological world of the late twentieth century. The current "declining force of membership" was
inconsistent with the survival of a system wholly dependent on
the playing of complementary roles by individuals and subsystems. Apparently, Vickers's emphasis on responsibility, commitment, and constraint struck a conservative note: He was not,
however, suggesting a simpleminded return to the past. The sense
of membership and responsibility that modern circumstances required was more austere and more demanding than anything the
Victorians had needed. The modern individual had multiple mem-
berships and had to balance commitments and obligations as a role
player in a host of overlapping systems. A sense of responsibility
adequate for modern circumstances depended on cultivating a
deeper sense of past and future, including the responsibility to
generations yet unborn, and on understanding the extraordinary
facts of modern interdependence.

Vickers's feeling of isolation was immeasurably increased with
the death in 1972 of his wife, Ellen, after a long illness. He wrote
to Adolph Lowe of "the corrosive loneliness of Ellen's absence, which
other presences and absences leave quite untouched, though a few
of them comfort" (J. Vickers, 1991, p. 86). He continued, however,
to be as active as ever, and during the 1970s, he was increasingly
drawn into the emerging specialism of futures research. The diffi-

culty of thinking about the future had, he argued, increased pro-
portionately with the power to change it. The problems of political
regulation confronting the modern industrialized world were in-
comparably greater than those two centuries earlier. Modern man
was dependent on large-scale organizations, whose costs in the
future must become both larger in total and more widespread. The
need for government intervention was particularly great at the end
of the twentieth century when so many dangerous linear trends
were approaching their critical limits and threatening, if unchecked,
to breed at enormous costs their own reversals. In these circumstances, ideas of cutting back the power of the state and relying
more on "automatic" market regulators—the ideas that continue to
dominate British and American politics more than a decade after
his death—were extraordinarily inappropriate (Blunden, 1994).

Vickers retained formal links with American universities into
his eighties. During 1975, he was visiting professor at both Berkeley
and MIT. His intellectual and personal impact, particularly on the
young, was described by three of the doctoral students who first
met him at this time:

> Sir Geoffrey was a significant mentor for us, and for many others a
> generation or two younger than he. He was also a formidable
> intellectual sparring partner, a lively conversationalist on an in-
> credibly wide range of topics, an indefatigable correspondent. And
> he was a delightful companion and friend who brought his consid-
> erable energy and acuity to bear on all the events of life, great or
> small. In all situations in which we saw him, he seemed to be fully
> engaged, as a whole person. This was exemplified in the way he
> introduced himself to our young children. Then in his eighties he
> knelt down to talk to them in a very direct and personal way. In a
> few brief moments he established a bond with them—simply by
> presenting *himself* to them. (Adams, Forester, & Catron, 1987,
> p. xiii)

The warmth of these friendships eased his comparative neglect by
the academic and professional establishment:

> Nothing surprises and delights me more than that I should have
> made more friends in the twenty-five years since I was sixty than

at any other time in my life. Nearly all those who befriend and accompany me now are in the generations of my children and grandchildren. Many are abroad, largely in North America. I owe largely to them what insight I have into the huge cultural changes of which my own life has been a tiny ingredient of both cause and effect. (G. Vickers, 1982a, p. 36)

His Berkeley lectures focused on the weaknesses of Western culture and epistemology:

My concern with culture developed largely through realising that the resistances to what I was trying to say were largely cultural and related to the two elements which we prize most in our contemporary culture. One is the scientific culture, which hates to admit the devastating variable "culture" either into subject matter or still more into its image of itself in so far as its prized objectivity allows it to have one. The other is the individualist culture which has evolved from the liberal tradition. (G. Vickers, 1979, p. 35)

Although the lectures were enthusiastically received, the resulting manuscript, called *Western Culture and Systems Thinking*, was repeatedly rejected for publication.

In 1977, unable any longer to cope adequately with living alone, he moved into a nearby residential home for the elderly. Sir Geoffrey, with his unfailing courtesy and thoughtfulness, was a much loved and respected resident. Although it seemed an unpromising intellectual environment to some of the academics who visited him there, he was not starved of stimulus. He continued his indefatigable correspondence. Young strangers came from distant places to discuss his ideas and to express their gratitude. Few people of his age had so many friends in the two generations younger than his own.

A collection of papers, including some delivered at Berkeley in 1975, were published under the title *Responsibility: Its Sources and Limits* (G. Vickers, 1980), and at the age of eighty-six, Sir Geoffrey embarked on the writing of his last book, *Human Systems Are Different* (G. Vickers, 1983). It has a note of urgency:

If the argument of this book has any validity at all, it is to suggest that all today's human populations, perhaps particularly those heirs of the Enlightenment who have so successfully pioneered the huge cultural changes of the last two hundred years, need now to achieve an even more radical reversal, a change not only in their understanding, as observers, of the developing situations in which they are trapped, but also a change in their appreciation, as agent and experients, of what those changes require of them. (p. 186)

In January 1981, Bayard Catron wrote from George Washington University on behalf of young American scholars who wanted to organize a Festschrift:

We want to acknowledge more than the power of your intellect. The character of the man, his warm and gentle humanity, his indomitable curiosity and zest for life—these have touched us. . . . None of us has known you throughout your several careers, and many have known you for less than one of your eight-plus decades. But having known you as a person as well as author, we understand ourselves and our culture better. (Open University, 1984, p. 38)

"No letter," he replied, "I have ever received has moved and pleased and comforted me more than yours. . . . This exceeds even the highest hopes which I privately nourished when in March 1955 we left London and the Coal Board" (G. Vickers, 1981, p. 38).

As his health deteriorated, he reflected much on his past life. It had often troubled him that his life lacked coherence, a sad reflection for one who believed that the making of a personality, the living of a life, was an exercise in the creation of form, the making of a work of art. Now, in the hospital at the age of eighty-seven, his life seemed more coherent than he had realized (J. Vickers, 1991, p. 221). He was glad to be alive.

Sir Geoffrey Vickers was admitted to the hospital in March 1982 and continued to dictate letters until the day before he died.

Among his papers were found notes for a projected autobiography started and abandoned in 1979.

I write . . . to express my grateful bewilderment at the course which my life has taken. . . . I would think it arrogant to postulate a Providence concerned to regulate my small affairs, when I see around me so many more deserving whom fortune has treated less kindly. But one can be grateful without a specific benefactor. So some of these episodes have found their way into this book because they stand out so vividly in my memory and in the hope that I can share the surprise and delight which they brought.

Behind all this lies the delight which I have always felt in being alive in this astonishing world. (G. Vickers, 1982a, p. 38)

Foreword to the 1983 Edition

KENNETH E. BOULDING

◈ WISDOM IS EASIER TO RECOGNIZE than to define, and one recognizes it in every chapter of this classic volume, which is just as wise today as when it was published in 1965. It comes from a rich and complex life experience coupled with the ability to generalize, plus the rarer ability to see all generalizations and descriptions as only shadows of the complex truth. Sir Geoffrey Vickers combined a very productive and varied experience in the "real world" of legal, political, and economic life with a wide knowledge of academic thought and writings about it. This work contains a critique of the more academic models of human behavior, both from economics and from psychology, inspired by reflection on a large and varied experience of it. The critique is perhaps more implicit than explicit, but the careful reader, brought up on the facile models of maximizing behavior in economics, or rat and pigeon behaviorism in psychology, will do well to detect it and ponder. Footnote 4 in the Introduction, in which Vickers outlines his differences with Herbert Simon, perhaps the most sophisticated theorist of the age, is especially worthy of attention. Vickers' experience taught him that the real world is an endless dynamic flux, that all goals are transient, that equilibrium is a figment of the human imagination, even though a useful one, and that our images of facts and of evaluations are inextricably mixed and are formed mainly in an interactive learning process that he calls "appreciation."

A delightful characteristic of this volume is the way in which it shifts constantly between the abstract principle and the concrete illustration. The most concrete of these, like the reports of three Royal Commissions in England in the 1950s and 1960s, may seem a little dated, though the problems that they discuss—traffic, education, and crime—are still very much with us. The anonymous case studies, which clearly come out of personal experience, emerge almost as little novels; Mr. Black, Mr. Green, and Mr. White, Mr. Deadletter and Mr. Redletter, spring vividly from the pages, turning us from colorless abstract theory to the colorful world of real human beings.

The reader should be warned that the easy style, the charming illustrative episodes, and the sharp aphorisms "—black or red figures in a profit and loss account—might be discriminated even by a well-conditioned rat" (p. 154) may quite unintentionally disguise the intellectual depth and significance of this volume. As the title indicates, human judgment and decision is indeed an art, a process of such complexity that it cannot be completely described by science. Nevertheless, science can illuminate and improve art, and art can illuminate and improve science, at least by making it aware of both its virtues and its limitations and cultivating the art of decent humility. This book is an exercise in the illumination of both the art and the science of judgment by each other, and its careful study should improve both. We may see our personal decisions and judgments in a new light, from the most insignificant to the most momentous. Certainly, if the powerful figures of this world whose decisions may affect the lives of all of us could catch the lessons of this volume, our chances of survival could be much enhanced. And those of us in the business of the theory and science of decision might edge our theories closer to the rich and complex reality that they so imperfectly represent.

To the roads I did not take
because I was committed to another;
and to those who trod those roads without me—

not in remembrance,
for I never knew these might-have-beens;
nor in regret,
for every "yes" implies a thousand "no's";
but in acknowledgement
of the uncountable costs
inherent in every choice,
which give an abiding mystery
to this book's theme.

Preface to the Original Edition

I HAVE SPENT MY LIFE in practicing the law and helping to administer public and private affairs; and I have thus had opportunity to observe and take part in the making of policy. The more I have seen of this, the more insistent has been the challenge to understand it both as a mental activity and as a social process, for it seems strange and dangerous that something so familiar and apparently important should remain so obscure. My enquiry into it has led me further than I expected. I have had to question sciences in which I am not professionally qualified and sometimes to supply my own answers, when theirs seemed ambiguous, inconsistent, or absent. I present the result with humility but without apology. Even the dogs may eat of the crumbs that fall from the rich man's table; and in these days, when the rich in knowledge eat such specialized food at such separate tables, only the dogs have a chance of a balanced diet.

Those who have helped me, knowingly or unknowingly, in one way or another, are far more numerous than I can acknowledge. I am especially indebted to seven friends who by their own writings or by their criticisms of mine, by the doors they have opened, by their encouragement, or in all these and more subtle ways have not only influenced the form and content of this book but have helped to maintain the inward pressure that has brought it to completion. It is typical of the exercise that the names that gratitude brings first to my mind—Professor D. M. MacKay, Dr. J. M. Tanner, Dr. Leonard J. Duhl, Professor John R. Seeley, Professor Adolph Lowe, Dr. J. H. Oldham, and Professor Michael Polanyi—should be those of a physicist, a physiologist, a psychiatrist, a sociologist, an economist, a theologian, and a philosopher-scientist and that these labels should so poorly express the nature of my debt to them or of their contributions to what I believe to be a common field. I do not, of course, by this acknowledgement, imply the agreement of any of them with anything I have written.

I have sometimes quoted from and more often reproduced in slightly altered form material that has already appeared in previously published papers of mine. These are listed in the bibliography. I am indebted to the editors of the journals in which they first appeared for permission to treat them so.

Goring-on-Thames
England
January 1965

Introduction to
the Original Edition

◆ FROM LEGISLATURES AND LAW COURTS, from cabinets and boardrooms, a stream of decisions issues and appears to mold the course of history. We attach great importance to this process, giving the greatest prizes that our society offers to those who seem to excel in it, be they statesmen, judges, military commanders, heads of business corporations, or princes of the church. In less exalted roles, the ability to make "right" decisions distinguishes the expert, whatever his profession, craft, or occupation; and a role that leaves no scope at all for this ubiquitous activity is rated as subhuman. If we consider the individual, not as holder of a particular role but as controller of an individual life, managing through the years a bundle of interlocking and partly inconsistent roles, as husband, father, employee, citizen, and so on—not to mention the unique and self-made role of being himself, insofar as this is separable from the others—we attribute the same importance to the serial acts of conscious choice that punctuate and seem to modify his course. Irrespective of any views or doubts we may have about the degree of "freedom" with which any of these choices are made, we can hardly escape the universal assumption that they are the expression of a mental activity that may be exercised with greater or less skill. I will call this activity *judgment*.

Concerning this activity of judgment and the decisions that partly reflect it, common speech and common practice make confident assumptions that are not to be justified or explained by anything yet to be found in any psychological textbook. Selection boards, for example, attach sometimes overriding importance to the capacity of rival candidates for "good judgment"; yet their estimation of this is a matter for their own judgment and if they differ and fail to reach agreement by discussion, there is no means by which any of their judgments can be *proved* right or wrong— even, I shall suggest, after the event. Judgment, it seems, is an ultimate category, which can only be approved or condemned by a further exercise of the same ability.

Again, decisions may be made not only with greater or less skill but also with or without "responsibility"; and though we often differ in our judgments of how skillfully another has reached a decision, we are quick to sense and seldom dispute whether he has made it "responsibly" or not. When members of a selection board or a board of directors or even a court of appeal, all with similar training and experience, reach opposite judgments on the same facts, we are seldom surprised; we may even commend the "sense of responsibility" that has led the minority to maintain their view against the pressure to conform. To suggest irresponsibility would be to suggest neglect of rules by which the least skillful, no less than the most skillful are expected to be bound. We thus imply that the activity into which I am inquiring is exercised within some framework of "rules," which deserves further enquiry.

Further, we recognize that decisions may or may not display "initiative." Everyone with experience of decision making knows that the more closely we explore alternative courses of action, the more clearly we become aware of limitations of various kinds that restrict the courses open to us. Sometimes decision making proves to be no more than the painful process of discovering that there is only one thing to do or even "nothing to be done." On the other hand, experience also recognizes situations in which the decision maker can in some degree impose a pattern on the future course of affairs rather than merely responding to its demands; and the difference between the two situations can be analyzed without becoming involved in a philosophical debate about determinism and free will, a dilemma that, as I shall suggest, is in any case in process of losing its horns. Unhappily, the limitations on our initiative in any situation are seldom equally apparent from within and from without. So it may be inevitable that we should sometimes expect far more of our governors and even of ourselves than is in fact open to them or to us and suffer in consequence unnecessary agonies of fury or guilt and that we should sometimes expect far too little and thus allow a high human function to be abdicated. Yet the extent of such errors might be reduced, if we understood the process better; and it is important that it should be reduced, for at the moment it imperils the whole working of our political system.

The ability to exercise initiative is a special aspect of the general skill implied by good judgment. Its study is complicated not only by the fact that the actual limitations on its exercise at any moment are hard to chart but by an even closer link between the skill and the limitations; for the scope for initiative is created and preserved largely by the way in which it is exercised. It follows that good judgment can be recognized only over a substantial time span. Tomorrow is already committed, but how varied, today, are the possibilities for ten, twenty, thirty years hence! They cannot all be realized, but perhaps one of them might be. For example, the extent to which competing claims for land use frustrate each other and limit our initiative in our ever more crowded island today reflects a century of past decisions; and our initiative or inertia today will help to determine the degree and kind of choice that will be open to the next generation. We are the architects of our children's opportunities, if not of our own.

This temporal process is twofold. Those who are engaged in a course of decision making soon become aware that each decision is conditioned not only by the concrete situation in which it is taken but also by the sequence of past decisions, and that their new decisions in their turn will influence future decisions not only by their effect on the history of event but also by the precedents they set and the changes they make in the way decision makers in the future will see, interpret, and respond to an event, a separate development that for the moment I will label the history of ideas. Thus, human history is a two-stranded rope; the history of events and the history of ideas develop in intimate relation with each other yet each according to its own logic and its own time scale, and each conditions both its own future and the future of the other.

Thus, judgment and decision, though mental activities of individuals, are also part of a social process. They are taken within and depend on a net of communication, which is meaningful only through a vast, partly organized accumulation of largely shared assumptions and expectations, a structure constantly being developed and changed by the activities it mediates. The individual decider can no more be studied in isolation than the individual decision. The mental activity and the social process are indissoluble.

This is the field that this book seeks to explore. Its primary aim is to describe, analyze, and understand the processes of judgment and decision, as they are encountered in business and public administration and particularly those exercises that we regard as contributing to the making of "policy." As such, I hope it will make some contribution to the practice and the teaching of these important, practical arts. In doing so, it makes use of concepts and ways of thought that, though common today in a wide variety of sciences, have so far penetrated only patchily into the thought of laymen—concepts that can perhaps be comprehended with least danger of misconception under the name of general system theory. I hope it may thus speed the naturalization in everyday speech and thinking of concepts that seem to me of the greatest usefulness and also help reciprocally to throw light on the meaning and limitations of these concepts. I have often been surprised to find that ideas I found difficult to grasp when I first met them in some scientific presentation spring to life of themselves when some familiar aspect of practical life is looked at with a fresh eye.

The decisions of public bodies and, in varying degrees, the mental processes that underlie them are more explicit than those of the individual mind. They are nonetheless the work of individual minds, and any analysis of them must reach conclusions or make assumptions about individual mental processes, as well as about the social and historical matrix that conditions and makes them possible. These conclusions and assumptions are relevant to normal psychology and seem to me to go beyond the present findings of that science. It is therefore a second aim of the book to suggest the findings relevant to individual and social psychology that seem to be implicit in the study of what I shall call *institutional behavior* and to suggest the possibilities of such studies as a field of psychological analysis and research.

The third aim of the book is by no means limited by its inadequacies in achieving the second. It is even more important in this field than in any other that the layman should constantly insist on the problems to which he wants answers, in all their complexity and should confront scientists with the assumptions on which he, the layman, is acting. He is thus likely both to speed the day when scientists will speak effectively to his condition and to diminish the risk that they in the meantime will persuade him to limit his stature and complexity to the measure of their concepts and techniques.

For in studying men and societies, the scientist, like the layman, is inescapably within the field of his own study; and in consequence, his views on men and societies are not mere observations. They are also agencies, certain to affect the subject of their attention and no less potent to stunt or distort it than to speed its development. A book which I shall often have occasion to quote defines its aim as "to re-equip men with the faculties which centuries of critical thought have taught them to distrust" (Polanyi, 1958). Whether the implication be accepted or not, it is clearly true that both science and philosophy, by the concepts of human nature that they use and propagate, can powerfully affect men's views of themselves, their possibilities, and their limitations and may thus alter what human nature effectively is. A mistaken view of planetary motion, though held for centuries, had no effect on the motion of the planets. They continued on their elliptical way, undisturbed by human preference for circular motion; and even when men discovered their mistake, they had no means to bring the course of nature into line with their aesthetic predilections. A too restricted view of human nature, on the other hand, even though only briefly ascendant, can significantly alter the expectations and hence the behavior of men and societies and may thus provide its own bogus validation.[1] This is always a danger, not least today; and this book is a contribution to what I hope will be a never ending resistance movement. A too ambitious view, though potentially no less dangerous, is more likely to disclose its own shortcomings.

My concern is primarily with decisions taken in the conduct of public affairs. These decisions are taken by individual men, acting alone or in small, face-to-face groups (boards, councils, committees), and they are the fruit of judgment formed by individual minds; but the individuals concerned are acting as governors, directors, controllers of some institution, and their decisions are approved or criticized for their effect on the regulation of the institution they control rather than for their effect on the personal fortunes of those who take them. I will call such decisions *institutional decisions*. The behavior of men acting in such roles I will call *institutional behavior*.

I need a way to talk and think about institutional behavior. The present state of the behavioral sciences does not present an agreed body of theory sufficient in my view to support an analysis at the level with which I am concerned; and some contemporary assumptions seem to me to be suspect. So in developing the conceptual model that I shall use, I have supplemented and sometimes departed from current orthodoxies. I shall state and try to justify these innovations. Insofar as they are not accepted as explanations, I hope they will be regarded as useful descriptions. I have tried to do full justice to the evidence, even though this involves great difficulties of explanation, rather than cut down the subject matter to fit an overall theory.

The evidence includes three dubious but inescapable sources. The first is documentary. The processes of institutional decision are documented, sometimes very fully. The most completely documented are the decisions of courts of law, in which the issues, the arguments, and the criteria, as well as the judgments, are recorded in the full consciousness that they are part of an ongoing process and with a view to their being used as such. Governing bodies of all kinds, however, sometimes document their decisions not much less fully. Their agenda and accompanying papers define issues, provide facts and appreciations supposed to be relevant, propose and forecast the results of alternative policies. Their minutes record decisions and sometimes reasons and dissenting views. It does not follow, of course, that what happened is fully explained by what is recorded; but it would need a high degree of cynicism to regard the record as irrelevant. Still more explicit are the proceedings of Royal Commissions and similar bodies, three of which I shall examine in some detail.

The second source of evidence, far from conclusive but not to be ignored, is language. In the present state of our knowledge, much of our understanding of the processes with which I am concerned is implicit in our language, rather than explicit in our theories. As Professor Peters (1957) has observed, "We know *so much* about human beings and our knowledge is incorporated in our language. Making it explicit could be a more fruitful preliminary to developing a theory than gaping at rats or grey geese." I do not subscribe to any derogatory implications that may lurk in the last six words. Tinbergen's (1951) account of the territorial behavior of sticklebacks is a distressingly exact description of a type of interdepartmental behavior endemic in many institutions; and I have often felt, when taking part in wage negotiations, that I was participating in interaction that would be more easily described in terms of ethology than of economics. Nonetheless, the rat in the maze and the judge on the bench display differences (as well as similarities) of behavior that cannot at present be contained within a single conceptual framework. No doubt even judges might sometimes behave in every respect like rats; but rats never behave in every respect like judges.

The third source of "evidence," if such it can be called, is experience. In all these matters, I have the inescapable limitation of being a "participant observer," so I may claim also such advantage as attaches to that controversial role. I am well aware that the illustrations and case histories that play so large a part in the book are radically conditioned by the fact that I have spent my life in such situations.

* * * * *

The arrangement of the book is designed to meet as fully as may be two inherent difficulties of presentation. First, those who, I hope, will read the book do not share a common universe of discourse. Many administrators and men of affairs have had no occasion to apply to their own activities concepts that are becoming familiar to scientists of widely different persuasions; and scientists, even social scientists, except in some well-defined fields, such as law and economics, seldom try to apply their concepts to the complexities of institutional life, though the increasing attention paid to business management is a welcome exception of rapidly growing importance. An attempt to write for both classes may fail to be acceptable to either. I have therefore addressed the book primarily to laymen; and where I expect that it will raise "sturdy doubts and boisterous objections" in the mind of the scientist but not of the administrator, I have left to the notes the task of acknowledging the difficulty and doing what I can to meet it. I have also avoided terms in scientific use, except where they have passed into the language of laymen and where I can use them with precision.[2] Where I have developed concepts for which no adequate expressions are in common use, I have so far as possible chosen words that science has not appropriated and that can be used for my purpose with the least extension of their normal meaning.

The second difficulty of presentation is common to all writing in the psychosocial field that is addressed both to laymen and to scientists of different persuasions. Any description of individual behavior must assume a whole set of sociological concepts about the effect on people of their membership of groups and institutions. Any description of group and institutional behavior must assume a whole set of psychological concepts about the way individuals think and feel. Neither set of concepts is yet adequately developed and agreed even among the specialists; and what they do agree has not yet penetrated fully into the thought and language of men of affairs. So whichever approach is put first is liable to depend too much on exposition that is to follow.

To minimize the difficulty, I have approached policy making first (Part I) as a mental skill. In Part II (Policy Making as an Institutional Process), I have distinguished various types of institutions and examined the effect that their differences may have on the policy making that takes place in them. In Part III (Policy Making in the Context of the Decision Situation), I have considered policy making in the context of actual situations that call for action and have analyzed the effect of such situations on the policy that they modify or evoke. In a very brief Part IV (Policy Making Within the Human-Ecological System), I have tried to present policy making in the context of the historical process from which it proceeds and that it tries to shape. These views, like four small photographs taken at various angles and distances of a process spread vastly through space and time, are, of course, utterly fragmentary and partial and would have been no less so had they been multiplied; for neither a comprehensive nor a unitary view of reality is within our compass. Nor have I made any rigorous effort to prevent overlapping, hoping that the degree of repetition that the arrangement involves may prove useful. What is familiar to the reader will be uninformative, even when said only once. What he may find new—and the hope that he may find something new is the only justification for writing or for reading—is unlikely to convey its load of information unless it is said at least twice. In particular, I have not hesitated to reiterate in different ways the attitude toward time that is fundamental to my view. Few would deny today that time is a dimension of the space in which we objectively and subjectively live; but even fewer, I believe, have yet acquired the habit or drawn the conclusions of taking it sufficiently seriously.

Of the examples, which are drawn from public administration, business, and government, some are imaginary. Case histories would have been more cogent and more satisfying; but to derive suitable case histories from all the fields involved would not only have been a most difficult task but would have involved insuperable further troubles. They could not have been sufficiently simplified without being distorted; nor could I, with actual case histories, have stated as facts situations, such as the state of a man's mind at a given moment, that cannot be certainly known, even though "the state of a man's mind is as much a fact as the state of his digestion." I will ask the reader to suspend, until he has read the illustrations, his judgment on whether I have used my storytelling license legitimately. Where I have been able to use detailed and public case histories, notably the three reports analyzed in Chapter 3, I have been glad to do so.

This book so often crosses ground charted by Professor Simon (1947) in his outstanding book *Administrative Behavior*[3] that I have thought it convenient to append a note summarizing what seem to me to be the most important differences of substance or emphasis between my analysis and his. The points on which I follow him are so numerous that it would be tedious to acknowledge them—or my indebtedness to him—in separate notes.

Notes

1. As, for example, did the psychological assumptions underlying the most "individualist" period of British legislation in midnineteenth century, such as the Poor Law of 1834.

2. The word *culture* deserves a special note, since it is extensively used both scientifically and in common speech with varying degrees of extension and precision. I use the term in a wide but, I hope, a precise *sense* to include any shared "appreciative system" (q.v.) to the extent that it is shared. Thus, the members of any group, however small, who share an appreciative system, share to that extent a common culture. For greater clarity, I sometimes refer to such common areas, when small and greatly overlapped by others, as subcultures, but I intend no difference in kind. Even the most well-marked cultures are not and should not be all-comprehensive. Scientists, for example, share a culture that is in some respects wider, in others narrower, than the national cultures to which they equally belong.

3. The most interesting differences between the classic analyses of this book and my own seem to be the following:

    a. I adopt a more explicitly dynamic conceptual model of an organization and of the relations, internal and external, of which it consists, a model that applies equally to all its constituent subsystems and to the larger systems of which it is itself a part.

    b. This model enables me to represent its "policymakers" as regulators, setting and resetting courses or standards, rather than objectives and thus in my view to simplify some of the difficulties inherent in descriptions in terms of *means* and *ends*.

    c. I lay more emphasis on the necessary mutual inconsistency of the norms seeking realization in every deliberation and at every level of organization and hence on the ubiquitous interaction of priority, value, and cost.

    d. In my psychological analysis linking judgments of fact and value by the concept of appreciation, I stress the importance of the underlying appreciative system in determining how situations will be seen and valued. I therefore reject "weighing" (an energy concept) as an adequate description of the way criteria are compared and insist on the reality of a prior and equally important process of "matching" (an information concept).

    e. I am particularly concerned with the reciprocal process by which the setting of the appreciative system is itself changed by every exercise of appreciative judgment.

PART I

Policy Making
as a Mental Skill

The Regulation of Institutions[1]

◆ IN GOVERNMENT AND BUSINESS, a distinction is often drawn between policy making and executive decisions—the first being designed to give direction, coherence, and continuity to the courses of action for which the decision-making body is responsible; the second designed to give effect to the policies thus laid down. The distinction cannot be clearly maintained between decisions, still less between decision-making bodies, but it is valid and useful as a distinction between two elements in the process of regulation. According to the view here taken, every decision-making body is to be regarded as a regulator of the dynamic system of which it forms part, but its scope for *regulation* and hence the meaning of that term is much more complex than at the simpler levels at which our concepts of regulators and regulation are commonly formed. This complexity resides chiefly in the presence of "policy making" as a constituent of regulation. So I will begin by examining the concept of regulation at the level of *institutional behavior.* This I can best do by means of an example. A major local authority maintains a variety of services—education, roads, sewage disposal, and so on. Each of these consists in maintaining through time a number of relationships, quantitative or qualitative or both. It must, for example, provide sufficient school places, year by year, for all its children who are at the time of school age; and it must also provide for them education of a quality and character acceptable to its citizens, to the inspectors of schools, and to its own education committee and officials. If we went from department to department, we should find in nearly all someone responsible for one or more of such relations, which I will call functional relations.

In some departments, however, we should find officials responsible for relations of a different kind. The aggregate demands for money made by all departments must be kept in line with total revenue and total cash resources. The aggregate staff needed by all departments must be maintained in number and in quality, skills, and experience by recruitment, training, and promotion, despite continual wastage. Office space must be adequate to house them. Operating departments need stocks of consumable stores, which must be constantly replenished to balance loss in use. Viewed as a dynamic system, the organization maintains itself by appropriating from its surround and using a continual intake of money, men, and materials, as a cow maintains itself by appropriating and using grass, air, and water. The analogy is close enough to suggest for these relations the name of metabolic relations. Some departments, such as finance and personnel, are wholly concerned with metabolic relations.

This network of relations, quantitative and qualitative, functional and metabolic, may be divided in another way. Some are internal, relations between departments and individuals within the organization; and some are external, between the organization as a whole and its milieu. There is a relation between the two sets. An animal must learn to digest the food it can find or to find the food it can digest, and it perishes unless in one way or the other or both it can match its internal needs and resources with its external demands and opportunities; and an organization is in like case. It must match its human resources, in skill, energy, and morale, with what it aspires to do or is required to do, or it must cut its aspirations or the demands upon it to the level of its resources.

Finally, the relations that the authority seeks to maintain may be distinguished as imposed or self-set. Some are given by the facts of the situation, such as the need to balance money-out by money-in. Some are given by external authority, such as the duties imposed by Parliament or by the executive. Some are imposed by its own commitments previously taken, such as contracts for works still to be completed or services provided or promised that can no longer be withdrawn. All these imposed relations, however they arose, have become limiting conditions, more or less mutually consistent, more or less capable of total fulfillment. Subject to this net of relations that have thus become, at least for the moment, inescapable, there may or may not remain scope for the authority itself to vary the relations, quantitative or qualitative, internal or external that it will seek to maintain. It may perhaps have scope to embark on a new educational experiment, to redevelop the town center, or to improve the conditions of service of its staff; to raise the rates, extend its provision for old people, or cut down its public transport facilities. The total volume of its resources, their distribution between different uses and the character of each use may all admit of change and development.

The distinction that I have thus drawn between imposed and self-set limitations distinguishes the ends of what is really a continuous scale. Some relations are inescapable. Others may be pursued or changed at varying "cost," an expression that, however measured, means essentially the loss of whatever possibilities the decision excludes, and within varying limits, including limits of time.

Thus the activity of the local authority consists in maintaining through time a complex pattern of relationships in accordance with standards or within limits that have somehow come to be set as governing relations. Its regulative function consists partly in maintaining the actual course of affairs in line with these governing relations as they happen to be at the time and partly in modifying these governing relations so as to "maximize the values" (whatever that may prove to mean) that can be realized through the pursuit of these relationships while keeping the aggregate of activities within the bounds of possibility. That element of the regulative function that consists in maintaining the course of affairs in line with the current governing relations I regard as the executive element. That element that consists in modifying the governing relations I regard as the policy-making element.

The policy-making element is becoming more important and less adequately provided in our society, as it must in every society that is in process of rapid change. A convenient example is the regulation of traffic—that is, the maintenance of an acceptable relation between road capacity and traffic volume. In a community where both the potential volume of traffic and the standard of acceptable congestion are static, regulation would involve merely the provision and maintenance of the road capacity that these two require. This would be an executive function, except insofar as it competed with other potential uses for limited resources of money, land, plant, energy, and skill; and since in a static society, the distribution of resources, even scarce resources, remains fairly constant and is well sanctioned by custom, policy problems would be minimal. In a community, on the other hand, in which the potential volume of traffic constantly increases, not least in response to improved roads, the attempt to preserve the relationship by increasing road capacity raises ever sharper problems of policy by its increased competition for resources, of which one at least, land surface, cannot be correspondingly expanded and soon shows diminishing returns.

So the problem, previously seen simply as one of road development, becomes for the first time a problem of traffic regulation, in that control of traffic is seen as a means of regulating the relationship no less legitimate than road expansion. This too, however, raises issues of policy, in that it disturbs other relations that are dependent on unrestricted road traffic.

Each of these dimensions has room for ingenious executive action. Britain in the early 1960s is well accustomed to arterial roads, bypasses, flyovers, underpasses as means of expanding road capacity; even the multistory road has made its appearance. In regulating traffic volume, it has experience of taxing petrol, limiting some types of transport by license, limiting and charging for parking space. More obvious and direct controls have not yet been tried. Yet already, as the Buchanan report on traffic in towns[2] has shown, executive efforts to solve the problem have changed its character by revealing that it cannot be solved so long as it is regarded as simply a problem of traffic regulation. This is itself part of the wider problem of relating the needs of transport in and through an area with the other needs of life within that area; and this is a problem of town planning in three dimensions. Thus, executive solutions pose new policy problems, no less than policy decisions call for new executive solutions.

We should not suppose that regulation in such situations *depends upon* human regulation. If left alone, it will regulate itself. Traffic, outstripping road capacity, will generate self-magnifying traffic blocks in which no vehicle can move and through which it is impossible even to walk. This self-defeating situation will both prevent and deter the further flow of traffic; and when the blocks have been cleared, a reduced volume will move for a time in relative freedom, which will soon attract enough traffic to generate another jam. The volume of traffic will stabilize, oscillating about a mean at which it is just sufficient to deter what the roads cannot handle; and in doing so, it will automatically eliminate first those users to whom it is least essential or who are least able to support its demands, its hazards, and its frustrations. The sole purpose of human intervention is to regulate the relationship at some level *more acceptable to those concerned* than the inherent logic of the situation would otherwise provide. The aspiration to "optimize" implies a whole world of human preferences and human faith in the possibility of judging one combination of satisfactions to be better than another and making the judgment into an effective governing relation. Thus, policy making assumes, expresses, and helps to create a whole system of human "values."

I have deliberately chosen a fairly complex example, in the local authority and its planning problems, partly to guard against the very real dangers of oversimplification. The example is, in fact, far more complex than has so far appeared; for every department, every subdepartment in the organization, and still more, every official and every councillor is a partly independent subsystem with its own governing relations not fully consistent with those of the system as a whole. For the moment, however, I will describe the institutional "regulator" as if it were a unitary mechanism and will so far as possible defer the consideration of its internal complexities until later.

I have chosen a local authority for this example because the various functional relations that it is set to maintain—education, roads, and so on—are explicit; their independence of each other is apparent, and their conflicts for precedence cannot be supposed to be settled by recourse to any built-in priorities. I believe, however, that this is equally true, not only of the other "public" bodies that I shall notice, the central government and the boards that control public corporations, but also of private undertakings operating for profit. The idea that in these last all governing relations are subservient to and can therefore be resolved into "maximizing profit" is, I shall suggest, a myth (see Chapters 10, 11, and 12). For even economic criteria are manifold; growth and stability have many dimensions. And apart from these, such undertakings are expected and even expect themselves to maintain a host of other relations, political, social, legal, and moral, in their multiple roles as producer, supplier, employer, land developer, earner of foreign exchange, and so on. I shall seek to show that the process by which conflicts between these are resolved is substantially the same as in the other examples. Even the courts, no less a regulator, exercise a degree of policy making and have to resolve conflicts between policies; for the inescapable function of the courts in developing and even changing the law by the very process of applying it is well recognized and forms a clear example of the relation between the two elements of regulation.[3]

The authority in my example may be regarded as a dynamic system of precarious stability. Its balance may be disturbed in either of two ways—and in practice is constantly being disturbed in both these ways. Total resources may shrink or grow, relative to current demand, making overall restriction necessary or expansion possible somewhere; and policy must decide where the restriction shall fall or the growth occur. Alternatively, the standards by which these services are judged may change, increasing or reducing the claim of any one relative to the others and demanding a redistribution of energy and attention over the whole field; and policy must decide what redistribution shall be made.

Any major change will reverberate through the whole system, affecting and affected by even such apparently remote variables as the personal ambitions of officers and the nostalgic memories of councillors; for an official's desire to increase his responsibilities and a councillor's wish to keep the old town as it was are also examples of governing relations—standards that help to determine whether a possible change shall be welcomed or resisted. What some see as a housing issue, others will see as a problem of road development, sewage disposal, or finance; as a threat to the former character of the town; or even as a matter of personal relations; and all these views are valid. How such disparates are resolved and the side effects of any resolution are the main theme of this book.

In observing such situations, we can usefully distinguish two strategies, which alternate with changes in the situation. When for whatever reason achievement is falling, relative to current standards, thresholds of acceptability have to be lowered, and a hierarchy of values develops which appears more obvious as things get worse. The system in jeopardy sheds first the relations least essential to its survival. As an organism in danger of death from cold restricts its surface blood vessels and risks peripheral frostbite to preserve its working temperature at more vital levels within, so businesses facing insolvency and nations facing invasion discard all but the simplest of their governing relations without hesitation or debate. An understanding of this protective strategy, however, will not suffice to explain what will happen when achievement is expanding in relation to current standards. What new, more exacting standards will structure the new possibilities? Expanding strategy needs its own explanation. An executive who is outstanding at salving undertakings in danger of dissolution, a statesman supreme at leading a country under dire threat, is not necessarily so successful at exploiting success. Certainly his performance in an expanding strategy cannot be predicted from his achievement in a protective one.

*   *   *   *   *

I have described policy making as the setting of governing relations or norms rather than in the more usual terms as the setting of goals, objectives, or ends. The difference is not merely verbal; I regard it as fundamental. I believe that great confusion results from the common assumption that all course holding can be reduced to the pursuit of an endless succession of goals. Some of the blame must be taken by the psychologists who have made "goal seeking" the paradigm of rational behavior. Rats, it is true, maintain their metabolic balance, which is a biologically given norm, by a series of excursions after food, each of which is a goal seeking; and some humans similarly maintain their solvency by periodic excursions after money. This, however, is by no means a sophisticated form of financial control, precisely because it shows a failure to appreciate relations in time; and an enhanced capacity to appreciate relations in time is clearly one of the distinguishing marks of our species. The most outstanding feature of regulation as practiced by governing bodies in industry or government is the trouble taken to observe the major variables as flows in the dimension of time.

Those who recognize the difference should not, I think, be content to mask it by giving to goal setting and goal seeking a meaning wide enough to include norm setting and norm holding; for goal setting is a distinct form of regulation, with its own specific mechanisms; a form less important, in my view, than norm setting but important enough to be separately distinguished. For example, a man who loves power—which is a specific relationship between a man and his milieu—both *seeks* power and *exercises* power. If he finds himself in a position in which his opportunities for exercising power are inadequate to what he feels to be his capacity, he will probably seek (consciously or unconsciously) a position of greater power. This element in his motivation may lead him, if a politician, to seek to become prime minister, as it may lead a scientist in industry to leave research for the path that leads to high executive office. For such aspirants, the prime minister's office or the managing director's chair are indeed goals, to be attained or not attained once for all; and the existence of such a goal will explain something of what they do.

But even before and still more after their attainment of their goal, the primary explanation of their activities is not the *pursuit* but the *exercise* of power. As they go through their daily work, chairing a difficult meeting, conducting a complex negotiation, they enjoy—among other things—maintaining that relationship with their milieu that *is* the exercise of power. This is of course no criticism of them, so long as it is within their role.

Most of these individual activities have indeed their own goals. The complex negotiation has an object; the difficult meeting must reach some conclusion; but these ends derive their meaning from the ongoing relations that they mediate. Each individual sale made by a salesman is the goal of a sequence of efforts, but to him and to his superior these are significant as constituents in the performance of a role, the exercise of a skill, and the maintenance of a rate of sales. Even to drive a car is always to maintain a set of spatial and temporal relationships, though it is usually also resorted to as a means of getting from A to B. To discharge a role, to exercise a profession, to live a life are, I suggest, even more obviously exercises in the maintenance of relationships in time.

Neglect of the norm-holding aspect of activity has produced that curious figment of the psychological textbooks,[4] the purpose-ridden man, an abstraction as odd in our time as the economic man was a century ago, though our culture, like that of our grandfathers, is all too well set to make the abstraction plausible. The purpose-ridden man's only "rational" activity is to seek goals; but since each goal is attained once for all, it disappears on attainment, leaving him "purposeless" and incapable of rational activity unless and until he finds another. "Satisfaction" is impossible to the purpose-ridden man or at least forms no part of his rational activity. He is allowed only a momentary "relief from tension." Even his goals are mediate, explicable in terms of more remote goals. Thus, the essential purposelessness to which the view condemns him is hidden behind an infinite regress. However "successful" he may be, however long he lives, some new "goal" flutters for ever just beyond his grasp.

This view I believe to be fallacious. It derives partly from the fallacy, to which the structure of our language may contribute, that men desire objects. They do not. The objects of our desires and aversions are not objects but relations. No one "wants an apple." He may want to eat it, sell it, paint it, admire it, conceivably even merely to possess it—a common type of continuing relation—in any case to establish or change some relation with it. *The goals we*

seek are changes in our relations or in our opportunities for relating;
but the bulk of our activity consists in the "relating" itself.

To explain all human activity in terms of goal seeking, though
good enough for the behavior of hungry rats in mazes, raises
insoluble pseudoconflicts between means and ends (which are
thus made incommensurable) and leaves the most important aspect of our activities, the ongoing maintenance of our ongoing
activities and their ongoing satisfactions, hanging in the air as a
psychological anomaly called "action done for its own sake." This
book, without denying that men sometimes seek goals (in the sense
already given) stresses a different and I believe more fundamental
and more neglected aspect of our activities, the maintenance of
relationships in time; and this is what I understand by regulation.

I must draw one other distinction also. It is generally agreed, I
believe, that even where conventional explanations in terms of
goal seeking are appropriate, they mask the perhaps much greater
amount of behavior that should be described as threat avoiding.
This is equally true of norm holding. For it is a feature of most
dynamic systems that if the relations to be regulated deviate from the
norm beyond a critical threshold, they suffer radical, self-exciting,
and often irreversible change. The animal dies, the skater falls, the
political party disintegrates, the business goes bankrupt; and thereafter the system dissolves or assumes some new configuration.
Each of the authority's constitutive relations, functional as well as
metabolic, operates with some such critical threshold. Road capacity and road user, if sufficiently out of phase, will generate self-
magnifying traffic blocks. Public order, sufficiently neglected, will
be taken over by the racket and the gang. The regulation of an
institution is too often governed—to the exclusion of the policymaker—by the need to avoid such threatening thresholds rather
than by the more sophisticated aim of norm holding.

The distinction is vividly exemplified by the familiar device
that road safety testing stations have taken over from the psychological laboratories. A chart on a rotating drum discloses a track
formed by two irregularly waving lines; and the operator, control-
ling a pointer by means of a wheel, must keep the pointer within
the waving track. Given sufficient preview and a sufficiently slow

speed, he can closely follow the center of the track; but as the speed increases or the preview is cut down, he feels the tension mounting; and he is well aware of the point at which he gives up his attempt to hold the center line and aims only to keep somewhere, anywhere within the track, away from its threatening boundaries—the point, that is, at which he becomes controlled by threshold, rather than by norm. A little more and all control is lost; and thereafter his best efforts may be worse than random. For there is a familiar situation in which to be systematically late is to be systematically wrong.

The techniques of control by threshold differ significantly from those of control by norm; and I accept only reluctantly the need to allow the expression norm holding to include threshold avoiding, except where the distinction is expressly marked. It would be too cumbersome to do otherwise, but the convention does not imply that either process can be resolved into the other.

Notes

1. In this and some subsequent chapters I have drawn on material that I first published in the 38th Maudsley Lecture, "The Psychology of Policy Making and Social Change" (Vickers, 1964b).

2. Containing (a) report of Steering Committee, chairman sir Geoffrey Crowther, and (b) report of working group, chairman Colin Buchanan.

3. This process has been extensively analyzed in the last fifty years (see, for example, Cardozo, 1921).

4. For example, the theory of action developed in Parsons and Shils (1951) as "a conceptual scheme for the analysis of the behaviour of living organisms"; yet it appears to conceive this behavior solely as "oriented to the attainment of ends or goals or other *anticipated* [italics added] states of affairs" (p. 53) and gives as an example a man driving his automobile to a lake to go fishing. The driving is described as action directed to the end "to be fishing," but the fishing would seem to escape from the definition of action, unless some further "end" can be discovered to which it in turn mediates. Few would accept the (possibly) caught fish as a sufficient end and none who did so could convincingly propound the end to which this in turn mediated.

To limit the concept of action in this way seems to me inconvenient. I prefer to accept a fisherman's assertion that he fishes because he likes fishing—more exactly enjoys maintaining that complex relation with the milieu in which fishing consists. Maybe he likes driving, too.

2

Appreciation[1]

◆ THE PROCESS OF REGULATION in its simplest form has been conveniently modeled by system engineers. An ongoing physical process, a ship at sea, a heat treatment plant in operation or what you will, is so designed as to change its state in response to signals; and it contains a subsystem (an automatic pilot, a thermostatic control) designed to generate the signals to which the main system will respond. The subsystem derives its signals by collecting information about the state of the main system—about the internal relations that constitute it, such as the relation between heat generation and heat loss or about the external relations between it and its surround, such as the direction of the ship's head—and comparing this with standards that have somehow been set for these variables. The disparity between the two generates a signal that triggers change in the main system, sometimes through the medium of a selective mechanism that chooses from a repertory of possible actions. In due course, the effect of the action taken along with all other changes that have happened in the meantime is fed back to the regulator through later information about the state of the system and thus contributes to further regulative action.

Thus, the desired relation is maintained through time by a circular process, which can conveniently be regarded as falling into two segments. In the first segment the actual course of affairs (or rather its relevant aspects) is compared with the norm, and information is gathered about the relation between the two. In the second segment, action (or inaction) is chosen as a response. The human helmsman for example, reads continuously from the compass card not only the current direction of the ship's head, relative to the course but also the rate at which it is swinging and the rate at which that rate is itself increasing or diminishing. These rates he compares with his learned knowledge of what they should be to steady the ship on her course; and this comparison provides the information on which he must decide whether and if so how much and how fast to turn the wheel—in other words, what signal, if any, he should give to the powered gear that controls the rudder, responses that must also be learned. Thus, the first segment of the process constantly sets a series of problems; the second segment as constantly provides solutions, right or wrong. The automatic pilot does the same, except that the rate of change appropriate in any given circumstances and the signal required to achieve it are normally built in. It would be feasible to design an automatic pilot that could learn these things for itself.

This system-engineering model usefully clarifies both the similarities and the differences between the kind of regulation that such systems are at present designed to achieve and the regulation of institutional behavior at the level described in the previous chapter. Human regulators also can usefully be conceived as revolving through the same circular process; and anyone seeking to understand regulation at either level will find his problems falling into three main groups. How does the regulator select, derive, and represent its information about the "state of the system"? How does it derive the standards by which this information is evaluated? How does it select and initiate a response? But in seeking to answer these problems, the inquirer into human regulators encounters questions that as yet seldom trouble the engineer.

The most obvious differences are in the first segment. Manmade regulators are usually designed to maintain a given relation by means of a given repertory of responses—a relation, moreover, that the repertory of responses, if skillfully used, is expected to be able to maintain. They are designed, in other words, for executive action in a situation in which "policy" may be taken as both "given" and feasible. Much regulation by men and institutions is on the same level. The human helmsman, for example, functions in a manner so nearly identical with that of the automatic pilot that a description of the process need hardly disclose whether the mechanisms involved do or do not include a human nervous system. For the human helmsman, no less than for the automaton, the course is usually given by a source outside the system, a navigator. Where the navigator's course setting follows rules that can be specified, as for instance in the changes needed to hold a "great circle" course, he too could be brought within the system and his function absorbed by the regulator, as the regulator of a homing missile includes the function of altering course so as to intercept a moving target. The relation to be found or held can be regarded as given, whether it is periodically "set" from outside the system; built in, like the setting of a ship's stabilizers; or calculable by the regulator by any specifiable process, however complex.

But the problems of policy making outlined in the previous chapter involve judgments of value made by processes and according to criteria that cannot yet be specified. Whether they are logically specifiable is a question that I will for the present leave open. These judgments are directed to the linked and continuing objectives of "optimizing" values in the realization of multiple, not wholly consistent policies within limits set by the requirements of dynamic balance and, at the same time, of maintaining this balance at the level most favorable to the optimizing process. So long as this dual process (which I will call *optimizing-balancing*) remains unspecified, the first segment deserves examination in its own right.

It is the second segment that has so far received most attention not only from system engineers but also from students of problem solving and its associated learning processes in animals and men;

and for such studies the uncertainties of the first segment need to be eliminated so far as may be. An experimental psychologist, for example, makes sure that his maze-running rats are so hungry that he can safely assume the abatement of their hunger pangs to be their chief concern. Koehler in his classic experiments with chimpanzees, excluded from their attention anything likely to present to them any problem other than the one he wanted them to solve—how to secure one tantalizing bunch of bananas just out of reach.

Similarly, in institutional behavior, when the object is not to study problem solving but to get a problem solved (or even to find out whether it is soluble within given limits) policymakers well know that the first essential is to present the problem clearly and simply to the problem solver and to hold it constant until he has exhausted his response to it. Such problems are often presented to a research and development department—for example, to design an appliance with specified features and capacities within a given price range. Nothing is more inimical to the process of solving *executive* problems than to change the specification of the problem or even to suggest that it might be changed. If the problem is very large and difficult—for example, to produce the first atom bomb— the problem setter is likely to establish an agency with this only as its task and criterion of success. In such a case the slightest hint that the policy that demands the bomb may be changed may be lethal to the morale and success of the executive enterprise. The solver of executive problems, problems arising in the second sector, must be protected from the uncertainties of policy making, so far as they might affect his executive task. Hence the concentration both of technologists and of business executives on the second, the executive segment of the circular process of regulation.

For the policy maker, on the other hand, the executive problem is not given; it is for him to decide what it shall be. This is *his* problem, a problem of a different kind, a problem of policy. He is, of course, free to range in imagination round the whole circle; indeed, he must do so, since the possibilities and limitations of executive action are among the forces that influence and limit his policy making. But the problems of the first segment remain distinct from those of the second. They too call for skill in problem solving and give rise to learning no less important, though less noticed and studied than the solving of executive problems.

This book, then, being chiefly concerned with policy making, will focus attention primarily on the first segment; the evolution and modification of the course, the norm, the standard, the governing relation that is inherent in every policy and the selection and ascertainment of the facts relevant to it. It will be concerned with the second segment only insofar as the two segments mutually interact, as they constantly do. The distinction is, of course, artificial—how artificial it is will appear ever more fully from the analysis that follows. It is nonetheless convenient. In considering the first segment in its own right, I need first a word to describe it and, as I cannot find one in the literature, I must invent one. I will call it appreciation, following the ordinary usage in which we speak of "appreciating a situation." Reviews of policy are usually preceded by such appreciations. The second segment I will call the instrumental segment, and the judgments to which it gives rise I will call instrumental judgments or instrumental hypotheses. These become executive decisions only when they have been in turn approved by appreciation.

An appreciation involves making judgments of fact about the "state of the system," both internally and in its external relations. I will call these reality judgments. These include judgments about what the state will be or might be on various hypotheses as well as judgments of what it is and has been. They may thus be actual or hypothetical, past, present, or future. It also involves making judgments about the significance of these facts to the appreciator or to the body for whom the appreciation is made. These judgments I will call value judgments. Reality judgments and value judgments are inseparable constituents of appreciation; they correspond with those observations of fact and comparison with norm that form the first segment of any regulative cycle, except that the definition of the relevant norm or complex of norms, like the identification of the relevant facts is itself a product of the appreciation. The relation between judgments of fact and of value is close and mutual; for facts are relevant only in relation to some judgment of value, and judgments of value are operative only in relation to some configuration of fact.

Judgments of value give meaning to judgments of reality, as a course gives meaning to a compass card. Information is an incomplete concept; for it tells us nothing about the organization of the recipient that alone makes a communication informative. This, as Professor MacKay (1964) has observed, is no criticism of a most valuable concept, developed originally by engineers concerned with problems of transmission, who could make assumptions or accept the sender's assumptions about the organization of the receiver. It remains important for the purpose of this book to recognize that a communication informs only a recipient who is so organized as to appreciate it and that its meaning to him will be governed by his appreciative organization.

The information given by a compass, for example, when fed to an automatic pilot has a meaning different from what it would have, if fed to an automatic device for keeping a running record of position by dead reckoning. To the automatic pilot, the changing direction of the ship's head is meaningful only so long as a course is set, and it changes meaning with every change of course. To the "dead reckoner" the course would be meaningless; and changes of direction would be significant only when combined with information about speed or distance traveled. Without some interest in direction, the compass would have no meaning for the eye or the automaton; and the nature of the interest determines what communications will be informative and how they will be used.

The difference between the engineering model of the first segment of regulation and the institutional model that I am concerned to develop lies primarily in the fact that in institutional behavior the concept of what relations should be regarded as regulable, the standards by which they should be regulated, and the ways of reconciling the inconsistent demands that they generate, are neither constant nor given but are themselves a function of the process that they are supposed to govern. Thus, of the relations that local government in Britain is expected to regulate in the early 1960s, many (for example, the supply and demand for housing and secondary education) were not regarded as needing regulation or capable of regulation a century before. Of those that were so regarded (for example, the relief of indigence), the norm has been radically reset—not merely the acceptable level of assistance but the whole concept of social obligation has radically changed. Even the possibility that rising norms and rising possibilities might provoke problems of reconciliation such as are illustrated by the Buchanan (1963) report were far below the conceptual horizon a few decades ago. Yet the process that has wrought these changes is the same historical process that they themselves have guided.

Policy making and execution, as I have already noted, describe phases in the regulative cycle, rather than different kinds of decision or decision maker. In human regulators, the two phases are notably interlocked; for the development of the power of appreciation makes it possible for executive action to be tried out hypothetically before it is submitted to the test of actual experience, and such hypothetical appreciation provides in fact by far the most abundant and cogent body of feedback to which such regulators respond. Each solution proposed by executive judgment is appraised, not merely as a solution to the problem that evoked it but also for its impact on other problems that it may make easier or harder of solution. Thus, the criteria by which one solution is preferred to another cannot be derived merely from the problem set. The "executive" even at the simplest level is never wholly relieved of the problem of optimizing-balancing, which is the hallmark of policy making.

*   *   *   *   *

It is convenient to illustrate this at a simple level, a level that at first sight is almost indistinguishable from the level of the helmsman. In any industrial plant, it is the function of some person or department to keep the supplies of raw materials at predetermined levels—responsible, for example, for ensuring that stocks of sheet steel are never, say, less than four weeks' or more than six weeks' supply at current rates of use. The buyer must adjust the rate at which materials flow into his store by reference to the rate at which they are currently flowing out, and he must be sensitive to changes both in the rate of user of the stocks and in his suppliers' times for delivery. Thus far, the function is typical of automatic regulation of a very simple kind. It could be modeled with a tank and a few pipes.

In fact, the buyer's function is much more complex. He must get good value for his money, yet keep good relations with his suppliers. He must be sensitive to changing nuances in the requirements of the users but only insofar as they can be contained within a practicable buying policy. He must try out new supplies and new suppliers without unduly disturbing uniformity of products and the goodwill of old established contacts. In these and other ways, he must reconcile the divergent requirements of disparate, qualitative norms, no less than the local authority in my first example. And he must do all this within the overall limitations of the funds available to him and of his own and his department's energy, skill, and time. Thus, like the policymakers at more exalted levels, his success consists in producing an optimal or at least an acceptable combination of solutions within the limitations of his budgetary requirements.[2]

These qualitative norms cannot be prescribed, as stock limits can be prescribed; nor can the degree of his success in meeting them be measured, as can the degree of his success in keeping his stocks within their prescribed limits. They constitute the unspecifiable content of his job, the element in it that, according to the researches of Dr. Elliot Jaques (1956, 1961) determines the weight of its responsibility and the true measure of its value. These norms and his performance against them can be recognized only by an act of judgment; and they are constantly so appraised by himself, his colleagues (especially the users who depend on him for their supplies), and by the manager to whom he is responsible. For the buyer has to regulate relations not only between flows of material but also between people; nor can the one be reduced to the other. Even with suppliers in an open market, relations of confidence are important; and they are still more important between the buyer and the users within his own organization, who depend on his skill but have no reliable means to judge his competence.

Insofar as the buyer's actions are directed to other human agents, as they almost all are, they carry a load of meaning greater than their overt content. An order withheld, repeated, or placed with a new supplier may operate not only to maintain or change the volume of steel sheet in store but also to convey a message of confidence or dissatisfaction, an invitation to cooperate, or even an unintended sidelight on the state of business in the buyer's undertaking; just as delay in payment for what he has ordered may operate not only to conserve the undertaking's cash resources but also to depreciate its credit. The buyer, in appreciating the probable results of his intended actions, no less than in interpreting what has actually happened, must regard all he does, no less than all he says, as a communication, the meaning of which is to be found only in its impact on receiving minds.

The stock limits, which were a datum to the buyer, were for the manager a product of regulative judgment. He wanted to lock up in stocks as little capital as was consistent with avoiding a stoppage in any section of the plant for lack of material. What stock levels would suffice for this could not be calculated with exactitude. They could only be fixed by an act of judgment, in which seriousness of risk and remoteness of risk were balanced by a mental calculus that has not been fully analyzed.[3]

This calculation, however, was only a small fraction of the disparate norms, quantitative and qualitative, to which the manager (far more than the buyer; hence his heavier responsibility) must produce an optimal or at least an acceptable ongoing response within *his* budgetary limits. Stocks of material were only one among many claimants for the capital at his disposal; and this in its turn was not a datum but to some extent a product of policy. The manager, like the buyer, has a host of relations, internal and external, functional and metabolic, that he must maintain as best he may. Among these manifold relations one is of especial interest in the context of this example—his relations with the buyer. I will follow these through two imaginary examples.

I will suppose first that at some point of time a wage negotiation in the steel industry began to create in the minds of steel users an expectation that steel prices would shortly be increased and an apprehension that steel supplies might be interrupted. Users began in consequence to increase their stocks; and suppliers, with increasing orders, began to extend their dates for delivery. At some point, these events, "appreciated" by the buyer (I will call him Mr. Black) set him a new problem. His normal procedures for maintaining steel stocks could no longer be relied upon, because of the uncertainty attaching to the delays that might intervene between *future* orders and their delivery.

The signal that alerted Mr. Black to this danger may have been pure hypothesis, suggested to him by following events in the steel industry. Alternatively, the critical signal may have been the first quotation he received in which delivery dates were actually increased, a signal instantly interpreted by him in the light of doings in the steel industry that he had already noted as likely to be relevant to him. Or again he may have been alerted only when repeated increases in delivery dates set him looking for an explanation. I will assume that Mr. Black, a competent steel buyer, was among the first to realize what was happening and likely to happen.

How in such a market could Mr. Black maintain steel stocks within the limits and discretions assigned to him? He explored alternatives that he had not used in the past and concluded that the best plan he could devise involved buying abroad at an enhanced price. This would exceed his authority, so he put his proposals to the manager. The manager thought the enhanced price too costly an insurance against the risk, as he assessed it and told Mr. Black to do his best with his existing suppliers, accepting the risk that stocks might fluctuate above or below the limits he had set.

In fact, there was no interruption of supply, and stocks did not stray beyond their appointed limits. The exercise, however, was by no means without effect. It affected the manager's appreciation of the buyer. To the manager, who was more remote than the buyer from these informative events and who had other preoccupations, Mr. Black's appreciation of the future course of the steel market was a welcome addition to the wider stream of information that flowed through his more complex net of evaluation; and in its timing, its accuracy, and its inventiveness it was in the manager's view a credit to Mr. Black.

The exercise also changed Mr. Black. He had explored market possibilities that were new to him but that would not be new to him again, even though on this occasion he had not used them. He had also changed his relation with the manager, increasing his own confidence in the manager and his sense of the manager's confidence in him.

I will add one further illustration, drawn from the same relationship. The manager, being responsible for the effective working of his organization, had the duty, among many others, of "appreciating" the performance of the buyer, not merely by his success in meeting the quantitative norms of stock control but also by comparison with those qualitative standards with which in the manager's view, he should conform. For a long time, the comparison of performance, insofar as the manager could notice and evaluate it, had corresponded closely with the standards that the manager regarded as satisfactory and had sometimes even exceeded it, notably on the occasion just described. This prolonged concordance had had results more positive than the mere "absence of a mismatch signal." "Match" signals are also informative; in this case, they had so built up the manager's confidence in the buyer that when later he noticed minor but recurrent shortcomings, they did not carry the same meaning for him as they would have done if the buyer had been newly appointed. Though more surprising, they were less alarming.

An observer endowed with the power to see the manager's mental processes displayed in detail would have seen these messages competing for his attention in a context in which they were first silenced and then muted by his confidence in Mr. Black. In due course, however, these nagging mismatch signals passed a threshold and won the necessary priority, not in the first instance for action but for attention. Something was wrong with the Supplies Department—wrong enough to need more detailed appreciation to find out what it might be. To this, the manager addressed his mind with the following results.

The buyer's performance had not changed; this was the trouble. The job had changed and so had the manager's expectation; and the buyer had not changed correspondingly. The undertaking had begun to buy a greater variety of materials and components than it formerly did; and the buyer had not only less experience of these new markets but less interest in them. In effect, though they had been added to him, he had never fully taken them over; and it was from these new areas of responsibility that the warning signals were coming. Moreover, the manager had imperceptibly raised his standards of what to expect from a supplies department; and this was due partly to his own progress, through study and experience, in the art of management; partly to a redistribution of his time and attention, due in its turn to the solution of other problems; partly to the intelligent performance of Mr. Black at the time of the steel crisis, which reset the standards by which the manager would in future judge his role in other fields beside steel. Through this combination of changes both in the nature of the job and in the standards defining its proper discharge, it had outgrown the capacity of Mr. Black. Thus, the regulator completed its first cycle. A disparity signaling—"Something is the matter" had set the problem—"What is the matter?" and the answer—"*This* is the matter" had set a new problem—"What to do about it?" A series of possible solutions to this problem were submitted to appreciation and rapidly eliminated.

Could the buyer (Mr. Black) be made equal to the new job by training, encouragement, warning, or a brief attachment to some other, highly developed supplies department? The manager thought not. Could he be replaced? An alternative (Mr. White) was available, somewhat inexperienced but capable in the manager's view of taking over and growing to the full stature required by the job without undue risk on the way—but how to make room for him? Transfer the existing buyer to another post? There was no suitable post. Discharge him? That would not be fair. Retire him on generous terms? He was too young; and any terms adequate to offset the hardship would set an intolerable precedent. What then? Carry on as before? No, that was no longer acceptable.

Within the familiar framework of reality and value judgment, the problem was insoluble. Instrumental judgment suggested an alternative. The manager might upgrade the supplies department and divide it into two parts; leave Black in charge of one half, containing the work he knew best; appoint White to control the other half; and place the whole under the general supervision of Green, a senior colleague who was soon to retire.

Appreciative judgment scanned the new proposal and approved. Black would retain all the work he could do well, and the undertaking would retain all his proved services. White would get an easier introduction to the work. The enlarged department would have the room for growth that it needed. When the new head retired, the post could be filled in the usual way. Black and White could be considered on their merits; either or neither could be appointed without disturbance of inner or outer relations.

The regulator had turned through its second cycle. *This* was what should be done. The solution posed a third set of problems. How to proceed and in what order? There were discussions to be held with Black, White, and Green before the change was made public. Black in particular must not misunderstand the communication that the change would convey to him. I need not follow the regulator in detail round its third cycle. The example has sufficed to show in the simplest form the main feature of institutional regulation—an endless dialogue between appreciative and instrumental judgment, in which appreciative judgment always has the last word, testing the solutions offered to it against judgments of fact or of value and rejecting them (that would not be practicable; that would not be fair) until an acceptable one is found. Judgments of fact and value can be distinguished even when both are present together. When the manager judged that "it would not be fair" to discharge Black, he had in mind that, as a matter of fact, it would be regarded as unfair by the staff and that this would injure the undertaking's reputation as an employer, perhaps even precipitate the loss of others who could less easily be spared. This was a reality judgment, although the facts judged included the value judgment of others. But he also had in mind "I the manager would regard it as unfair. It would not conform with my idea of what is to be expected of the undertaking as an employer and of me as its manager"; and this is a judgment of value, the application by the manager to his own projected action of standards accepted as valid by him. The distinction is one that I shall have many occasions to illustrate and underline.

Thus, even in this simple example the normal executive duties of both buyer and manager involved them constantly in that optimizing-balancing process that I have defined as the essence of policy making, stressing the fact that policy making and execution are aspects of the same regulative process.

The instrumental judgment depended in each case on proposing some change in the agent's usual way of seeing and valuing the situation. To regard it as *possible* that foreign steel, though more expensive might have become in the circumstances the best to buy; that the buyer's proved gifts might apply only to part of his job; that the Supplies Department might be so reconstructed as to contain its present head within one part of it—all these involved an element of *innovation* in some preexisting set of readinesses to see and value the situation in one way rather than another. This power of innovation had its far-reaching effects not only on the solutions reached but also on the "readinesses" that underlie both reality judgment and value judgment.

Notes

1. Parts of this and later chapters amplify an analysis that I first attempted in "Appreciative Behaviour" (Vickers, 1963a).

2. The difference between seeking the optimal and seeking the acceptable is important. Although I have referred throughout this book to "optimizing," I believe that the process consists in the progressive elimination of alternatives that are judged "not good enough," until one "good enough" is found. This result is not necessarily optimal. In a jumping contest, the bar is progressively raised until all competitors but one are proved not good enough; and the survivor, being good enough, is consequently "best." This result, however, follows only so long as all the competitors are allowed to attempt every jump. In examining possible solutions to a policy problem, we often review a series in order of familiarity and stop as soon as we find one that seems acceptable. If a familiar response seems good enough, why should we spend time trying out others? Professor Simon (1947) has coined for this exercise the useful verb "to satisfice."

3. The most substantial attempt known to me is by an economist, Professor G. L. S. Shackle (1952). An extension of his analysis to political choices would, I think, be fruitful.

Three Case Studies
in Appreciation

ROYAL COMMISSIONS AND SIMILAR BODIES provide examples of appreciation that have the advantage of being matters of public record. They are appointed not merely or even primarily to recommend action but to "appreciate a situation." By exposing what they regard as the relevant facts and their own value judgments thereon and the processes whereby they have reached their conclusions, they provide the authority that appointed them and also all who read their report with a common basis for forming their own appreciations and, it is to be hoped, with a model of what an appreciation should be. They are thus not only analytic but catalytic; and the knowledge that they are expected to be so leads them to expose their mental processes with a fullness that other public bodies seldom equal and are often at pains to conceal.

I have chosen three such reports, differing widely in subject matter: the Buchanan (1963) report on traffic in towns, the Robbins

(1963) report on higher education, and the Gowers (1953) report on capital punishment. Each is concerned with a basic problem of regulation; the problem of how to assimilate a major change with the greatest net gain (or least net loss) of "value" while preserving the balance of the system. The first is concerned with the impact of greatly increased demands for traffic movement; the second with the impact of greatly increased demands for higher education; and the third with the impact of a demand for a change in a critical provision of the penal law. Of these impacts, the first falls primarily on the physical system that both generates and must accommodate traffic; the second on the educational system; and the third on the penal system. But as the reports show, their impacts cannot be thus canalized. It is interesting to observe how similar are the mental processes made explicit in the three reports.

The terms of reference of the Buchanan committee were "to study the long term development of road and traffic in urban areas and their influence on the urban environment" (Buchanan, 1963). The report begins by establishing that, failing restrictive measures not yet dreamed of, the number of motor vehicles in Britain may be expected to double in ten years and treble in little over twenty years, while their users may increase even more rapidly. The result will be to overwhelm the city street as now conceived, even as a traffic carrier, as well as multiplying the injuries to amenity already caused by motor traffic—danger, intimidation, noise, fumes, visual intrusion, and squalor. This comprehensive reality judgment is assumed even by the committee (careful as they are not to impose their own value judgments on others) to be negatively valued by their fellow countrymen. Even those who attach little value to environmental amenity or who are prepared to sacrifice it all for "better traffic" may be assumed to rebel at a process of development that must be self-defeating even in terms of traffic alone. The report shows that the relation between roads and traffic, still more the relation between traffic and the other activities of human life will not regulate itself at any acceptable level or evoke such regulation by any regulative devices now in use. So a case is made for more ambitious regulation.

The next phase of the enquiry is to find some more adequate and comprehensive way to think about the manifold relations involved. The conflict is reduced to the interaction of two variables by the following analysis:

1. Traffic is an aggregate of individual journeys, virtually all of which are from buildings to buildings and are generated by the activities in those buildings. Their density is a function of the density of buildings; their pattern a function of the spatial relation of these buildings to each other.

2. All buildings need some degree of accessibility. All buildings also need a number of environmental characteristics, to some of which motor traffic is inimical. The conflict involved in reconciling traffic needs and other needs can be expressed as the conflict between accessibility and good environment.

3. Urban traffic movements take place through streets that still serve the multiple needs that they served in medieval times—vehicles in transit, vehicles arriving and departing, pedestrian traffic, retail trade, and personal intercourse, to which parking has now been added. This is an historical legacy, not a law of nature. Dwellings also contained not long ago relatively undifferentiated space. "As recently as the seventeenth century all sorts of human—and even animal—traffic flowed through the salons of Versailles" (Buchanan, 1963, Steering Committee report, para. 38). The use of space between buildings, no less than within buildings, could and should be differentiated so as to minimize the conflict between accessibility and good environment.

4. The conflict, even if minimized, will remain. A given minimum of environmental value implies an upper limit to the amount of accessibility. How high this limit may be depends on the tolerable upper limit of a third variable, cost.

These four propositions state the problem with admirable clarity and perfectly exemplify the "optimizing-balancing" problem involved in policy making.

The conflict between accessibility and good environment is today, as the report shows, sharper than it need be. Unless reconciled by radical redesign, it will cross one of those thresholds already noticed and result in the progressive deterioration of both terms of the relation. Redesign, however, can only expand the area within which choice is possible. It cannot remove the need to choose—or let events choose for us—what the balance shall be.

The report proceeds, with a wealth of concrete illustration, to bring home these generalizations. Actual traffic flows are analyzed, especially the dominant one generated by the diurnal need of people to move from home to workplace and workplace to home. "Through" traffic is distinguished as a separate and relatively soluble problem that complicates but does not create or alter the problem of a city's self-generated traffic. Examples are given of the separation of vehicular traffic from other uses of a city's "outdoor" space—some by horizontal, some by vertical planning. Her Majesty's Stationery Office, freed from its usual logistical restraints, decorates the broad margins of the pages with telling diagrams and photographs that scarcely need their captions. The report is a major piece of public education and makes clear the dimensions in which education is possible.

It educates the reader's *reality* judgment, stressing the necessary relation between the amounts that can usefully be invested in motor vehicles on the one hand and in facilities for their use on the other; describing the relative orders of magnitude of the factors involved, including the time factor; exploring the degree of certainty attaching to the various forecasts; and inviting him to consider what towns will be like on the basis of present trends and what they might be like on the basis of trends that might be achieved. In doing so, it helps him to break through limitations imposed by his tendency to *see* things in their now familiar categories—to see streets for example, as necessarily serving all the diverse purposes that they serve today.

Further, it educates the reader's *value* judgment—tentatively, as befits a government committee in a society that tolerates the manipulation of its values more readily by private than by public agencies. The committee limits its own value judgment on priorities to the proposition that good environment *matters*; it has some *value*; accessibility cannot be *all*. When expressing its faith in the potentialities of towns it goes further: "Of this there can be no doubt, that there are potentialities for enriching the lives of millions of people who have to live in towns beyond anything most of them have yet dreamed of" (Buchanan, 1963, Working Group report, para. 66). Text and illustrations combine to expose the reader to representations of what is and what might be and invite him tacitly not merely to value but to share the committee's valuation. Will you really put up with this? Would not that be worth striving for? In doing so, they help him to transcend limitations imposed by his tendency to *value* things in familiar ways—to accept what he supposed to be inescapable, to cling to what he believes to be indispensable, without examining those habitual valuations.

Finally, it educates the reader's instrumental judgment by setting a problem before him in its full complexity and showing him some of the innovations already in use—main shopping streets in cities turned daily into pedestrian precincts by barriers of removable posts; precincts and buildings based on a platform high enough above ground level to accommodate all vehicular traffic below; and so on. Such conceptions presented to minds not yet familiar with them, open doors wider than are needed for their own entrance. They help to usher in the concept of traffic architecture, the concept that access to buildings should be as much a function of design as the facilities for circulation within them.

I am concerned here not with the merits of the report as such but with its significance as a step in policy making. It is an admirable example of appreciative judgment; I will draw from it two conclusions that will be of continuing importance to this study.

First, what difference did the report make? Like every effort of appreciation, it posed a problem in regulation and elicited possible executive solutions that it in turn appreciated. It revolved through this circular process sufficiently to identify the main relations to be regulated (a wider set than at first appeared) the kinds of measure that regulation would involve and the scale of effort that would be required. Pursued further—and the covering report of the Steering Committee pursues it somewhat further—this would lead to progressively more concrete conclusions about the institutional arrangements needed to support the necessary executive actions, the method of finance, and so on.

This, however, was not the only aspect of the report. It also enlarged and changed for its readers—doubtless also for its members—the mental organization of which their appreciative judgments are a temporary expression, those readinesses to see, to value, and to respond to situations in familiar ways that, while they last, exclude the power to see other possibilities. I will call these readinesses of the mind its *appreciative setting*. The exercise of appreciative judgment does more than produce an executive solution. It also changes the appreciative setting of the mind concerned, perhaps in fields remote from those of the actual judgment—as Mr. Black's abortive plan changed his own and his manager's appreciative setting in regard to each other, no less than in regard to the undertaking's steel supply. This is the educational significance of the mental activity I call appreciation, which is an exercise always in self-education and usually in the education of others also. Since regulation in contemporary societies involves the cooperation of ever more people in sustaining policies of ever greater range and cost, the educative value of appreciations, such as the Buchanan report and the dialogue to which these publications gives rise is of major importance and accounts for their increasing use.

How needful and how difficult is the educative task appears even from the comments of the Steering Committee, a separate committee appointed by the minister to comment on the report and draw conclusions for public policy.

Referring to limitation on the urban use of vehicles as one possible component in the regulative process, the Steering Committee commit themselves to two significant comments. "Distasteful though we find the whole idea, we think that some deliberate limitation of the volume of motor traffic in our cities is quite unavoidable. The need for it simply cannot be escaped" (Buchanan, 1963, Steering Committee report, para. 30). The committee does not explain why "the whole idea" of limitation should be "distasteful" to it. Individually, we must assume that each of these eminent men, in the regulation of his personal life, had long since accepted the fact that limitation is inescapable and indeed necessary to the creation of form. As experienced men of affairs, they must also have realized that limitation is essential to the regulation of human institutions. I derive the impression that their "distaste" for limitation in this connection reflected a long-entrenched value attaching to the economic system of Britain in the nineteenth century, that strange epoch when the populations and technologies of Western peoples were expanding among unused resources and unoccupied spaces so vast that the idea of self-limitation was temporarily lost, and the arduous goal of choosing and realizing a "good," at the cost of all it would exclude was comfortably hidden behind the so much simpler objective of aggregating "goods."

The impression is strengthened by a later comment on the limitations that attach even to the possibility of limitation. Of these

> perhaps the most decisive is that a car-owning electorate will not stand for a severe restriction. It is a difficult and dangerous thing in a democracy, to try to prevent a substantial part of the population from doing things that they do not regard as wrong. (Buchanan, 1963, Steering Committee report, para. 31)

Since the Steering Committee members accept the report unreservedly, they presumably accept also its conclusion that unless regulation on a scale unprecedented is introduced at once, the car-owning electorate will have to stand for something more than a severe restriction. (It is standing for it or rather sitting for it already in many public places.) So the committee's comments presumably mean that the electorate will not stand for any restriction *imposed by authority*, rather than by the blind course of event. And the ground for this judgment is that in a "democracy" people think that state interference should be limited to the prohibition of things that are "wrong." The judgment may well be realistic, when applied not to any "democracy" but to our own today; but the value judgment of which it is a realistic appraisal is itself under fire and in course of change in many contexts.

The regulation of our society requires increasingly the prohibition of acts not because they are morally wrong but because they are socially inconvenient, and it thrusts onto the courts the task of enforcing these prohibitions as part of the criminal law. As Barbara Wootton (1963) has recently pointed out, this confuses a concept of crime and punishment deeply embedded in the consciousness of both judges and laymen and leads to incoherent and ineffective enforcement of the law in this area, of which "traffic offenses" form an important part. Clearly "a democracy" whose citizens do not regard it as wrong to break traffic laws, however necessary, will not enjoy the pleasure and convenience of car owning as far as it otherwise might; but to assume it incapable of learning any better seems to me defeatist. (The avoidance of income tax was once regarded very much as the avoidance of parking regulations now is.) Legislation in such matters is only one of the triggers of cultural change, and cultural change is a possibility that the Steering Committee seems to me to underrate.

On the need and possibility for organizational change the Steering Committee has no such reservations. It is clear that existing institutions could not carry out work on the scale required, and it recommends the creation of executive agencies, central and regional. Although the committee describe these truly as bodies "for which there is no precedent," both they and the reader feel themselves on more familiar ground in this part of the report. Public corporations acting as executive agencies have a long history in Britain and elsewhere. The mind has little difficulty in picturing these corporations—much less, at least, than in picturing the towns that they would create.

Finally, the Steering Committee comment on the cost. The true cost, they observe, is "the real burden of labour and materials that would be entailed" (Buchanan, 1963, Steering Committee report, para. 53). The money cost would be greater, since so much of the money cost would result from the purchase of land. Raising and paying out the money would present economic problems distinct from those involved in canalizing so much labor and materials to this use. It would, however, earn some indirect return in the increase of revenue from motor and fuel taxation. It is noteworthy that this monumental capital expenditure is never described in the report as an investment, nor is any reference made to the values of land and buildings that these developments would create or to the return that these might yield, as distinct from the return to be squeezed from the increased traffic. Something seems already to have muted the report's clarion call to regard vehicles and the accessibility they need as only one element in the planning of cities as a fit setting for all the activities of civilized urban life. That something is the inertia, necessary yet dangerous, of established ways of seeing and valuing what is and what might be.

*   *   *   *   *

Like the Buchanan committee, the Robbins committee was required to consider the results of an explosive increase in demand. The expected rate of increase in the demand for higher education, as estimated by the committee, was about the same as the expected rate of increase in motor vehicles as estimated by the Buchanan committee—nearly double in ten years, nearly treble in twenty years, with an even sharper rise in the first five years. The committee, however, was in the happy position of concluding that this demand not only should be met in full (a value judgment) but could be met in full (a reality judgment). The expansion would involve heavy physical development but far less than the rebuilding of our towns; heavy institutional development but on familiar lines. The budgetary problem was marginal, for higher education's share of the national budget, 0.8% in 1962, would need to grow to no more than 1.9% in twenty years. As the committee cautiously remarked, "It is quite conceivable that there are items in the present composition of the (national) budget that on calm consideration may be deemed less urgent than a better educated population" (Robbins, 1963, para. 636).

Nonetheless, the committee showed itself highly conscious of budgetary problems. Its definition of "real cost" is significantly different from that of the Buchanan Steering Committee. "The real cost of anything is what has to be foregone in order to have it." It devotes a whole section to "education as an investment" and stresses throughout that one main effect of expenditure on "higher education," most of it being current expenditure, is to maintain a national asset, "human capital," which is essential even to the merely economic well-being of a community such as Britain in a competitive world. It is at pains to discuss the reality of the return from the investment and the reasons why it cannot be measured. At some point, diminishing returns might set in but "there is a strong probability that the country would have to go a good deal beyond what is contemplated in our recommendations before the return in terms of social net product could be said to suggest general over-investment in this sector."

The terms of reference of the committee were

> to review the pattern of full time education in Great Britain and in the light of national needs and resources to advise . . . on what principles its development should be based. In particular . . . whether there should be any changes in that pattern, whether any new types of institution are desirable and whether any modifications should be made in the present arrangements for planning and co-ordinating the development of the various types of institution.

The committee was thus concerned with the redesign of an institutional rather than a physical milieu, and none of its recommendations, with one exception, required its readers to make a revaluation so radical as that required by the Buchanan report, in its estimate of accessibility as a "good" that every urban environment must limit in order to optimize all its values. Indeed, it sets no difficult problems of valuation as such. That higher education should be available for all who can benefit from it and wish to do so, that it should be almost wholly financed by public funds, that the bodies that receive these grants should be free as they are now to decide how to spend them, that individuals thus freely educated should owe no formal obligation to the society that had done so—all these basic values are either taken for granted or asserted and justified, and none of them struck a controversial note.

Nonetheless, the Robbins report invites the reader to accept a radical rearrangement of its subject matter: "For the greater part of their history the universities which were more or less independent of the state, dominated the landscape of higher education" (Robbins, 1963, para. 14). Their isolation had been eroded, partly by their increased dependence on state support (canalized though it was through the University Grants Committee), partly by the rise of near-university-level, technical colleges; teacher training colleges; and other institutions that had grown up within the "state" system of education. The time had come in the view of the committee to group together these institutions of "higher" education. This involves a mental adjustment of a peculiarly difficult and complex kind. Institutions previously recognized as part of the state system of education must be taken out of that category, grouped with others (the universities) that have hitherto strenuously and successfully resisted such grouping in a new category called "higher education" that must then in turn be related more closely than before to "secondary" education.

This logical step had its dangers and can be discussed as an educational and as an organizational issue. I am concerned not with its merits but with its psychological and more precisely its epistemological implications. The reader is invited to change his categories of thought and that in a more radical and painful way than anything involved in the Buchanan report. It is not unduly difficult to subdivide the contents of a given concept, to replace, for example, the concept of a street by a number of concepts each providing for one or more of the many functions of that multipurpose space. It is much harder to regroup the objects of our attention in new categories that straddle the boundaries of the concepts they replace. Administrators know the difficulty in another form; in reorganizing institutions, it is easiest to subdivide, more difficult to combine, and most difficult to carve up and regroup the constituents in a going concern. The difficulty illustrates and is perhaps related to the more basic psychological difficulties attending the growth of the categories that underlie our judgments of reality.

A complex net of values is attached to the concept of the university. Any change in this concept—in particular the attempt to include in the category institutions from a category hitherto sharply distinguished—implies a threat to these values. Behind the discussion of merits and demerits, this threat adds its often unidentified note of warning. It was this that made so significant the question whether higher education as newly defined should be the responsibility of the minister responsible for other education or of some other minister. Whichever the recommendation, it would carry a threatening message to numbers of its most concerned readers—in the one case the threat of an intention to "isolate," in the other the threat of an intention to "level down." No words can neutralize such implications. It is significant that this is the only aspect of the enquiry that elicited a dissentient report.

The report, like all such exercises, is not merely a plan for a reorganization of our institutions. It is also a plea for the reorganization of our thought.

One other aspect of the report deserves attention from the point of view of this enquiry. The report recognized that the expansion that it proposed depends on an adequate supply of teachers. Since an increase in the numbers of students produces almost automatically a corresponding increase in the number of *potential* teachers, the committee saw no reason to suppose that their plans would in the long run demand an increase in the proportion of graduates needed by the teaching profession. They recorded, however, that at the time of their report, recruitment was growing more difficult, the proportion of highly qualified teachers in schools was falling, and the emigration of academic professionals, especially to America, gave ground for serious concern. They stressed the need to make teaching in higher education sufficiently competitive both in its rewards and in its conditions of work and the ways in which this could be done; but in their estimates of expense, they make no provision for these changes in direct and indirect inducements, nor did they refer to the difficulty of ensuring that universities would or could make these qualitative changes in condition of work, even if the money were available, at a time when they would, as the report recognized, be overstretched to meet the demands of increased quantitative standards. This was clearly the bottleneck where, especially in the immediate future, the optimizing-balancing skill of the policymaker would be most sharply called on, both at government level, in giving higher education a degree of precedence that must leave a lasting impression on it, and in the universities, in reconciling quantitative and qualitative demands. It is possible for a reader to feel that the report does not fully face the most critical area of true cost, namely the problem of ensuring that the potential teachers of the immediate future do what the report wants them to do, to the exclusion of "what has to be foregone in order to have it." Their hesitancy in this regard parallels the hesitancy of the Buchanan Steering Committee, when faced with regulation demanding a cultural change that cannot be directly achieved by reorganization.

* * * * *

The Royal Commission on Capital Punishment[1] (Gowers, 1953) was required

> to consider and report whether liability under the criminal law in Great Britain to suffer capital punishment for murder should be

limited or modified and if so to what extent and by what means, for
how long and under what conditions persons who would otherwise
have been liable to suffer capital punishment should be detained
and what changes in the existing law and the prison system would
be required, and to enquire into and take account of the position in
those countries whose experience and practice may throw light on
these questions.

Thus, the commission was not concerned, like the Buchanan
committee, with a reorganization of the physical milieu or, like the
Robbins commission, with a reorganization of the institutional
milieu. It was concerned with the reorganization of a small but
important part of the penal law. This was occasioned not by an
expected influx of murderers (as the others were occasioned by an
expected influx of motor cars and of students) but by a change in
the valuations current in society. Opposition was growing to the
death penalty as such, and this new standard of value was shoul-
dering its way into the closely organized, traditionally sanctioned
ways of classifying and valuing offenses embodied in the criminal
law and in the social conscience in which that law must rest. The
change was not universally accepted; opinion was divided. The
government of the day wished to make some gesture of acknowl-
edgment toward it, without fully accepting it, and at the same time
to extend and clarify the public debate on it, which was unusually
impassioned.

So it appointed the Royal Commission on Capital Punishment
with terms of reference designed to exclude a recommendation on
or even a discussion of the *abolition* of the death penalty for
murder.

The commission prefaces its report with a statement of what it
has done, in words that should make a psychologist's imagination
boggle.

> Our duty . . . has been to look for means of confining the scope of
> (capital) punishment as narrowly as possible without impairing the
> efficacy attributed to it. We had . . . to consider . . . how far the
> scope of capital punishment . . . is already restricted in practice and
> by what means; and whether those means are satisfactory as far as
> they go . . . how far capital punishment has . . . that special efficacy

which it is commonly believed to have. We had . . . to study the development of the law of murder and . . . to consider whether certain forms of homicide should be taken out of that category and to what extent the liability . . . might be restricted on account of . . . youth or sex or . . . provocation . . . the extent to which insanity . . . should . . . negative or diminish criminal responsibility . . . whether murder should be redefined . . . whether any defects . . . could be better remedied by giving either the judge or the jury a discretionary power.

and so on; leading to the conclusion:

We thought it right to report at some length . . . in the belief that, *irrespective of our recommendation* [italics added], it would be useful . . . to place on record a comprehensive and dispassionate picture of the whole subject.

The nature of appreciative judgment could not be better illustrated or defined.

By far the greater part of the report is devoted to describing all relevant aspects of the situation as it is and as it might be, by applying to a great variety of fact and opinion, partly conflicting, the selective, critical, and integrating mental activity that I have called reality judgment. This is interspersed with comments expressing the commissioners' own approval or disapproval, their value judgments. Each section ends with recommendations for action, with instrumental judgments.

The reality judgment is voluminous and complex. What homicides fall within the legal definition of murder? What kind and degree of insanity exclude the offense; what kind and degree of provocation reduce it to manslaughter? How varied are the motives and circumstances attending these crimes and the personalities of those who commit them? What is the purpose and what the effect of death or any punishment in such diverse cases? What are the respective roles of prosecutor, judge, jury, and home secretary in deciding which of those convicted shall hang? To these and many other questions answers are offered, definite or tentative, with whatever historical background is needed to make the present explicable.

The report has a double story to tell—the story of the relevant events and the story of the relevant ideas—and it moves easily, unconsciously between the two. The numbers and details of murders committed, of convictions, reprieves, executions belong to the world of event. The attitudes of men to murder and to the death penalty, the interaction of these two in giving murder a special status among crimes, these belong to the world of ideas, a world no less susceptible of factual report. Between the two worlds is an infinity of subtle, mutual connections that the commissioners must disentangle as best they may; for these interactions lie at the heart of the problems committed to them. What is, what should be, the relation between criminal responsibility as a legal fact, defined by the common law; responsibility as a medical fact, defined, they are assured, by the criminal's neural organization at the time and thus no less factual than the law but assessable only by the often divergent judgments of psychiatrists; and responsibility as a normative judgment passed by men on men, a standard of what *should be deemed to be* the scope and limits of their responsibility, yet a standard not without effect on the actual state of minds that know they are to be judged by it.

Based though it is on the present and the past, the reality judgment is concerned primarily with the future, which alone can be affected by any change now made. The death penalty could be limited by changing the definition of the offense or by subdividing it into "degrees" or by admitting a discretion as to sentence. The reality judgment must arrive at an assessment of the probable effect of these alternatives, collecting what evidence seems relevant about the experience of other countries that have abolished, relaxed, or reinstated the death penalty and about the problems attending the long-term custody of prisoners convicted of crimes of violence.

Some of this evidence is significant in two distinct ways. The commissioners, having collected the views of police officers on whether abatement of the death penalty will increase violent resistance to arrest, must evaluate these statements of opinion both as evidence of what is likely to happen in the world of event and as evidence of what is actually happening in the world of ideas. For the apprehensions of the police about the effect of a change in the law, whether well or ill founded, is both a fact and a force in the present situation and one that may indirectly alter the effect that such a change will actually have—for example, the willingness of police officers in Britain to continue to work unarmed.

The evidence on which the commissioners found their reality judgment varies vastly in certainty and in character. Statistics and estimates; opinions, often discordant, on matters both of fact and of value; the views of different authorities, past and present, on the legitimate purposes of punishment; the views of psychiatrists on human responsibility and its impairment by mental illness—all this and more goes into the mill and out comes the reality judgment, balanced, coherent, urbane, a mental artifact that only familiarity robs of the wonder that is its due.

The report is also sprinkled with the commissioners' own value judgments—usually expressed as agreement with value judgments found as a fact to exist in the community but nonetheless their own. Insanity *should be* a defense to murder. The then existing rules defining insanity for this purpose were narrower than they *should be*. Among the sane who are convicted of murder, culpability varies so much that they *should not* all be sentenced to the uniform, extreme, and irreversible penalty of death. The abatement of this penalty *should not* be left to so great an extent to the home secretary. It *should not* be left to the judge; or (for different reasons) to the jury. It *should be* expressed in the law itself. In these and a dozen other contexts, the commissioners, going beyond the recording of other people's value judgments, commit themselves to value judgments of their own. Whence came the norms that produced these value judgments?

The answer is simple but subtle. The commissioners used the norms that they brought with them to the conference table; but these norms were changed and developed by the very process of applying them—by the impact of the reality judgment that they focused; by the impact, attrition, and stimulus of each commissioner on the others; and by the exercise of their own minds as they applied them in one way or another, on one hypothesis after another, in the search for a better "fit." As an illustration, consider their debate on the use of the home secretary's power of reprieve.

It was their value judgment that, among people convicted of murder, culpability varied so much that punishment should also be variable. This, they realized, could be achieved (within their terms of reference) only by elaborating the definition of the crime or by giving someone discretion to vary the penalty to suit the facts. The first alternative they found in practice to be immensely difficult. The second was already in operation, in that nearly half those convicted of murder were reprieved on the recommendation of the home secretary. Was it "satisfactory" or even "proper" that so large a discretion should be vested in the home secretary? Eminent witnesses were divided. To make the home secretary "an additional court of appeal, sitting in private, judging on the record only and giving no reason for his decision" said some, "does not fit into the constitutional framework of this country." The Archbishop of Canterbury objected on different grounds.

> It is intolerable that this solemn and deeply significant procedure should be enacted again and again, when in almost half the cases the consequence will not follow . . . a mere empty formula is a degradation of the law and dangerous to society.

Other distinguished witnesses found it not at all intolerable. The late Lord Samuel suggested that "to maintain a degree of uncertainty as to what would happen in marginal cases may be very useful in retaining a deterrent effect on potential criminals."

The commissioners' appreciative judgment was that the home secretary's discretion was "undue"; but the only less objectionable alternative seemed to them still too repugnant to recommend. So their appreciative judgments on the point were expressed without any recommendation for executive action. Such recommendations as they did make, they admitted, "would go very little way toward solving our general problem" (i.e., how to relieve the executive of this undue responsibility). They concluded that

> if capital punishment is to be retained and at the same time the defects of the existing law are to be eliminated . . . the only practicable way of achieving this object is to give discretion to the jury to find extenuating circumstances requiring a lesser sentence to be substituted.

This appreciation, though without an executive recommendation and indeed all the more on that account is perhaps the most important part of the report; for it amounts to a finding that there was no satisfactory halfway house between the existing state of affairs and the *abolition* of the death penalty. Their terms of reference precluded them from recommending or even considering abolition; yet a major contribution of their report to the appreciative judgment of their contemporaries was to support the movement for abolition that had in fact occasioned their appointment. The report made some recommendations for action. Some were adopted in the Homicide Act, 1957; some were ignored. Yet if all had been ignored, the major importance of the report as an appreciative judgment would have remained the same. The state of the commissioners' minds on the subject of capital punishment, after they had made their appreciation, was different from what it was when they began; and this change, communicated through the report, provoked change, similar or dissimilar, in greater or lesser degree, in all it reached, from serious students to casual readers of newspaper paragraphs, and thus released into the stream of events and into the stream of ideas an addition to the countless forces by which both are molded.

Yet their terms of reference, on the face of them, required them only to recommend means to a given end.

Note

1. The following summary of the report is taken from the paper "Appreciative Behaviour" (Vickers, 1963a).

4

The Appreciative System

THE THREE REPORTS THAT I HAVE EXAMINED deal with widely different matters and were occasioned by widely different situations, but they all exemplify the mental process that I have called appreciation and provide material for a closer analysis.[1]

Appreciation manifests itself in the exercise through time of mutually related judgments or reality and value. These appreciative judgments reflect the view currently held by those who make them of their interests and responsibilities, views largely implicit and unconscious that nonetheless condition what events and relations they will regard as relevant or possibly relevant to them and whether they will regard these as welcome or unwelcome, important or unimportant, demanding or not demanding action or concern by them. Such judgments disclose what can best be described as a set of readinesses to distinguish some aspects of the situation rather than others and to classify and value these in this way rather than in that. I will describe these readinesses as an appreciative system. I call them a system because they seem to be organized as a whole in ways to which I will return, being so interrelated that a change in one part of the system is likely to affect and be dependent on changes elsewhere. I will describe the current state of such a system as its *setting*, as we speak of the setting of a man-made regulator, to describe the governing relations to which it is for the time being set to respond (though with the mental reservation that in human systems this setting is to some degree self-set); and I will describe the settings of several such systems as an *appreciative field* when I am concerned with the way in which they interact with each other.

These readinesses have to be learned; and like all learning, they are necessarily limiting, as well as enabling. They facilitate further learning consistent with the patterns that they create; but they create "unreadinesses" to see, to value, and to respond in ways inconsistent with those patterns. The readiness to conceive a street as a multipurpose space, to identify higher education with universities, to regard murder as a closed and homogeneous category of event are in various ways impediments to the mental readjustments that the relevant report advocates.

Limiting though they must be, such readinesses are precious; for without them, we could not see or value or respond to *anything* in *any* way. Even physical perception depends on learning perceptual categories by which to classify experience. The child learns to recognize cows in all their variety by their correspondence with some generalized schema in which "cowishness" has come to reside; yet the very schema was developed by the experience of seeing actual cows and will be amplified and if need be corrected by its further use. The medical student cannot read a pulmonary radiograph until experience of many has built up an interpretative schema; nor can he build up a schema except by exposing himself to individual experiences.[2]

Perceptual schemata are only one class of concept, all of which are built up in the same way. "Street," "university," "murder" are not data but concepts defining categories of experience that it has been found convenient to group together. Each schema derives its meaning both from the experiences that it subsumes and from its relation to other concepts similarly developed. Changes that would

shake this conceptual system are resisted with vehemence propor-
tionate to the extent of the threat; and the extent of the threat
varies, as I observed in relation to the Robbins (1963) report, with
the nature of the change involved. It is minimal when the change
is by differentiation within an established concept; greater when
it comes through the recognition of a wider category under which
several established concepts can be subsumed; and greatest when
it involves the dissolution of a concept and the distribution of its
contents among others.

The mutual relations that link these readinesses into a system
are threefold. They form part of the system by which the individual
makes sense of the *observed* world in which he lives and its
configuration in space and time. They form part also of the system
by which he makes sense of the *communicated* world that he shares
with his fellow men. They form part, too, of the system by which
he makes sense of his *experienced* world and hence of himself.
These distinctions are, of course, unduly sharp, but I find them
convenient. When all three systems reinforce each other, change
is at its hardest. A contemporary of Galileo who accepted the
heliocentric system had to reinterpret the evidence of his senses,
revise his ideas of creation, and subscribe to what his society
regarded as a dangerous heresy. He was lucky if none of these
demanded overt change in his behavior or his conversation so that
the confusing leaven could be allowed time to work its changes
out. Some of the equally radical changes of our own day do not
allow us so comfortable and prolonged a period of latency.

A highly organized mind is one that comprehends the variety
of experience in a number of conceptual patterns, overlapping but
not mutually inconsistent. A flexible mind is one that readily alters
its conceptual patterns so as to assimilate change without a pro-
hibitive increase in incoherence. These mental skills have and will
always have their limits, though these will be greatly enlarged,
when our society has come to regard its appreciative system and
those of all its members as precious, irreversible but always unfin-
ished works of art.[3]

The development of an appreciative system, at once enabling
and limiting, is the inner history of an individual, an organization,
and a society. It may have psychopathological features, such as

undue rigidity or *irrational* structures—few wholly escape such blemishes—but even if it had none, it would remain an artifact, a unique interpretative screen, yielding one among many possible ways of interpreting and valuing experience.

Although both reality judgment and value judgment are involved in appreciation and are indeed inseparable concepts, I have found it convenient to distinguish between them; and I find it equally convenient to distinguish the underlying settings that they express; for the facility with which the appreciative system can change depends in part on the extent to which the reality setting is charged with "value." To conceive a city center in which all the functions of a street except vehicular circulation, parking, and access to buildings are raised several feet into the air, requires an effort of visual imagination, for which individuals may be most variously gifted, but it does not greatly disturb our valuations; for streets as such are relatively neutral concepts in terms of value. Universities on the other hand carry for most people sufficient positive value to imply a potential threat in an even partial assimilation of their status with that of institutions not similarly valued. Murder carries a much more intense, though negative, charge and is thereby fortified against conceptual change.

These charges have become attached to these concepts because the concepts exemplify relations that are thus valued. A value system, however, has also its own concepts that are of wider generality—for example freedom. Among the many common connotations of this concept in Britain today is the one that the Buchanan (1963) Steering Committee defined—the absence of any attempt by the state to restrain the individual from anything that he does not regard as "wrong"—wrong being another concept with a highly specialized meaning in our contemporary culture. Thus, resistance to the idea of traffic limitation, naturally unwelcome in itself, is fortified by resonance through the whole value concept of freedom, while the idea of "traffic architecture" encounters no such barrier to its access, except insofar as it awakens the still pejorative implications attached to the concept of "planning."

I find it convenient to regard an appreciative system as a net, of which weft and warp are reality concepts and value concepts. Reality concepts classify experience in ways that may be variously valued. Value concepts classify types of relation that may appear in various configurations of experience. I will develop this model later.

Among the most important facts that we have to appreciate are the appreciative settings of our fellows. What I have called the history of ideas is neither more nor less than the development of the appreciative systems that govern historical agents, including those that we ourselves share and that, consequently, we must use in the process of appreciation. The possibilities and limitations, hopes and dangers, that attach to the attempt of an appreciative system thus to appreciate itself are not yet charted. It is an ancient exercise of philosophers, but it is only recently that cultural anthropologists began to explore this hall of mirrors, and the rest of us are as yet by no means at home in it. In consequence, business executives and physical scientists—though seldom politicians or civil servants—still sometimes tend to regard the appreciative judgment of persons other than themselves as facts of a second order of reality—only "what people think," as opposed to "what actually is." It is true, of course, that judgments of reality need the most objective verifications of which they admit, but this is much less than is commonly supposed. There is no more basic reality than the appreciative settings of our fellows—except, for ourselves, our own. It is for this reason that I refer to findings of fact as judgments, no less than to our valuations and our proposed executive solutions.

The value judgments of men and societies cannot be *proved* correct or incorrect; they can only be *approved* as right or *condemned* as wrong by the exercise of another value judgment. The budget of the local authority in my first example shows a particular distribution of resources between objects as disparate as sewage disposal and the care of the old. By what criterion can conservatives or reformers prove that resources now devoted to this should be reallocated to that; or that the total resources available for public spending by the authority should be increased or reduced and the residue in the private sector change correspondingly? There are abundant arguments that our further "appreciations" may distinguish as legitimate or illegitimate (a judgment of value) and as likely to be more or less cogent (a judgment of reality); but there are no "external," "objective" criteria (in the narrow sense that we have come to attach to the term) to which appeal can directly be made. In the endless political debate on such matters, which include most of the most vital valuations of our time, each disputant can only expose to the others those aspects of the proposal that he thinks most likely to bring the others' appreciative settings into line with his own. If no change results, he can accuse his unconvinced opponent of inhumanity or irresponsibility, of being out of date or deviant, even of being unable or unwilling to "face facts," but not of placing an "illogical" value on the facts faced.

We need not conclude that views on these matters are merely a matter of personal taste; the entire political dialogue of the world—that is, its endless debate about policy—would be palpably futile if this were so. Nor need we—or, I think, can we—conclude that they are "given," however unconsciously, by our economic or other interests, unless we penetrate much more deeply into the process of which our interests are both products and generators. Marx's influence could not possibly have been so great if the views they changed or displaced had been as "determined" as his theory asserted. We have to assume, as I shall try to show, an inner criterion, self-set and constantly reset by every exercise—as the value judgments of the commissioners about capital punishment and those of their fellow countrymen were affected by the actual process of their appreciation. This self-determining process is the main subject of this book.

Reality judgments are more susceptible of "proof"; yet if we examine the reality judgment of the commissioners, how few, in fact, are provable, even after the event. Some are estimates of probability. In the event, the improbable may happen; but the estimate is not thereby proved faulty. Some are of facts essentially unobservable and never clearly demonstrable, such as the state of people's opinions; and of these a special and extensive class are facts that are changed by every reported observation—as public opinion is changed by every published report, purporting to describe its state (see MacKay, 1964). The word *judgment* is appropriately used even of reality judgment; for the more complex the subject matter, the more the relevant facts are matters of judgment.

Moreover the relevant facts are necessarily only a selection of all that might have been noticed. They are selected for their "relevance"—to what? To the value judgment that makes them interesting and significant. Their selection no less than their validity is a matter of judgment.

Instrumental judgments are commonly supposed to be demonstrable as right or wrong at least (if they are acted on) after the event. Unhappily, this too is fallacious. The more complex the situation in which we act, the less verifiable by experience is the effect of our own actions and inactions. For the information derived from feedback is of two kinds. It tells us the trend, up to the moment of last comparison, between actual and norm. It may or may not tell us something about the effect of our own would-be remedial actions in the past; for these may return for judgment so long after the event and so intermixed with other more important variables as to give us neither confirmation of the past nor guidance for the future. Moreover, unlike experimental rats, our blundering alters not only ourselves but our maze; so we never run the same maze twice. Who can prove that even the most disastrous foreign policy had *results* that were *worse* than those of some conceivable alternative? Even our executive judgments come ultimately to the bar of appreciation. Yet as our own judges in that ultimate court of appeal we show remarkable assurance—reminiscent, sometimes, of that apocryphal judge who silenced a protesting counsel with, "Mr. X, this court may sometimes be in error; but it is never in doubt."[4]

The terms that I have developed in this chapter are intended as conveniently simplified descriptions of the skills involved in policy making. Two of these are familiar. To represent to oneself—or to others, as the commissioners do—the present state and probable future course of relevant events is a familiar exercise, and when we see it supremely well done, we recognize excellence in the capacity to comprehend and analyze a complex situation extended in time, to assess the outcome of multiple, causal interactions, to apply appropriate time scales, to comprehend uncertainties, most of all perhaps to simplify without distorting by excluding the inessential. This is the skill I have called *reality judgment*. We recognize also as a skill the ingenuity that produces apt solutions to the problems set by such surveys of "reality," calculated to change the pattern of expected relationships by responses perhaps never tried before. This is the skill I have called *instrumental judgment*. We recognize that both these can to some extent be learned; and we accept, when we reflect on it, that in learning we include both assimilating useful information and techniques and developing skills in their use.

We are less accustomed to regard valuation as a skill, which needs and admits of learning; but I find it necessary to include this also in an analysis of policy making. Men, institutions, and societies learn what to want as well as how to get, what to be as well as what to do. They learn not only new valuations but also increased skill in valuing; and they learn these things by the activity of appreciation. Since our ideas of regulation, like our associated ideas of adaptation, were largely formed in relation to norms that can be deemed to be given (at least for the time span involved), they need to be radically revised in relation to norms that change with the effort made to pursue them.

These three skills are closely related. What I have called reality judgment begins with the selection of what is relevant; and this relevance is a matter of valuation. It involves predictions based on alternative suppositions; and insofar as the likelihood of these alternatives can be affected by the agent, they provide material for instrumental judgment. I have already stressed that the three labels denote three aspects of one mental activity. It is nonetheless useful to distinguish them, if only because the skills are different. In the next three chapters, I will discuss what seems to me their most important aspects—prediction, innovation, and valuation.

Notes

1. This chapter and, indeed, the whole development of the concept of appreciation may be taken as a contribution to the science for which Professor Boulding (1961) in his well-known book, *The Image*, proposed the name of *eiconics*, though I would hope that this branch of epistemology will not be limited by the implications of the word *image*.

2. I am indebted to M. L. Johnson Abercrombie's (1960) interesting study, *The Anatomy of Judgment*, for a summary of the findings on this point.

3. This is nowhere more needed than in the current attempts of predominantly white Western states to adapt their appreciative systems so as to include dark-skinned fellow citizens in a manner that will prove workable, internally consistent, and acceptable to all concerned. The first step is to recognize that this is an operation much more complex than the elimination of "prejudice" and the acceptance of "fact." An appreciative system so revised as to be acceptable will be no less a work of art.

4. It is important, I think, to accept the fact that purposeful and calculated action takes place even when the conditions necessary to regulation appear to be absent. What techniques come into play in these circumstances is a question deserving a more careful answer than I can attempt here. I tentatively explored the question in two earlier papers—"Stability, Control and Choice" (the ninth Wallberg Lecture, Vickers, 1956b) and "Positive and Negative Controls in Business" (Vickers, 1958a), a paper published in the *Journal of Industrial Economics*.

5

Prediction

◆ THE POWER, EXEMPLIFIED BY THE REPORTS, to make what I have called reality judgments, is strange and would be startling if it were not so familiar. These mental artifacts are derived from observations and (far more) from communications by mental processes often complex and prolonged, resulting in inferences, forecasts, estimates, and conclusions, which may be stored and further processed to an extent still unknown. It would not be relevant to this book to discuss (even were I competent to do so) how far the neural processes by which these things are accomplished can be modeled by the digital and analogue computers that the system engineer can now command or conceive in theory. I shall assume only that we have today no adequate reason for refusing to believe in our capacity for doing any of the things that we manifestly do. This is itself no small advance.

The skills involved in forming reality judgments include skills in originating hypotheses ("suppose we did so-and-so"), and this anchors these also to the instrumental judgment. The solutions proposed by the Buchanan (1963) and Robbins (1963) committees and the Gower (1953) commission, like those proposed by the manager in the earlier example, depended on this capacity for representing to themselves—and relying on the capacity of others to represent to themselves—possible realities that do not yet exist and may never exist. This aspect of reality judgment I will pursue further in the next chapter. The use of reality judgment is not, however, confined to such innovating initiative. Its basic use is to supply a predictive picture of what is going to happen next. Even the helmsman regulates his wheel movements not by reference only to the current deviation of the ship's head but by reference to forecasts of its future movements, derived from current information by methods subtler than extrapolation. Similarly the local authority regulates its building program by comparing its expected results when completed with the demands on it that are to be expected then and thereafter.

This power and need to make and respond to a representation of the future is characteristic of all human behavior; and though it is to be found in some degree among other creatures, it seems to have attained in man a new dimension of significance. Psychologically, I believe that this power deserves far more attention than has yet been given to it, as a constituent both in human capacity and human vulnerability. If indeed humans have grafted on to an age-old biological capacity for "action now" a more recently evolved capacity for envisaging a future to which only limited adjustments can as yet be made, we should expect that the enlarged capacity would bring increased stress and increased capacity for error as well as increased power.[1] And if this were so even in static societies, we should expect it to be far more so in the self-exciting and self-changing societies in which we live today.

The static societies of the past depended on prediction in varying degrees. Agriculture became possible only when men learned to recognize and respond to needs not apparent in the immediate circumstances of time and place—for example, the need not to eat their seed corn. The farmer's life is full of *latent urgencies*, times for ploughing, harrowing, sowing set by needs still many months away. Over some forgotten span of years, these needs were worked out, by intellectual effort as well as trial and error, and the discipline needed to meet them was slowly built into the pattern of life, each season calling for its own contribution. In our time, the latent urgencies are more demanding and less repetitive. The Buchanan (1963) report and the Robbins (1963) report are unusually ambitious efforts to forecast major changes soon enough to respond to them. Each of them emphasizes the *latent urgency* of the situation. Action must be begun years, even decades before the situation that it is to meet is presently visible. The last possible moment for effective response may pass long before the need for it is even noticed. That situations of this kind develop ever more frequently in these days is evident from the frequency with which such special machinery is set up to appreciate them. This results from a combination of two opposite trends—on the one hand, increase in the speed and frequency of major changes in the physical, institutional, and cultural milieu; on the other hand, increase in the time needed to mount adequate responses to such changes. It may well be that in all the more important spheres of corporate life, such as those covered by the Buchanan and Robbins reports, the minimal conditions for effective regulation have already ceased to exist.

The scale of prediction can be better observed in a more common context. The steel buyer in an earlier example, before the crisis in which we discovered him, was conducting his affairs on the basis of a set of confident predictions, many of them too confident to be conscious. That markets available to him today would be available tomorrow, that contracts made last month would be fulfilled, that steel delivered would correspond with what had been ordered—all these and many more working assumptions underlay his daily activities. None of them was absolutely certain, but each of them was certain enough to act on. As week followed week, actual experience confirmed these expectations and strengthened his confidence in relying on them.

The signal that alerted him to the likelihood that some of these assumptions might cease to hold, may have been (as I observed earlier) actual, repeated experience of their departing from the expected—say, of continually lengthening delivery dates. Alternatively, the signal may have been given simply by change in his predictions, based on his appreciation of the probable effects of negotiations in the steel industry. The second is a more refined operation than the first. It involves responding to an inner representation, derived from a variety of information by a complex mental process; and this is neither so easy nor so common as we tend to suppose. It may be, as I observed earlier, that the appreciation of trends did no more than alert him to the possibility of change and turn his attention to the field in which actual changes would first be seen—to give him, what in psychological language would be called a "set," a narrower concept than what I describe as a "setting."[2]

In any case, the comparison of the actual course of events, as it unrolls, with the previous forecast has a double effect. It confirms or revises the regulator's expectation of the course of events. It also confirms or shakes his confidence in his power of prediction or in the range of its reliability. It may have either effect without the other; and the second may be more important and far-reaching than the first. Through the first, he only corrects his predictions. Through the second, he may learn to predict better or may learn the extent to which he can hope to predict at all. The ongoing process of predicting and correcting by experience is in itself a cyclical process of problem setting, problem solving, and *learning*.

For the steel buyer, the subject of the predictive judgment is a set of variables largely beyond the control of the predictor. He may predict but he cannot control the course of the steel market or (except marginally) the policies of steelmakers. All he can do is to change his own policies to match changes or expected changes in the milieu. This might be described as the classic case of biological adaptation. The agent must adapt himself to the situation; he cannot adapt the situation to himself.

I will next take an example where prediction relates to the expected outcome of the predictor's own behavior.

A contractor tendering for a building contract plans the manifold operations needed to complete it and phases them in time in the most economical way. Since experience tells him that such contracts seldom go wholly according to plan, he makes some allowances both in money and time for contingencies. Nonetheless, the variables that he has to estimate, such as the prices and dates of delivery of materials, the availability of labor, even the time likely to be needed to get necessary approvals and consents, are for the most part predictable within sufficiently narrow limits to be worth predicting.

I will suppose that his tender is accepted. He plots on charts the planned course of his operations; and month by month he plots against them his actual achievement. If performance falls behind the plan—or even is shown by prediction to be likely to do so—he is alerted to the need to correct the deviation; and the first step will be to find out where, among all the constituents of the plan, the deviation is occurring, whether the cause is transitory or continuing, curable or not. His plan operates as a norm in two senses; it represents both what is to be expected (given everyone's best efforts) and also what is to be desired. And again, concordance and nonconcordance of plan and performance have a double meaning for the contractor. They confirm or disprove that the operation is "going according to plan"; and they confirm or question the validity of the plan. If operations cannot be brought into line with the plan, the plan must be altered to bring it within the possibility of performance. For it is the resultant of many planned operations phased in time to ensure that men, money, and materials should be ready when and where they are wanted, and failure of one operation may require the rephasing of many others.

I turn now to a third example, yet a little more complex. An engineering firm planning a new model of some appliance, specifies the requirements on which its designers are to work, knowing that the resultant product cannot reach the market for, say, two or three years. It plans and phases the operations that in that period are to turn specifications into prototype and thence into a product assembled from a host of components, each designed, manufactured, or bought and fed into the assembly line as required—the tool designing, the testing, the publicity, an operation at least as complex as that of the building contractor. But unlike the contractor, it must also forecast the demand for the product in the market as it will be some years hence in competition with other products most of which are unknown, are indeed in the same state of planning on the drawing boards of competitors. Thus, the engineering firm regulates its course according to a norm that is not only itself predictive but that derives its validity from wider predictions about the development of the market and the activities of competitors, predictions that contain wide margins of error. In many markets, the only thing that the firm and all its competitors can predict with certainty is that some, at least, of them will be proved wrong; for few markets are so elastic that they could absorb the aggregate of what every supplier would regard as success.

In such a situation, each supplier needs flexibility in those points on which prediction is most uncertain—in particular, freedom to vary output to meet demand and design to suit preferences. These, however, are the points on which mass production is least flexible. The resultant conflict is not confined to the field of competitive mass production.

In the regulative cycle, the making of any response involves the commitment of resources for a period of time; and the importance of a response may be measured by the minimum size and duration of the commitments that it involves. This minimum is rising. The size and duration of the commitment that the engineering firm must make to produce *any* new model in replacement of an existing model is greater than it was with the manufacturing methods and machines of fifty years ago. Equally, the size and duration of the commitment needed to make *any* adequate response to the situation disclosed by the Buchanan (1963) report is greater than that required by either the planning problems or the traffic problems of a few decades earlier. The tendency is natural, indeed inevitable.

On the other hand, the situations that invite these more massive commitments do not allow us a correspondingly longer time in which to plan them. On the contrary, they are themselves the product of an increasing rate of change in all the major variables affecting the relations that we want to regulate. If in our crowded island, motor cars and would-be graduates (to take only the two variables thrown up by my examples) are expected to triple in twenty years, it is inevitable that the commitments involved in any adequate response should be far greater than were needed when these variables were changing slowly or not at all and (probably) far beyond the capacity of institutions developed in response to a much slower rate of change. It is inevitable also that they should make unprecedented demands on our (biologically recent and socially very untried) capacities for responding quickly to un-precedented situations present only as predictions of the mind.

Whatever other limits there may be to our capacity to respond to such a challenge, one limiting condition seems obvious. We must at least believe our own predictions. It is, however, a disquieting feature of our situation that in many fields change is becoming not only more rapid but more unpredictable. The Buchanan committee explores carefully the question whether within twenty years the motor car may have been replaced by some wholly new form of personal locomotion; and although they think this possibility can be excluded for the purpose of their report, they cannot *prove* a negative, and the persuasiveness of their judgment is affected by the general climate of opinion about prediction in the field of technology. That within twenty years the cheapest fuel in Britain may be gas made not at all from coal is a prediction seriously made today that was unreal twenty years ago.

Technological change, important as it is, is neither the most important nor the least predictable change of our time. That in the early 1960s only two areas of Africa would not consist politically of independent African states, that the German currency would be stronger than sterling or the U.S. dollar—these are two examples of change not predictable in the 1940s and imply the certainty of changes by the 1980s that are not predictable now. The regulative problems posed by the Buchanan (1963) and Robbins (1963) reports arise within a small, relatively predictable area of a large and unpredictable future; and even some of their predictions may go astray. The Buchanan report accepted a projection made in 1962 that the population would increase by some 50% in forty years; yet in 1949, the Royal Commission on Population predicted that by that time the population would already have begun to decline. Both necessarily depended on assumptions about volatile variables, notably the average size of families.

In the unpredictable area of life where "wisdom lies in masterful administration of the unforeseen," rigidity is to be feared and flexibility is to be prized; and this is the source of the dilemma that faces would-be regulators, whether in the boardroom of a small enterprise or at the center of government. Massive change demands massive commitments and hence no small element of rigidity. Unpredictable change demands flexibility. Change both massive and unpredictable makes inconsistent demands for rigidity on the one hand and flexibility on the other and poses the most basic policy choice of all, the choice of what to regard as regulable. For the decision to retain liberty of action and hence flexibility by deferring commitment is in fact the decision to regard the situation as for the time being too uncertain to regulate, a decision that may be wise but that has its own costs.[3]

This threatening situation is itself capable of adjustment in three dimensions, two of which have as yet scarcely been tried. The first is in improving and increasing the use of prediction, where this is possible. There are limits to this; for variables differ inherently in their predictability. The demand on British elementary schools five years hence is very much more predictable than the demand on British prisons at the same date. All the factors that determine the first are known and fairly predictable; almost all the factors that determine the second are not known and may be inherently unpredictable. Where a basis for prediction exists, we are much better placed than we were to make the prediction and determine its degree of probability.

The second possibility is the acceptance of risk. It may be that commitments as vast as our present atomic power program or even the groundnuts scheme were rightly undertaken on the basis of assumptions known to be doubtful and ought to be written off without recrimination as well spent insurance premia if the critical assumptions prove to be wrong. This would require not only much greater clarity of thought than is now apparent in national policy making but a radical change in the atmosphere in which political dialogue is conducted.

The third possibility, still hardly tried, is to increase the predictability of the future by limiting the sources of uncertainty, in particular the rate of change. Of the variables that control the future course of any relation we may want to regulate, some are the results, direct or indirect, of human action, and some are not. It might be supposed that those that resulted from human action could most easily be controlled by human decision and that, as the importance of these grows, relative to that of the independent variables, the situation would become more easily regulable. Hitherto, this inference has been constantly disproved, though it lives on in the persistent cliché that improved technology gives mankind greater control over the environment. This facile equating of power with control has still to be dethroned in the popular and the political mind, even though scientists are now well accustomed to think of regulation as limited by the adequacy not of energy but of information.

Yet the fact remains that the course of variables that are originated or modified by human action could be made much more predictable than they are if we seriously wished to hold them constant or control their rate of change. This is indeed the obvious thing to do and must, I think, become increasingly necessary. It is resisted only because in our culture change has become such a sacred cow that any overt interference with it can still be proposed only after expiatory incantations. The Buchanan Steering Committee, contemplating the restriction in the use of vehicles declared, "We find the whole idea repugnant." They agreed nonetheless that it would be necessary. It may be that technologists and politicians will in time face the repugnant idea that the use of supersonic aircraft will have to be limited to mitigate the resultant "carpet of sonic booms." The acceptance of such specific needs, however, will always be too little and too late, until policymakers realize that all activities are ultimately self-limiting and mutually limiting and that the "optimizing-balancing" role of the policymaker is precisely to impose a more orderly and acceptable set of mutual limitations than would otherwise result.

The rate of change in a system and the degree to which change is predictable set limits to the extent to which the system can be regulated. Within these limits, the extent of regulation possible depends on the type of regulation that is acceptable. Each has its own possibilities and limitations, and the regulator's choice will always be a political choice, a choice of policy, since different choices set different norms both for optimizing and for balancing. These choices, however, will be less confused by irrelevance, once the limitations and requirements of regulation are clearly understood. To anticipate another example to which I shall return, the nationalization of the British coal industry changed the method of regulating the main constituent relations of the industry both internal and external. Thereafter, some things became easier that had been difficult or impossible, and others became more difficult than before. These changes were implicit in the change of regulator. An understanding of what the new regulator was designed to do and what it could be expected to do was essential both to the judgment whether it should be established and to the judgment whether, when established, it was working satisfactorily. Such an understanding in that and any other field depends on understanding the conditions and limitations of the regulative process.

In two fields, prediction has secondary effects so important and peculiar that they need separate consideration. The building contractor and the manager of the engineering firm, having plotted the course that they intend their operations to follow, communicate to their subordinates what is expected of them. These communications make a difference to those who receive them; they set standards of success. They thus alter the behavior that they predict. One of the difficulties to which this gives rise is the difficulty, endemic in business, of distinguishing between budgets and targets. The standard set by prediction is the standard of the most probable. The contractor, the manager may hope to do better than the most probable. They may know from experience that unless everyone tries individually to do better than the most probable, the ultimate outcome of the whole effort will "most probably" be less. It is, however, difficult in a regulative process, to combine the norm "what is most to be expected" with the norm "what is most to be striven for," especially when there is a substantial gap between the two. The detailed difficulties that arise from this need not be pursued here. The important point is that a communicated prediction changes the situation and the prediction must take account of the probable effect of this change. This effect is not confined to the subordinates of the regulating body. As Professor Seeley (1963) has pointed out, it distinguishes the role of the sociologist and the psychologist from all other scientific roles.

The effect on a man of predicting *his own* behavior is still more complex. In the absence of an authenticated model of this familiar process, I will state what I assume it to be, using as an example the thought processes of the manager who found it necessary to reorganize his supplies department. I shall regard this for convenience as falling into four stages.

The first stage led to the manager's identifying a "need to do something" about the supplies department. An appreciation of the relevant facts disclosed that some of the relations that this department was required to regulate were straying unacceptably from what the manager thought they should be. This involved the manager, because his role, as he conceived it, required him to keep this regulator in working order. The resultant stream of signals claimed more of his attention for the supplies department and awakened in him what I will call a "sense of default." For it concerned the regulation of *his own* behavior, as well as of the undertaking.

The second stage led to the manager's identifying what seemed to be a practical plan of action, after exploring many alternatives. This created a further change. His mental acceptance of this plan, though known at present only to himself, changed his sense of default into a condition of incipient action, endorsed his confidence in himself as a solver of such problems, and gave the still private solution a new status in his running forecast of the future. It could still be changed but at the cost of disturbance to his own state greater than this would have caused before.

The third stage, involving the preliminary talks with Black, White, and Green, added the important new factor of communication to others. The merits of his plan depended on his estimate of the response to it of these three men. Discussion with them might disclose that his estimate was wrong. If so, he could still withdraw; but he could not return to the position he had left. His plan and his change of plan would both then be known, and this knowledge would change the appreciation settings of those concerned. There are situations in which the most tentative mention of a change makes the *status quo* untenable; and although in our culture, such situations are far commoner than they need be, they cannot be wholly eliminated.

The fourth stage is the stage at which the proposal is actually put into effect. An instruction goes out to all concerned, changing the organization of the department, prescribing new roles and allotting them to new role holders. This is the first and last bit of executive *action*, as commonly understood. It is, however, by no means the first bit of activity or the first bit of commitment. The manager's commitment to this course of action to the exclusion of others had been growing since he embarked on the first stage and it was probably complete by the beginning of the third. With his commitment, grew his assurance in including his own proposed action and all its results in his representation of what was going to happen; and this in turn helped to increase his commitment.

Notes

1. I developed this point further in a paper on "The Concept of Stress" (Vickers, 1960).

2. A *set* is an awakened readiness to notice one among many aspects of the milieu. A *setting* is a number of latent readinesses, awaiting arousal.

3. Such decisions may also be politically impossible to make in cultures that, like those of Western societies today, find the confession of impotence intolerable.

6

Innovation

THE MIND PEERING INTO THE FUTURE and asking, "What is going to happen?" inevitably asks as a sequel—"What are we going to do?"—and answers to either type of question set further questions of the other type. So I will turn now to consider questions of the second type, which call for what I have called instrumental judgment. A problem has been posed by some disparity between the current or expected course of some relation or complex of relations and the course that current policy sets as the desirable or acceptable standard. The object of executive judgment is to select a way to reduce the disparity.

The simplest way to reduce such disparities is to change the standard that creates them, and this is a common and most important form of adaptation. It may be conscious, as when the manager abated temporarily his requirement that steel stocks should be kept within the limits previously required or when the building contractor revised his operational program to bring it within the scope of the possible. It may equally occur unconsciously, as the manager unconsciously raised his standards of what to expect from his supplies department, an example none the worse for exemplifying a raising rather than a lowering of standards. These changes in policy, and their relation to changes or stabilities in the valuations that underlie them, I have chosen to regard as exercises of value judgment and to exclude from my concept of instrumental judgment; and I will defer the consideration of them until I deal with value judgments.

Apart from changing policy, there are in principle two ways in which an agent can influence the course of his relations with his milieu. He can alter the course of affairs in the milieu, and he can alter his own course in relation to them. It is convenient, however, to distinguish a third form of adaptation, which may greatly enlarge the possibilities of the other two. The agent may reorganize his appreciative system so as to bring within his view (and thus within his reach) a wider or different set of possible responses. If the agent is an institution, it may further reorganize itself by changing the mutual relations of its members—(a) by changing its organization, as the manager changed the organization of his supplies department; (b) by changing what may loosely be called its culture, in particular, the mutual expectations and self-expectations of its members; or (c) by changing its personnel. All these are avenues of possible innovation.

The first form of innovation needs further subdivision. The "external course of affairs" includes developments both of the physical and of the social milieu—for example, both the physical developments of towns and roads and the social pattern of urban life and road user. To alter the social milieu requires techniques totally different from those needed in altering the physical milieu, so they need to be considered separately, despite their close connection.

In this chapter, I will consider first the innovating skill required to exploit any of these sets of possibilities and, in this connection, the function of the planner. I will then develop a little further the distinction between manipulating the physical and the social milieu.

To explore any of these fields of possibility requires in some degree that skill in innovation to which I have already referred—

the ability to envisage as possible what has not yet been experienced in fact. Koehler (1939) has described the flash of apparent insight with which the apes in his experiment came suddenly to see that the hooked stick in their cage might be used as an extension of their reach; the boxes, if piled one on another, as an extension of their height. This experience is as familiar in daily life as in a research and development department. I recall an occasion during the war of 1914-1918 when, as an inexperienced subaltern, I was told to arrange hot baths for my company in a Flemish hamlet devoid of any man-size receptacles for holding water. I was familiar with the sight of the company "limbers," horse-drawn vehicles each consisting of a linked pair of square, wheeled containers covered with tilts; but it did not occur to me, until bluntly prompted, to take the containers off their wheels and push the tilts inside. That a wheeled vehicle was a collection of bits and pieces, of which the wheels might for some purposes be irrelevant; that tilts tailored to keep rainwater off a protruding load would serve equally well, pushed into the empty container, to keep bathwater in—these were leaps of the imagination, which, like Koehler's less successful apes, I failed to make. It involves a mental skill, depending, it would seem, to some extent on natural endowment but certainly capable of development by learning.

This power to rearrange in imagination the constituents of some familiar object of attention, so as to see them in a changed relationship and another context is one of the skills of instrumental judgment. Car parking requires large, vacant spaces. In towns, where car parks are most needed, the only large vacant spaces are the roofs of buildings. So why not *think* of parking cars on roofs? Because in Britain, where flat roofs have hitherto been unusual, we are accustomed to think of roofs as a *lid,* not a floor, and of cars as belonging to the land surface on which they move. To *think of* a car park on a roof means for most people, at the date when I write this, to enlarge their familiar concept both of a roof and of a car park—even in some degree of a car—though once the suggestion is made, there is no reason why it should not be quickly assimilated.

Whether the idea, once suggested, should be adopted is, of course, another matter. No one can be logically sure, still less can anyone, however convinced, prove to another, that the experiment of a car park on a roof, when carried out, however carefully, on the mind's stage alone, has disclosed all the objections, snags, and side effects that will arise in a full-scale operation on the ground. So projects that can be tested in practice only on a grand and irreversible scale need an entrepreneur combining vision, prudence, persuasiveness, and wealth on a scale seldom found together. It is right that such proposals should have to overcome an inertia greater than is inherent in more conventional or less costly projects; right also that the decision whether to implement them should be taken by minds other than those that conceived them. It is on the other hand important, and in our day more important than ever, that the innovating skill that conceives such projects shall be encouraged and developed and that all should accept and prize the innovating function and should be aware of and discount the innate tendency to smother the unfamiliar at birth.

Skill in innovation is not, of course, confined to reordering the physical milieu; it comprises also the ability to envisage the possibility of organizational and social change. The public corporation has a long history in Britain. Each step, from, say, the founding of the Port of London Authority in 1908 to the establishment of the New Towns corporations under the New Towns Act of 1946, records a series of innovations, none of them a radical break with tradition but amounting in the aggregate to a major change, to which the proposals of the Buchanan (1963) Steering Committee add their quota of innovation. The degree of innovation involved is not always obvious at first sight. The manager reshaping his supplies department changed its pattern to one no less conventional and familiar than the old: The innovation lay in using a change, well justified on its own merits, to create a new post, more limited in scope but not reduced in status, for the manager who had been left behind by the growth of his own department.

Innovation in organizational and social concepts has played a major part in history and its importance increases. Not long ago, it required an imaginative leap to conceive a world without slavery; still more recently, it needed a leap no less great to conceive a Britain not dependent for its government on the existence of a class of financially independent citizens. Our own day is equally confined within similar limitations that become visible only as they break down. For example, judges in criminal courts commonly sentence, even when the verdict is left to the jury. Why? The function of finding that an offense has been committed and the function of deciding how to deal with the offender are radically different functions, requiring different training. Why not confine the judge to the first (with or without the cooperation of a jury), and leave the disposal of the prisoner, his treatment, and the date of his release (within a maximum laid down by the judge) to a different institution, differently staffed, trained, and oriented? Once the question is asked, a flood of fruitful dialogue is released concerning the purposes of punishment and its possible scope, the relative rights of criminals and their fellow citizens, the training of the judiciary, and a host of other aspects of our contemporary appreciative setting, questions that cannot be answered or even asked without changing that setting. Yet today in Britain there must be many who are unaware of this as an area of controversy and who would be surprised to learn that such a separation has been part of the legal system (for example) of the state of California for fifteen years.[1]

A history of institutional innovation would include many of the more dramatic moments of growth and change in political and social history and would throw some light on the interrelation of social and institutional changes. Florence Nightingale was a notable organizer, but the basic change that she attempted and achieved was the creation of a nursing *profession,* a body of people radically different in what others expected of them and in what they expected of themselves from those engaged in the same occupation before her time. This cultural change was partly the result of organizational changes in the character and staffing of hospitals and partly of "education," conscious and deliberate within the schools of nursing, undesigned and spontaneous among the general public, when attention was direct to the facts and the possibilities.

From the smallest business concern to the organization of the United Nations, institutional and cultural innovation rather than physical and technological organization offer the major scope and the major need for regulation; for the major limitations on the policymaker today are not physical or technological but institutional and cultural. In this context, institutional change is significant not only for its own sake but as a means of producing cultural change— almost the only means that our culture allows to society. I have already pointed out how warily both the Buchanan Steering Committee and the Robbins (1963) commission avoid the issue of cultural change induced otherwise than by change of institution. I shall return shortly to consider the possibilities of increased control over cultural change.

The increased importance of innovation explains the increased importance of the planning function, a function that may be played by the policymaker himself but that today is increasingly separated in the realm of major policy. Planning is the central role in the production of that stream of instrumental hypotheses on which executive judgment depends, and it is much more inescapable and important than is commonly accepted.

The final executive decision can only be a choice between concrete alternatives. The policymaker may reject them all and bid the planner think again, but he cannot himself propound a new alternative, except by himself assuming the role of the planner. So any alternative that the planner suppresses or fails to notice goes unconsidered by the policymaker and may indeed be lost for ever. This danger is latent not only in decisions based on formal planning. It is latent in all decisions.

Theoretically, it may be that the only fully rational way of deciding is to weigh all the alternatives open and choose the "best" (see Note 2 in Chapter 2). Rational or not, this is not, in my experience, the way in which most decisions are made or the way in which many of them could be made; for the alternatives are too many and the time is too short. The more general course is rapidly to narrow the choice to a manageable number by a process that I have still to examine and then to range round the regulative cycle until a solution is found that passes as "good enough." Only if nothing good enough is found in the short list so casually made are other possibilities seriously considered. Hence the critically important role of the planner. It is he alone who gets a hearing for innovation.

The critical role of the planner is well exemplified in those provisions of British administrative law that provide for enquiries to be heard into objections raised by the public against decisions of a minister—for example, against a decision to acquire a site by compulsory purchase for some public purpose, say rubbish disposal. In such cases, the validity of the purpose to be served is usually admitted. The objection is to siting it at X. This objection, however, could only be logically upheld by comparing the decision—"site at X"—with the other possible alternatives or by criticizing the procedure by which the ministry did so. Did the ministry explore the relevant area with proper care? Did it identify all the alternative sites? Did it compare the chosen site with alternative sites with proper care and by proper criteria and reach a proper judgment? These are the real questions at issue, but they are not before the tribunal. They are buried in the files.

It would be possible, though not easy, to devise a public inquiry into relative merits of a short list of alternatives. The public would then have the opportunity both to inquire into the only issue with which it ought to be concerned and to educate itself in—as well as help to form—the criteria involved in these decisions of policy, which so fully exemplify the "optimizing-balancing" process. Failing this most desirable reform, such public inquiries will continue to give scope for the expression of local self-interest but not for the engagement and development of that informed sense of the public interest on which planning at any adequate level must depend. Yet even if the reform were made, it would not ensure that the list of alternatives was in fact exhaustive; nor can even the minister assure himself of this before he exercises his power. It depends on the skill of his officials; and not merely on their skill but on the unexpressed criteria by which they select or exclude sites from their consideration. The whole subsequent consideration is built on a foundation that escapes inquiry. And so for the same reason do our personal judgments.

It is the merit of an enquiry such as the Buchanan (1963) report that it exposes the assumptions of fact and value and the subsequent mental processes that lead to the final conclusion. Its assumptions may be incomplete or faulty; its processes may be unsound. It cannot prove that they are not. But by exposing its assumptions and processes as fully as possible, it invites the criticism or the approval of every mind willing to follow these steps with the care with which they were originally taken. It does in fact precisely what administrative inquiries of the kind I have mentioned fail to do. It cannot do more. It facilitates rather than blocking or misdirecting the dialogue on which institutional regulation depends. This is the most the planner can do. It is also the least that the policymaker should require him to do, for this dialogue is critically important and at present critically inadequate.

*   *   *   *   *

The policymaker is dependent not only on the planner but on three other roles that circumscribe what he can usefully decide. He is dependent on those who will execute his plans, on those who have the legal or practical power to veto them, and on that much wider body whose confidence and concurrence is in fact needed to make them effective. Thus, in British central government, a Cabinet decision depends for its implementation (among other things) on the departments that will be concerned with its execution. It needs the concurrence of at least a majority in Parliament (whether formally or informally expressed) and of certain individuals, for example, members of the Cabinet not otherwise concerned who will share collective responsibility for the decision and whose resignation, if they were overridden, would not be acceptable. And it needs sufficient acceptance among those who as electors can make and unmake governments and who as potential lawbreakers can frustrate any policy that depends on their mass compliance.

These three roles can also be distinguished as limiting or enabling the policy making of any other policy-making body in industry or elsewhere. Viewed from the standpoint of the policymaker, these may be regarded as aspects of the social milieu, of which policy must take account. Plans for the implementing of policy must include plans to secure the necessary cooperation or compliance from these role players or to insulate it against their interference. To regard them so and only so would be a cynical and inadequate (though not an unusual) attitude in a policymaker; for these "aspects of the social milieu" are also, otherwise viewed, part of the policy-making system, contributing to, as well as affected by the policy that issues from the policymaker. The communication that enables each of these groups to maintain a sufficient measure of dialogue with the policymaker is essential to the policymaker, no less than to all those whom the policy will affect. I will nonetheless consider these other role players for the moment as part of the social milieu, over against the policymaker. For it is usually the case—and it should be the case—that any adequate policy innovation embodies a plan that will *not* be acceptable to them, unless they can change their appreciative system sufficiently to appreciate it; and the major agency of such a change can only be the plan itself, regarded as a *communication*.

The difference between the physical milieu and the social milieu is that the first can be modified only by the transfer of energy, in other words, by physically pushing it about, while the second can be modified almost only by the transfer of information. The distinction, though obvious and elementary, has been so overlaid by past habits of thought that it may be well to make it abundantly clear.

The use of physical force (the transfer of energy) can modify the behavior of men negatively by killing them or restricting their freedom of physical movement. All other changes in the social milieu are affected by acts of communication (the transfer of information). Even the threat of death or imprisonment, however immediate, can only inform, persuade, or deter. This basic difference between human and physical interaction, though obvious enough, remained latent and confused until science learned clearly to distinguish information flow from energy flow as a mediator of change.

Communication may of course be used as a weapon no less than weapons of war. It may be used as a unilateral instrument of coercion. It may be irresistible. When so used, it may be convenient for some purposes to class it with forms of physically induced change and to distinguish it from the communication that mediates dialogue and other forms of human intercourse. This, however, is not the distinction that I am concerned to draw here. Even the most inhuman brainwashing operates in a manner utterly different from the bulldozer. Nothing about its use can be learned from a textbook on mechanics. Like any other form of communication it can only inform, persuade, or deter.

I have so far regarded the reports analyzed in Chapter 3 primarily as exercises of mental skill. I will now consider them primarily as communications. As mental exercises, what they did could be summarized as description, prediction, supposition, and valuation. Regarded as exercises in communication, the same aspects of the activity may be summarized as stimulation, education, and persuasion.

Regarded as a communication, the first effect of any of these reports on a reader is to direct his attention to its subject matter. His attention once given must involve him in three activities each of which will cause some measure of largely irreversible change. It will add information to his memory store, change his conceptual structure and exercise his appreciative skill. I will include all these changes under the name of education and they are indeed the changes that education is designed to bring.

They are closely connected. It is through the effort to assimilate information that the recipient develops his conceptual organization and his appreciative skill. The nature of the change varies with the information; some information, important in itself, can be assimilated with virtually no change of conceptual organization or development of mental skill. Other information is worth assimilating only for its impact on conceptual organization and mental skill. These distinctions are familiar enough to educators, who can produce and measure accretions to the memory store more easily than improvements in conceptual development and appreciative skill but who know well enough that the latter is the truer measure of their success. These distinctions are not, however, relevant only to education proper. Every attempt by one to influence another by a communication is, whether deliberately or not, an essay in education. It needs to be guided both by an appreciation of the memory store into which it will fall and of the appreciative system by which it will be interpreted, and it will in some degree affect both. The reports I have examined were clearly designed to do so. That the City of Coventry has extensive car parks on its roofs, as is vividly shown in the Buchanan (1963) report, is not interesting as a piece of information in its own right, except to those expecting to park a car in Coventry. Its "educative" effect lies in enlarging, for those readers unfamiliar with the idea, their concepts of roofs, car parks, town planning, and other related ideas. This change will probably persist long after they have forgotten where they first met the new idea exemplified. By contrast, to someone going to Coventry by car, the address of a car park and directions for reaching it would be of equal importance, whether the park, when reached, proved to be on the roof or underground.

I have so far touched only the fringes of a vast subject that is central to this study. Institutional and social change may be less readily noticed than physical and technological change, but it is no less important. Changes in the one, designed or undesigned, produce formidable changes in the other. Our failure to recognize relations between the two is a danger. It is a paradox, as Norbert Wiener (1950) observed,

> that the people who control the fortunes of our community should at the same time be wildly radical in matters that concern our own change of our (physical) environment and rigidly conservative in the social matters that determine our adaptation to it. (p. 56)

The paradox has grown no less striking or less dangerous in the twenty years since he made his comment. In this chapter I am concerned only to point out that innovation, designed and undesigned, takes place not only in the physical world that we observe but in the conceptual world that directs and interprets our observations. This conceptual world, insofar as it is shared, comprehends our culture and our institutions. I shall explore it more fully when I consider policy making as an institutional process and as part of a wider and less conscious social process. Yet even regarded purely as a mental skill, policy making includes skill in communication—not merely in communicating information or triggering action but in a continuing process of dialogue that changes the appreciative settings on which it relies and that is often designed to do so.

These changes affect the value judgments, as well as the reality judgments, of the parties to the dialogue; and this also is often their main intention. The authors of the reports, however objectively they expressed themselves, were persuasive and could not have been otherwise. Before leaving the analysis of policy making as a mental skill, I must define a little further the terms that I shall use in describing value judgment, a subject that is still overcast by the curious implication that any study of "values" must be unscientific. Many years have passed since Koehler (1939) published a famous series of essays under the title *The Place of Values in a World of Fact.* Today, much scientific speculation in the behavioral sciences is properly devoted to the nature of fact in a world of values. For since the object of conscious regulation in human affairs is (as I observed in Chapter 1) to secure stability in a form that is judged to be "better" or at least more acceptable than would otherwise result or more ambitiously to "optimize" the possibilities latent in any situation, the dominance of governing human values must be taken for granted in any study of the process; and it is these values that select and in part create the "facts" that are to be observed and regulated.

Note

1. The problem is well surveyed in Jaffary's (1963) *The Sentencing of Adults in Canada.*

7

Valuation

◆ AMONG THE FACTS OF LIFE that present themselves to our reality judgment, none is more conspicuous than the fact that our fellows make value judgments and the value judgments that they in fact make. The most convenient approach to the value judgment is therefore to approach it first as a matter of fact. This is especially easy in the field of institutional behavior.

I return, as an example, to the local authority discussed in Chapter 1. Among the relations for which the authority is responsible is the complex of quantitative and qualitative relations that constitute the education service. If we were to ask the members of the Education Committee, the officials of the department, and a sample of the parents concerned in what ways they would like to see this service altered or improved (without regard to budgetary limitations), we should uncover in most of them an "ideal" representation of the service, in which accommodation, staffing ratios, quality and training of staff, content of curriculum, and extracurricular activities left, in the judgment of the appreciating mind, nothing to be desired, having regard to the numbers, character, and needs of the children for whom the council is responsible.

This standard, which I will call an "ideal norm," is the judgment of an individual mind, and it is clearly a judgment of value. As a standard, it is not unitary, for each individual judgment will be to some extent unique. It is not necessarily self-consistent; the full benefits obtainable from a highly "permissive" type of education cannot be combined with all the benefits to be obtained from a more "directed" pattern, yet a single mind might include the benefits of both in its "ideal." It is certainly not static. Even the most modest aspirations commonly shared today would be found to be far ahead of even progressive aspirations fifty years ago—for example, the value judgments recorded and shared by the Robbins (1963) report concerning the right of all who can benefit by it to free higher education. Nonetheless, this composite and moving "ideal norm," explored in a given content of time and place would usually be found to contain wide areas of general agreement. Some of these have formal expression in the Education Act of 1946, committing itself, as it does, to two major changes at an unspecified future time, which twenty years later have not been achieved.

Similar "ideal norms," more or less controversial, self-consistent, transient, and remote, could be identified as matters of fact in relation to each of the other functional relations for which the council is responsible, for health, welfare, roads, sewerage, planning, and so on.

Below the level of these ideal norms is the set of standards that the council has decided to accept as the best realistic governors of their efforts within the time span for which they plan, having regard to their total expected resources and the total expected claims upon them. This set of standards constitutes the council's current policy. It, too, is multiple, controversial, and subject to change, but it should be self-consistent and attainable. It also is the result of a complex value judgment, the judgment of relative priorities that seeks to "optimize" the total value of the achievements possible in all the fields concerned. This is the standard that operates as a norm in the regulation of current action, yielding, when compared with actual performance and estimated trends, those signals of match and mismatch on which regulation depends.

The distinction between ideal norm and operative norm or policy is, I believe, important, both theoretically and practically. The capacity to keep in view dreams that cannot yet be realized, is, as I observed earlier, a precious capacity of the human mind but only so long as that mind can distinguish the mismatch signals that it generates from those that call for "action now." Policy is the operative norm, yet the ideal norm is not without current effect. It supports policy against the eroding action of other operating norms that seek to grow at its expense—that seek for example, to make the imperfections of the highways more dominant than the imperfections of the schools—and it stimulates and guides the raising of the operating norm set by policy whenever resources permit.

The full realization of all ideal norms is, must be, and should be impossible, both because they are bound to be to some extent mutually inconsistent and because their full realization would require far more than all the resources available—and would continue to do so, however much these resources were increased. This still unwelcome conclusion follows from the fact that every decision is and must always be a choice made in conditions of scarcity. Hitherto, economics alone has formulated its calculus on this basis, and in consequence it is sometimes assumed that only economic decisions involve the idea of comparative cost. This assumption is false. As the Robbins report observes, every choice, economic or otherwise, excludes whatever "must be given up in order to have it" and this giving up results not merely from the incompatibility of many desirable relations but also from the fact that every activity claims its quota of time and attention—in brief, of life—and this, unlike energy or information or even physical resources, is not expansible. Moreover, the wider the field of choice, the more acute becomes the condition of scarcity. For subjectively, scarcity is the relation between what is potentially realizable and what the individual can actually realize, and it increases not only with the shrinkage of the latter term but also with the widening of the former. In a society in which every career is open to everyone, it is still true that no one can choose more than one—or at least more than one at a time. His exclusion from attempting the others has become his choice instead of his fate.

The value judgments of institutions are expressed partly by their policies and partly by such other expression as they give to what I have called their ideal norms. Each throws light on the other. Policy decisions are taken in a concrete situation in which the cost of each possible decision must be faced and real priorities are thus more likely to be disclosed. On the other hand, the limitations of the situation may itself deny expression to some strongly held valuations. The discussion of values in the three reports summarized in Chapter 3 provides a convenient starting point.

The Gowers (1953) commission, it will be remembered, arrived at a critical value judgment regarding the exercise of the home secretary's discretion to recommend commutation of the death sentence. This, they found, was "undue" and they regarded it as unacceptable, even though they could find no alternative that they could recommend. The reason for this negative value judgment is clear from the report. The home secretary, they held, was acting as a court of appeal. This classification—a reality judgment—carried automatically a negative value judgment; for a well-established norm provided that the executive should not assume judicial functions so as to give relief against the finding of the courts; and another norm laid down rules of procedure for judicial bodies, which the home secretary was manifestly not following. These valuations followed automatically from the way in which these activities were "seen."

The decision thus to see it was a judgment, rooted in past history and not without influence on the future. The proximate cause seems to have been the frequency with which the home secretary was intervening in the course of justice. If his interventions had affected only a small proportion of cases, instead of nearly half, he might have escaped classification as a court of appeal and been seen as an appropriate embodiment of the Crown's prerogative of mercy.

Even his intervention on the present scale would not have been so condemned, if the culture still accepted, as it once did, the concept of the Crown as the fount of justice, as well as the dispenser of mercy. The whole body of legal rules that lawyers know as equity was built up under the chancellor (as "keeper of the King's conscience") to mitigate the formality of the common law, and the two jurisdictions were formally fused less than a century ago. Nor would his intervention necessarily have been so condemned if sentence had ceased to be regarded as a judicial function, as perhaps it soon may; for then the home secretary's intervention in the matter of *sentence* would have been in a field no longer regarded as the prerogative of the judge. And of course, the whole debate would have been meaningless in a society that did not place a high value both on justice and on consistency. It is only recently that either quality was expected from the holders of power, either by others or by themselves. Justice and consistency in their turn are concepts that can be given a concrete meaning only in a defined society, though their meanings in different societies can be related to each other.

Thus, the entire appreciation was rooted in the culture within which it was made. This is in no sense a criticism of the report. On the contrary, it was only by being thus rooted that it could and did influence the culture from which it sprang. It is neither possible nor desirable that such a body or any body should make value judgments otherwise than from within a social-historical situation and about a social-historical situation. This does not imply that social-historical situations may not have much in common or that the valuer speaking from *within* his own culture may not be its most radical and effective critic.[1]

This example gives a glimpse of the appreciative *system*, into which the commissioners were vainly trying to fit a restricted death penalty. Changes in the public attitude toward the death penalty had for some time been reflected in changes in the action of the only component in the system that had a wide measure of discretion, namely the policy of the home secretary. This change, when examined by the commission, seemed itself inconsistent with other norms, such as those defining the "proper" relations of the executive and the judiciary, of judge and jury, of crime and punishment. Each of these norms was itself the product of history and was further modified by the new installment of "history" represented by the debate focused by the commission. Each of these norms was highly valued. No change within the commission's terms of reference would curtail the unacceptable extension of the home secretary's powers without deviating unacceptably from some other norm. To enlarge the function of the jury in such cases was a change that the commissioners could not recommend, except as an alternative less undesirable than a continuation of the *status quo.*

We may draw the conclusion that consistency is itself highly valued, at least by our contemporary culture.

The commission on capital punishment was itself set up in response to an appreciative judgment, a growing sense of dissatisfaction with killing as a punishment. The causes and course of this disquiet, which had been growing for several decades, I will not attempt to trace here, except to point out that it was primarily a cultural change in the concept of responsibility for self and for others that was advancing unevenly, was still incomplete, and hence was a focus of controversy. The committee on higher education (Robbins, 1963) was prompted by a cultural change equally striking but much more widely accepted—the value judgment that higher education ought to be freely available to all who could use it and would accept it. The committee on traffic in towns (Buchanan, 1963), by contrast, was prompted not by a new aspiration arising from cultural change but by a threat to the established value of free movement, arising from the multiplication of physical means to move about. But as I pointed out in Chapter 4, these enquiries, no less than the enquiry into capital punishment, uncovered equally disturbing threats to the *coherence* of the value system. To realize the new values, even to retain the old, new institutions and new cultural attitudes would be needed; and these possible innovations were themselves valued, not merely as means to these specific ends but as changes in relations that were valued in themselves and as precedents for changes perhaps still more radical. The extension of planning control, the unified development of urban areas conceived in three dimensions, the assimilation of universities and technical colleges as providers of the national requirement for higher education—all these involved cultural and institutional innovation that could be accepted only at the cost of restructuring and revaluing previous conceptual structures.

In Chapter 4, I referred to the appreciative system as a net, of which reality settings form the warp and value setting the weft. The more closely woven and coherent the net, the greater the disturbance wrought by any change. It is no accident that this century has seen unprecedented—sometimes disastrous—efforts to design an appreciative setting on a national or even supranational scale. The attempt of the Third Reich to impose a "nationalsozialistische Weltanschauung" was the most notorious but not the only example. Every national system of education molds *and must necessarily* mold the appreciative system. The safeguards against its abuse—and the standards that define abuse—can reside only in the culture itself and in its other institutions. The situation that evokes these manifestations, so strange to an eye accustomed to the "liberal" values of fifty years ago, has already begun to appear and will be summarized in the next chapter.

So far, I have described value judgments as matters of fact; and so they are to all except those who make them. For these, however, they have a different status; or at least we assume them to have, by analogy with our own experience. At this point, we encounter a peculiar complication that affects our interpretation of every observation we make and every communication we receive about other human beings. *We know what it is to be ourselves in a way in which we know nothing else*; and insofar as we assume that other humans have experiences like our own, we extend to them a whole range of assumptions that we may have no other evidence for making and that in any case we could not make, unless the basis for them were provided by our own experience.

Referring to the manager debating with himself whether to terminate the engagement of Mr. Black, I described him as reaching a double conclusion. He concluded that if he did so, the rest of the staff would regard his action as "unfair"; this was a judgment of fact about the probable functioning of other men's regulators in a certain hypothetical event. He also himself felt that it would be "unfair." This was a judgment of value, arrived at by comparing his part in the hypothetical event with a standard accepted by him. The working of his regulator was no less a fact than the working of other men's regulators, but it was not observable as a fact by him. *For him it was not a fact but an act, fact only after the event.*

Equally to me and to any readers who accept the distinction I am drawing, the distinction, presented as a matter of fact, is convincing only because we ourselves have experienced the making of such valuations as an *act*. It would otherwise be barely explicable.

I shall therefore assume the capacity for making value judgments as an activity of the mind that minds similarly endowed can infer from the behavior and communications of others but that they can interpret only in the light of their own experience. Proceeding within this inescapable limitation, I shall distinguish two kinds of value judgment.

The manager found within his appreciative setting—or he developed in it by the very act of appreciation—standards of obligation toward employees that were in conflict with the hypothetical proposal to discharge the buyer. These standards may have been associated with his role as a manager or with some more comprehensive or subtler role. At all events, they were standards to which he felt committed and that obliged him to go on seeking for a more acceptable solution. Similarly the commission on capital punishment, performing what looks like a far more ambitious exercise in abstraction with apparently equal ease, compared the current practice of the home secretary with the "constitutional framework of the Country," found that it did not "fit" and therefore condemned it. The constitutional framework of the country was a standard to which they were committed. I need not at this point engage in any psychological speculation about the origin or the mechanism of these "internalized" standards. I will only accept their existence as a fact and give them a name. I will call them *commitments*.

Commitments do not, however, comprehend all value judgments. The Buchanan (1963) committee pointed out to their compatriots that the buildings they used could not enjoy unlimited accessibility *and* optimal environmental conditions and would soon enjoy little of either, unless the users collectively chose which of various possible combinations they would prefer and planned accordingly. No "commitment" obliged them to prefer less noise to more accessibility above any given threshold. They were exhorted only to take those steps that would maximize their enjoyment of their environment or at least check the maximizing of their "disenjoyment," which their own unregulated activities would surely achieve. They had, therefore, simply to decide what they would prefer.

The distinction between value judgments of this kind and those based on commitments, is, subjectively, common enough. A hungry man choosing his dinner may hesitate between beef and mutton. He likes both; both are available, but he can accommodate only one. Which on this occasion would he prefer? His companion, training for a race or on a diet restricted by his doctor, may hesitate equally between the delicious but forbidden lobster à la Americaine and the dull but permitted steamed cod. Both are in a state of conflict and indecision; but the conflicts are clearly different. The first has merely to decide which he would prefer. The second must decide between a commitment and an enjoyment. Again, I will not speculate on the underlying psychological mechanisms. I will only mark a distinction so ingrained in common speech and experience that I cannot dispense with it, the distinction between commitment and enjoyment.

What I have called judgments of reality and judgments of value must account between them for situations that we use four sets of verbs to describe. What we can and cannot do, must and must not do, should and should not do are distinguished from what we want and don't want to do in ways that are subjectively familiar but not always easy to define. I hope this formulation will make the distinction clearer. What others expect of me I recognize as a fact by a judgment of reality. What I expect of myself I define by a mental act, which is a judgment of value. I cannot describe institutional behavior, any more than the behavior of men at a dinner table, in terms of commitments alone, and for its other constituent I can find no more apt term than *enjoyment*.

Men are energy systems, active by definition. They need to discharge, no less than to generate energy at a rate within the limits appropriate to their kind. Questions in the form, "Why is he doing that?" are misleading unless both asker and answerer supply the suppressed termination, "Why is he doing that *rather than something else*?" We have in common speech a variety of ways in which we can answer such questions; for example,

- "because that is what, at the moment, he wants to do";
- "because that is what he feels he ought to do";
- "because he thinks that will have results that he wants or feels he ought to bring about";
- "because that is what in the circumstances he is accustomed to do";
- "because that is what his role requires";
- "because that is what someone asked him to do";

and so on. Of these, the first and second appear as separate though not necessarily conflicting categories, while the remainder can be readily subsumed under one or other or both of them; and it would cramp the description even of the examples already given, if I did not mark the distinction.

Note

1. The view presented here and elsewhere in this book seems to me to offer an answer to the dilemma posed by Professor Seeley (1963). How can a sociologist make a radical criticism of the culture to which he himself belongs? The sociologist, as I suggest, like everyone else, belongs to many cultures, none closed; and his particular net of overlapping acculturation is unique to him. The endless interaction of these provides and demands criticism more or less radical from everyone capable of independent thought. See also p. 69.

8

The Limits of the Regulable

THE PICTURE OF INSTITUTIONAL REGULATION that has emerged so far, though complex, is still incoherent and incomplete. I will summarize it so far as it goes and draw some conclusions about the limits of the regulable.

To the helmsman, the compass shows the actual position of the ship's head with negligible delay; and shows it continuously, so that rates of change can be noted. The course is also continuously represented. The helmsman's possible responses, which are limited to movements of the wheel, are translated into rudder movements within seconds; and these in turn make an almost immediate contribution to the ship's behavior and hence to the stream of information flowing from the compass. Thus, the regulative cycle revolves continuously several times a minute.

These conditions of regulation are optimal and rare. Nonetheless, they might be insufficient. To take an extreme example, they would be both useless and inept to control a canoe shooting rapids—useless, because conditions would require quicker responses, based on different predictions; inept because in such circumstances the variables to be controlled would have changed. Regulation in such a case would be directed largely, perhaps wholly, to avoiding capsize, swamping, and impact, thresholds in relationships that the helmsman of a liner can usually ignore. The experience of regulating a national economy or a business corporation is sometimes more analogous to shooting rapids than to steering a great circle course, and the most intractable controversies about regulation often arise from unrecognized differences as to which in the circumstances is the more apt analogy. Yet the two examples are points on a continuous scale. A helmsman taking a small sailing vessel through a tide race may find himself uneasily balanced between the two.

Institutional regulators work in very different conditions. The multiple relations to be regulated and the norms (whether static or moving) at which they should be kept are themselves for the most part matters for decision. The actual state and possible course of these relations are imperfectly known and still less perfectly predictable. The means of affecting their course are drawn from a repertory not fixed but constantly enlarged and restricted by developments, both in the physical and in the conceptual milieu— developments partly caused by deliberate innovation. Their selection depends far less on past experience, far more on experiments carried out hypothetically on that obscure combination of analogue and digital computers with which the brain appears to provide us. To implement these responses requires extensive agreement and cooperation among many people, often remote from each other, who must consequently perform identical operations or trust and accept the results of those performed by others and who have learned that most sophisticated habit of responding to such predictions. These collective responses, even when selected and initiated, may take decades to complete and return for judgment in varied contexts and often unrecognizable form over more than one future generation.

Clearly, institutional regulation is possible only within limits. It is convenient to classify these limitations under three heads:

logical limitations, limitations of skill, and what I will call institutional limitations.

There are first logical limitations. The regulator must be able to compare actual with norm, both presently and with some measure of prediction. It must have within its actual or potential repertory some response that would reduce the disparity and that could be made to take effect in time. It must have some means of devising and selecting this response with better than random success from among all possible alternatives and some means of putting it into practice. Each of these conditions may be absent and impossible to create.

For example, apart from the difficulty of prediction, it is by no means easy for an institutional regulator to know even the present state of the variables concerned. Indeed, all its factual information speaks from a past date. Business corporations collate their statistics of sales, orders, stocks, creditors, and so on weekly or monthly in arrear; and some significant information emerges only from the annual accounts, which are seldom available less than three months after the end of the year to which they relate. Information about the milieu, such as the activities of competitors or the state of the economy may be less accessible and longer delayed. Generally speaking, the larger the institution, the more scanty and delayed is the information available to it relative to its needs.

Where changes in the relations to be regulated are themselves regular and repetitive, like the swinging of a ship's head, appropriate responses become coupled to the changes and do not require special exercises in prediction; but the institutional regulator must deal with changes that are not regular or repetitive. Even the buyer anticipating the disturbance in the steel market needed to forecast a situation unlike any that had faced him since he became responsible for regulating his undertaking's stocks of steel. The situations explored by the Buchanan (1963) and the Robbins (1963) reports are far more radically new. The enlargement in scale of institutional control and the speeding of the rate of change reduce the value of information about the current state of affairs and depreciate the value of past experience. It has been said that soldiers start each war perfectly prepared to win the previous one. The observa-

tion applies not only to soldiers but to all who have to learn from
nonrepetitive experience, administered in massive doses between
intervals fraught with change. This uneasy condition is becoming
increasingly common.

Learning takes place only in individual minds, and its possibilities are closely linked with the human life cycle. Death is as
necessary as life. It is on the one hand a thought overwhelmingly
strange that the whole expanding corpus of human knowledge
must be relearned about three times in each century; but it is an
even stranger reflection that the revolution of the generations that
makes this necessary also makes possible the innovations that
open the door to new knowledge of all sorts and that come,
generally speaking, from the new minds of each generation. In an
organization, the need to refill posts constantly emptied by retirement, transfer, or promotion is a major continuing anxiety, but it
is also the sole source of the essential, recurrent opportunity to
introduce new minds, new ideas, new energies, and new capacities
for learning. The same is true on a grand scale for life on the planet.
One of the major parameters of the human scene is the rate at
which the generations of men succeed each other. This rate is
falling, while every other rate of change is rising, a fact that must
surely set narrowing logical limits to the possibilities of adaptation
in general and in particular to that aspect of it that is the subject
of this book.

The conditions I have described put an increasing premium on
the power to predict and to respond to prediction; but even in
theory the future is predictable only to a limited extent, and this
places a further, narrowing limitation on the possibilities of regulation. For it excludes responses that cannot be made effective
within the period that prediction can cover with enough assurance
to provide a basis for action.

These logical limitations, then, may be summed up as follows.
Regulation is possible, even in theory, only when the regulator is
theoretically capable of initiating some action that is more likely
than not to be regulative, when it becomes effective, in the situation that will then exist and further, when the regulator has some
better than random means of recognizing what this action is. There
has seldom, I think, been a time when the field in which regulation

is even theoretically possible has been so narrow as it is today when compared with the field in which it is currently supposed to be possible. This gap between reality and assumption is due partly to the effect of the increasing rate of change in depreciating experience and hampering learning and partly to the exaggeration of hopes through the delusion that increased power must of itself bring increased control. On the other hand, there can seldom have been a time when, even within the limitations of the situation, so many possibilities of regulation lay unused through failure to develop and use the requisite skills.

For the logical limitations of regulation are not independent of the limitations of our skill. With imperfect skills, the scope for regulation is even more limited. These skills can be developed, and their exercise can define and even enlarge the boundaries of logical limitation.

Skill in reality judgment, including prediction depends on three main factors; first, on its understanding of the process to be predicted, in particular on the power to abstract regularities, akin to natural laws, on which to base prediction; second, on the capacity to collect, store, and process relevant information; and third, on the theoretic predictability of the process itself. Of these, the second has made spectacular progress in the last two decades and is still clearly in its infancy; but its value is limited by the first, which moves much more slowly, and the third, which continues to outdistance the other two. So net progress at the present time is dearly negative.

Skill in instrumental judgment holds out greater hope, though at greater risk. Technical skill in manipulating the physical milieu grows apace but can only create a world ever less predictable, understandable, and controllable, until it is used deliberately as an instrument of regulation. This involves a new concept of growth that is only now beginning to emerge in the applied sciences of social behavior though it has long been familiar to biology. The physiologist distinguishes readily between normal growth, a miracle of regulation achieved by mechanisms just coming into view and the proliferating, self-destructive anomie of the cancerous cell; but the distinction is still novel and suspect in Western economic (not political) thought. It is welcome that "national growth targets;"

that striking innovation in Western political norms, should now be conceived, sometimes at least, as norms bounded *on both sides* by dangerous thresholds.

Far more important, though more suspect, is increasing skill in manipulating the institutional and cultural milieu. As I have already pointed out, institutional and cultural factors, far more than technological factors set the problems and limit the solutions of our time. We could indeed, if we so wished, create a world less unpredictable than ours today and institutions better adapted to produce collective action on a scale more massive yet under the control of a policy more flexible than we can at present achieve. But this, I believe, would demand an institutional and cultural setup not yet attained by any developed or developing country and not guaranteed or even promised by *any* existing political system. It is, I believe, the major problem to which every developed and developing country is seeking a solution, moving forward, with whatever starting handicap or advantage, physical or cultural, its history may have endowed it. It seems probable to me that whatever viable solutions are reached by any of them, including my own, will have more in common with each other than any of them has with the ideology from which it started.

It would seem then that of all the skills involved in the regulative process, skill in value judgment is the most promising and the most important, as it is also undoubtedly the one least clearly distinguished. Artificial as it may be to isolate this aspect of appreciation, I find it necessary in order to rescue it from its usual fate of being overlooked.

I have defined the policymaker's skill as a continuing exercise in a dual process of "optimizing" and "balancing," within a situation that does not, cannot, and should not admit the full realization of all contemporary "values." This skill may be described under five heads.

Most obvious is the skill of the balancer. Any ongoing program of activity is contained by inescapable, though not constant, limitations of physical resources, energy, skill, and time. Policies that exceed these limitations by even a little may suffer shipwreck. The successful policymaker avoids such disasters partly by realistic appraisal of risks and limitations; but this controller's expertise is combined in the successful policymaker with a constant intensity of valuation, without which far less would be realized.

Again, the policymaker's skills include skill in integrating in one solution aims that seemed at first incompatible—as the manager contrived to free his supplies department from the limitations of its manager without losing the manager. This is an instrumental skill, but it is developed to the heights only under the tension of the policymaker's intense and constant valuations, which resist more resolutely than other men's the sacrifice of any of them for the sake of an easy solution.

A third element in the skill of the policymaker is skill in determining priorities, a need that no amount of integrative skill can wholly displace. "What matters most now?" is a question constantly renewed, in circumstances constantly changing. Its answers must be related to the needs of the minute yet must not be mutually self-defeating in the longer term. It is a valuational choice, based on a subtle appreciation of the effect that changes of priority will spread through the system. It requires of the policymaker a rare measure of mental discipline, at the service of an unerring sense of time.

Since policies are framed within a wider net of aspirations and apprehensions than can be fully realized, a fourth element in the valuational skills of the policymaker is the skill required to deal with those "ideal norms" that are not currently included in policy, including the skill to keep them alive without allowing them to interfere with "action now"—the skill, in brief, to keep his dreams on ice.

Finally, we need to distinguish that singular and most essential skill, the skill to develop this pattern of aspiration and apprehension from which policy is drawn—in brief, the power to dream. However we may explain it, let us accept as a description of the most familiar fact in history that men sometimes get ideas into their heads and that these ideas make a difference. More exactly and in the terms that I have been developing, innovations occur in the appreciative field and spread from their originators to others. Potentialities, formerly ignored, are noticed and become potent as norms, and often the proximate cause can be traced to the individual who first saw what might be and prized it as what should be and cried "Look!" and caused his fellows to see and to value, and in time to realize, what he first saw. History has its dramatic examples, but we need not look further than the Buchanan (1963) committee, allowing this creative vision to disturb the lucid waters of their official prose. "Of this there can be no doubt, that there are potentialities for enriching the lives of millions of people who have to live in towns beyond anything most of them have yet dreamed of."

And in all these fields of skill, the most essential element is the skill to learn. Any skill, as I am using the term, is a potential capacity of the organism, present at birth only as a potentiality capable of development up to limits that we may assume to exist but that perhaps we seldom reach, development that may perhaps be speeded to rates and raised to heights that we have not yet realized. A first step in this development is to recognize as a skill not only instrumental judgment but also appreciative judgment, not only know-how but also know-what.

*   *   *   *   *

Throughout these chapters, I have tried so far as possible to treat the institutional regulator as if it were unitary—"the policymaker" of previous paragraphs. This convenience I must now discard. As I acknowledged in Chapter 1, the institutional regulator is far from unitary. Policy is not only a mental skill. It is an institutional process, and this, too, imposes limitations, as well as enlarging possibilities in the regulation of human affairs. In Part II, I will discuss policy making primarily as an institutional process.

PART II

Policy Making as an Institutional Process

9

Institutions as Dynamic Systems

◈ IN PREVIOUS CHAPTERS, I have described and illustrated what seem to me to be the minimal assumptions that we need to make in order to explain what we claim to do in the course of policy making. Even if they are not accepted as psychological explanations, I offer them as convenient descriptions that refine the assumptions of common speech in ways both practically useful and scientifically probable. In particular, they remind us that the world in which policymakers, like other people, effectively live is a mental artifact, largely but never wholly shared by its inhabitants, whose main social function is to inherit it, preserve it, develop it, and pass it on.

Policy making in institutions, however, depends not only on these individual skills but also on limitations and facilities inherent in institutional life. It is an institutional process, a function, in part, of the nature, structure, and history of the institution concerned. To this aspect of it I now turn.

The skills of policy making are exercised, in the context of this study, by men playing some institutional role, as cabinet ministers, business executives, town councillors, company directors. The structure and function of the organization within which they are acting and its relations with other institutions powerfully affect what they will regard as standards of success, as well as defining the scope of their discretion and the extent of their power. Moreover, the structure and function of these institutions and their mutual relationship are not static but are, on the contrary, in increasingly rapid change, partly as a result of policy-making activity. I have to find ways to describe this mutual process, ways sufficiently simple to be manageable yet adequate to distinguish its most important elements.

This presents a familiar difficulty. We can, on the one hand, regard organizations as entities that can be studied in their own right. We can compile a natural history of organizations, classifying them by types and seeking regularities in their behavior. This makes visible some important realities but obscures the fact that even at the highest levels of the largest organizations, appreciations are made and decisions taken by individual men, who are always more—and less—than the embodiment of one institutional role. Alternatively, we can focus attention on the individual regarding his institutional role as only one among many factors that condition the course of his judgment and the extent of his power. This preserves us from the dangers of postulating group minds and common wills but masks institutional realities and overstresses individual autonomy.

The only way to minimize this difficulty is to adopt *both* views, remembering that no viewpoint can give more than a partial insight into any reality. Institutions determine the distribution of power in our society; they also express and preserve different, often divergent cultural heritages. They deserve to be studied in their own right. Yet the individuals who embody them are not wholly their prisoners or their puppets. Indeed, the most far-reaching control possessed by any society over its future is the power to remake its institutions.

In the rest of this chapter, I examine the institutional landscape and describe the *similarities* that all organizations have in common as dynamic systems. In Chapter 10, I note the historical process that in my view is increasing the scope of what I shall call political choice and correspondingly reducing the relative importance of what I shall call market choice and is thus imposing on the regulative bodies of *all* institutions the need for more complex appreciative judgments. In Chapter 11, viewing organizations primarily as energy systems, I classify them by reference to the various ways in which they generate the resources they need to survive and grow. In the next chapter, viewing them primarily as information systems, I classify them by the nature and extent of the controls to which their governors are subject through their formal and informal accountability. In Chapter 13, I view the same scene from the point of view of the policymaker, looking outward on the world with which his institution is in constant interaction and he himself in constant dialogue, looking also inward on the constituent relations that enable his institution thus to act as a whole and on the dialogue that mediates these inner relations also; and I inquire how far these differences of institutional form and relationship affect what their policymakers regard as conditions and criteria of success. I make no apology for the fact that these viewpoints are not consistently held. We need to be adept at passing from one to the other, never forgetting which one we are for the moment using. None needs this skill more than the policy-maker.

*   *   *   *   *

Our institutions, in the broad sense in which I am using the term, include the organs of central and local government, government agencies, public corporations, business enterprises, cooperatives, trade unions, universities, political parties, charitable foundations, churches, clubs. Their functions, like their forms, are of bewildering variety. A random reference to an alphabetical list confined to public institutions juxtaposes the Foreign Office and the Forestry Commission. A random dip into the register of limited companies would yield equally rich variety. Between them, these institutions not only provide nearly all the goods and services we collectively and individually use but also take nearly all the decisions about what shall be provided and regulate nearly all the relations that are important to us, from keeping the peace to keeping a job.

Lawyers will be interested in this variety of form, economists in this diversity of function; but sociologically, the significant differences are fewer in number, different in character, and less in importance. The most striking feature of all these institutions, sociologically, is their similarity. For they are all dynamic systems, dependent for their continuance on the regulation of relations, internal and external, functional and metabolic, such as I have already described in various contexts.

Professor Waddington (1960) has provided a very useful and general definition of an organization.

> Groups of elementary constituents [who] may be entering into close relationships with each other build up complex entities, which then enter into further causal relations with each other as *units*. It is this fact of the integration of groups of constituents into complexes which in certain respects act as units which is spoken of as an organization.

When we apply this definition to human society, we can identify five dimensions in terms of which organizations may be described.

The first is the dimension of *duration*. The coherence of social units may far outlast that of their transient human constituents, though this coherence is not inconsistent with constant change, which itself is often due to the replacement of one individual by another. Yet this coherence is vulnerable, and its vulnerability may be related to its duration. For organizations, as for individuals, both youth and age have their strengths and their weaknesses. An organization that has developed closely integrated and mutually supportive internal relations may be both more resistant to disturbance and also more limited in the directions in which it can develop further without falling apart.

The second dimension I will call the dimension of *extension*. The integration of units into larger units, which in turn enter into further combinations, might theoretically be continued indefinitely; but clearly, there must be limiting conditions to be observed if one of these integrated aggregates is to function successfully both as a whole and as part of a larger whole, and these conditions may be expected to grow more exacting with every additional level in the hierarchy. For each level must depend on the successful internal functioning of every unit at every level below, as well as on the readiness of all these units to maintain the external relations that integrate them (more or less strongly) so as to form the next level above. In politics, this sets the problems that hinder the approach to world government, the working of all federal governments, and even the maintenance of active yet cooperative local *and* central government in a small unitary state. In public and private administration, it sets the same problems of centralization *and* decentralization (each the name of only half a problem), though rather less intractably, since the area within which integration is required is smaller. Individuals grouped in work teams form sections of departments in industrial plants, each of which may be aggregated with others in one of several divisions to compose a single, great industrial concern. Within the organization, every "relating" is an external relation from one viewpoint, an internal one from another; and at every level, internal and external relations must be mutually responsive. Even so simple a matter as the ability of the undertaking to complete a contract in time may depend on the ability of a department to produce some component by a given date; and this in turn on the capacity of a tool-designing section to incorporate a modification, which again depends on the willingness of draftsmen to work overtime. At every level, the part played by a subsystem depends on the systematic relation of its own constituents.

A third dimension I will call the dimension of *fragmentation*. As Professor Waddington (1960) points out, such constituents may behave as units in some respects but not in all. They may be, and indeed usually are, integrated simultaneously into several different larger units. At each level of the hierarchy just described, the units have relations with others outside their own hierarchy, with suppliers, customers, bankers, and so on; and each of these relatings plays a part in some other system. Membership of a trade union is for each of its members only part of his external relations; membership of the department that employs him is only one other among his many roles. Yet within their respective fields, the members of the union and the members of the department "act as a unit." Here again, as in the multiplying levels of the hierarchy, every addition to the number of roles increases the risk that situations will arise in which the constituents may find themselves caught in conflicting roles, as in fact they often do. Western cultures rely to an unusual, perhaps an unprecedented extent on the willingness and ability of their members to play multiple roles, most of them less sanctioned by society, less distributed by tradition, less constant in content, and less assured in tenure than are the roles of more stable societies.[1] Naturally we pay a price for this in personal and social instability—or at least we "incur" a price. The full account has not yet been paid or presented or even computed.

A fourth distinction is worth noting. Some of these hierarchic relations rest on what I will call *authority* and some on *contract*. The chain of dependence between the head contractor for some immense civil engineering project and the smallest subcontractor may have as many links as intervene between the shop floor and the managing director's office in a huge industrial plant or between the humblest civil servant and Whitehall; and in both cases, the relation rests ultimately on contract. Nonetheless, there is a difference, which I will note here and examine later when I discuss the nature of authority. This difference also, I shall suggest, is a difference of degree along what may properly be called a dimension.

Along a fifth dimension we may measure the *strength* or *integrity* of an organization. The word *system* easily acquires too precise a content; for the constituents of Waddington's (1960) units cohere not only "for some purposes" but also in varying degrees. The tendency to preserve form, which is characteristic of systematic relations, may be marked or faint. It is a matter of convenience whether we regard some configuration of relations as stable enough to deserve the name of system, just as it is a matter of convenience where we draw the interface between a system and its surround. To describe it as a matter of convenience does not mean that it is arbitrary or illusory. We must decide what relations we will group together for attention for the particular purpose we have in mind and over what time span we will examine them; but if we choose wrongly for our purpose, omitting some variable essential to the behavior we are observing or including too much irrelevance, we shall learn nothing from our study except (perhaps) our mistake.

*   *   *   *   *

Not all systematic relations are deliberately "organized": indeed, these that are so organized are exceptions, evidence of human effort to impose on the net of systematic relations in which we are entangled some order other than that which it would otherwise have. The mixture of deliberate and spontaneous, strong and weak elements that compose this "net" may be illustrated by a glance at one small sector of the contemporary scene.

A football team exists by reason of the fact that its human constituents have accepted and learned the complex mutual expectations involved in playing this team game; and within each team exist sets of specially "close relationships," such as those that enable the forward line to function for some purposes as a whole. These internal relations constitute the members of a team and enable them, as a team, to engage with other teams in a series of matches, each of which is a systematic relation in which the mutual responses of each team to the other, as well as the mutual responses of each player to the others, sustains the characteristic activity called football. Without these external relations, no one could know what the internal relations of each team are, for they can be displayed only in action against another team, similarly organized—when, incidentally, they perfectly exemplify the alternation of what I have called protective and expansive strategies (see p. 31). The matches taken together may constitute a series that decides a championship and thus a relation of higher and lower, rising and falling between the competing teams. Each of these matches and the series as a whole is also the focus of a relationship between each team and its supporters and between the total set of teams on the one hand and those who watch football on the other. This relationship in turn is, from one point of view, a functional relation that locates professional football as a constituent of the entertainment industry, while from another viewpoint it is a metabolic relation that supports the players and provides the grounds.

A history of football, tracing its development from an anarchic pastime to an organized, professionalized, commercialized sport would record the successive emergence of regulative centers, each evoked and set by the needs of the past and each an agent in the further development of the process that gave it birth.

Viewed as dynamic systems, organizations differ significantly along the dimensions that I have described, but these differences are differences of degree and correspond scarcely at all to the differences of form and function that attract the attention of law-yers and economists. They are slight when compared with the similarities that all such systems share and that it is the purpose of this chapter to stress. The function of the policymaker is basi-cally conditioned by the nature of the systems that it is his function to regulate. The mutual interaction and dependence of these sys-tems in time is the historical process within which the policymaker functions and that he aspires to direct. The more clearly the historical process is seen, the bolder this aspiration appears. It is becoming even bolder and more difficult because of a historical development that I trace in the next chapter.

Note

1. This dominance of designed, as distinct from traditional role is, I believe, of greater importance to the working and the understanding of Western societies than is commonly recognized. It is also of comparatively recent growth. A society that powerfully sanctions the obligation of role-playing while leaving wide freedom to design and change the roles to be played, has obviously developed a new and powerful flexibility of adaptation.

10

Political Choice
and Market Choice

FOR MORE THAN A CENTURY, a change, manifold yet coherent, has been manifest both in British institutions and in their policies. It has been noted and described as political, economic, social, and moral, and in each aspect it has been hailed and speeded by some, hated and opposed by others. It focuses all the quasi-antitheses of our day—freedom *or* order, private enterprise *or* public service, independence *or* interdependence. Dicey observed it acutely and described it lucidly in 1905, yet without, in my view, fully realizing its driving force. It has produced the welfare state and the mixed economy as we know them today—or rather as we knew them yesterday, for both are changing too fast for any comprehensive appreciation to be less than years in arrear. Any description of this many-sided change must be a selective simplification; it is none the worse for that if the selection is aptly and adequately made for the purpose in hand. The one that I shall offer seems to me apt for the purpose of this book. It also has the merit of enabling issues charged with emotional dynamite to be discussed in relative serenity.

I will distinguish those situations in which an individual chooses for himself from those in which one chooses for many. The first kind of choice I will call *market choices*; for whether or no they are made by purchase in a market, they are choices made by the chooser between alternatives, each of which has a cost, if only the giving up of the others; and it is made to satisfy *himself* as fully as may be, having regard to the cost to *him*. The second kind of choice I will call *political choice*; for the choice is an exercise of power over the many and each of the many who are "chosen for" can influence the choice only by exercising such power as he has over the chooser or by himself struggling into the chooser's seat of power.

One way of regarding what has happened and is happening in Britain and in the greater part of the world (though not yet in the whole world) is to regard it as incidental to an increase in the volume, the relative importance, and the difficulty of political choice.

This increase has come about in several ways. It has arisen primarily because the many who have always been affected by the choices of the few have become increasingly able and ready to insist that their manifold interests be taken into account. This is what has made political choices difficult. Tyrants of all kinds, from absolute monarchs to city bosses, have little difficulty in "choosing for the many," so long as the many are ready to acquiesce in or are impotent to protest against whatever is chosen for them; but as the many struggle to make power responsible and in proportion to their success, political choice becomes involved in all the problems with which this book is concerned.

This is not only the story of political democracy. Industrialists, for example, as they designed their plant and processes, have always chosen for their workers the conditions of their work; but they have become generally conscious of the need to take this into account, as a condition if not as a criterion of their success, only as the power of organized labor, combined with the changing norms of the culture, required them to do so.

This increase in the responsibility of those who make political choices (who choose for the many) has not arisen solely through the insistence of the many who are chosen for. An increasing volume of political activity and hence of policy making is devoted to meeting the needs of those who can neither choose for themselves nor influence the choices that are made for them—the needs of children, of the sick, the aged, the underprivileged whose political influence is weakest—most of all perhaps the needs of future generations still unborn. If we are content that our age should have seen this increase in mutual sensitivity and foresight, we shall not deplore the fact that it widens the area and increases the complexity of political choice, but we should take note that it does so.

A further increase of "political" choice has arisen through the emergence of new demands by the many that can be satisfied only by a monopolist provider. We can all choose our own motor cars, but a single authority must plan and provide our roads. Such situations multiply partly through changes in the expectations and hence in the demands of the many, partly through their increased sensitivity to the demands of each other, and partly through the increasing physical limitations of our ever more crowded island. Yet another contribution to the increase of political choice has come from the natural development of the market itself. In one area after another, competition and the technological advantages of size have left the producers so few, so powerful, and so closely associated as increasingly to unify in that field the makers of the choices that affect the many and to mute the market signals by which the many can exercise their wills or even express their wishes.

These examples are domestic; external relations show the same trend. The planet, like the island, becomes ever more crowded; the demands of its inhabitants on each other increase; and so, even more significantly, do the unintended effects on each other of everything they do. More integrated machinery is needed, not merely to meet its increased demands but even to preserve the satisfactions that it has. Economic, political, financial, even cultural stability depend increasingly on external, as well as internal relations; and, as they become more precarious, add new norms and limits to the problems of the policymaker.

The market mediates transactions that are reciprocal; but the transactions that we can afford to regard simply as reciprocal diminish. The transactions of land owners and land developers affect their respective fortunes to an extent that is trivial compared with their effect on town dwellers and road users and numberless other third parties today and tomorrow and a century hence. The ancient legal maxim that bids us use our own in such a way as not to harm our neighbor is long since out of date. We affect our neighbor, probably for good *and* ill, by whatever we do with it, perhaps even by owning it at all. The distinction, once so serenely drawn between the private sector in which the individual could do as he pleased and the public sector in which common choices must be made, is shrinking toward the vanishing point.

Political choice is characterized not merely by the extent of the power that the few exercise over the many but also by the kind of influence that the many exercise over the few. At one extreme, this is simply the threat of revolution; at the other, it is the unconscious appeal to cultural norms held in common.

Whatever the nature of these relationships between the choosers and the chosen for, one feature is almost always common. The many cannot opt out of their relationship, except (in those rare cases where it is practicable) by leaving the society in which it arises. The dissatisfied road user cannot make a better road himself, nor can his need call out some new entrepreneur to meet it. Like the parent of a child in a state school or a patient in a state provided hospital, he can express his criticism and urge his views only through political channels—that is, through whatever channels of power or influence connect him with the authority that provides the service. This is equally true of those who use services provided by public or private monopolists against payment by the users. To anticipate a later example, the rate at which the British telephone service expands and improves is a political decision, governed by the amount of capital resources that the government decides to apply to it, having regard to its other requirements and commitments; and those who wish to change that policy can act only politically.

The contract of employment was once regarded as typically one in which a man chose for himself ("a market choice"), even though the bargaining position of the parties might be unequal. The development of what is still called collective bargaining has transformed this into political choice, though this is still half concealed behind the old name and the old conceptual schema. National wage negotiations take place between two partners in what is in effect an indissoluble partnership; each partner must choose for many and is under constant pressure from the many for whom he chooses. Whatever be the nature of this endemic power struggle, it is as remote as can be imagined from those choosings, each for himself, that took place on what our grandfathers understood as a free market, a phenomenon that today we have to search for. It is significant that in negotiating with their employees whole industries are expected to deal as monopolists, although they would break the law if they dealt as monopolists with their customers.

* * * * *

That these changes have occurred is written in the history of events; but their meaning is to be found in the history of ideas, and this has caused them to be appreciated in a way that later ages and even other cultures today may well find extremely odd. It is precarious to try to summarize this complex interaction of events and ideas, but I must make the attempt, because it seems to me profoundly important to an understanding of the current setting of the institutional system in Britain and elsewhere. It is also the most relevant example of the power of an appreciative system to determine what meaning the facts of life shall bear.

The past two centuries of history is an astonishing record of the growth of responsible political power. Concentrations of political power have arisen beyond all past dreams; nonetheless, there has been on the whole an increase both in the acceptance by the power holders of their responsibility toward the many and in the control and influence of the many over the holders of power. This in itself should surely be a source of satisfaction, even though the resultant problems of policy are more exacting and intransigent.

This, however, is not the only theme of these last two hundred years. Our ancestors in midnineteenth century were not only concerned with the age-old problem of making political power responsible. They wanted increasingly to do away with it, by setting each man free to choose for himself; and they believed that they had found a way to do so beyond the dreams of any previous age. For several decades already they had been exploring the possibilities of the greatest automatic regulator of human affairs ever devised by man—a free market in goods, services, capital, labor, and ideas and free access to the market for all; and they had then barely begun to discover its limitations.

It is hard for us to recapture the sense of liberation, even intoxication, with which, in the first half of the nineteenth century, many English minds accepted the revolutionary idea that the wealth of men and nations was freely expansible without limit, through human labor, enlarged by power, guided by technology, and optimally distributed, relationally and internationally, through the automatic agency of free competition. This is how it appeared to a well-informed Englishman, Joseph Priestley (quoted in Bury, 1912):

> Nature, including both its materials and its laws, will be more at our command, men will make their situation abundantly more easy and comfortable, they will probably prolong their existence in it and will grow daily more happy . . . thus, whatever was the beginning of the world, the end will be glorious and paradisiacal beyond what our imaginations can now conceive. Extravagant as some people may suppose these views to be, I think I could show them to be fairly suggested by the true theory of human nature and to arise from the natural course of human affairs.

This faith was no mere prescription for economic expansion. Its enthusiasts believed that it would in time eliminate national frontiers (which they deemed irrelevant) and wars (which they deemed irrational and therefore unnecessary) and would unite the world in the Great Commercial Republic, which would ensure indefinitely progressive peaceful change in the direction of the self-defined well-being of each and all. A quotation from a much admired utterance of 1845 brings back its messianic fervor.

> When that mighty power who spread abroad the heavens, fixed suns in their central positions and rolled the planets in their orbits . . . binding all together by the principle of gravitation and thus

united it to other systems throughout all the infinity of being—when that Power fashioned this earth of ours, it made a reflex of the combined, harmonized and mutually dependent system which is exhibited to the astronomer when he gazes in the heavens. It endowed one climate with one species of fertility and another with another . . . constituting climates sunny or moist in all their diversities, and gave the luscious vine to grow upon the banks of the Rhine and the Rhone and enriched the spice islands with their fragrant products. It spread the broad and vast prairies of America, sufficient to grow corn for the whole world's consumption, planted the tea groves of China, endowed the sugar cane with its sweetness and gave Britain its coast, minerals and industry and by these, as by the mutual dependence of the heavenly bodies, it said—"All these belong to each other! Let their influence be reciprocal, let one minister to another; let the interest of each be the interest of all and let all minister to each." They are one in wisdom and beneficence and show forth as resplendently as the starry heavens the glory of a benevolent Providence.[1]

We should not convict the speaker of stupidity or conscious hypocrisy; many of our own age's public utterances may seem as odd to a generation less remote from ours than ours from his.

There is no doubt that men of that and the succeeding generation believed that they possessed a truth of universal application and incalculable power. In 1851 the Prince Consort, opening the Great Exhibition said,

Nobody who has paid any attention to the peculiar features of our present era will doubt for a moment that we are living in a period of most wonderful transition, which tends rapidly to accomplish that great end to which all history points—the realization of the unity of mankind.

I believe that no such faith had animated these islands since the days when the cathedrals were built, that no vision of last things had so powerfully possessed men's imaginations since they ceased to expect the Second Coming.

One aspect of this faith is especially relevant. It was faith in a natural process, proceeding automatically from human nature and the natural course of human affairs. Man's part was not to guide the process, which was neither possible nor necessary but to create the conditions for its free functioning. Liberty was the condition and self-interest the driving force of the process, and increasing happiness would be its result.

Everyone today can see the fallacious assumptions behind this conception of the process; they were criticized at the time and still more by the end of the century. Yet they persist in ways that still confuse our understanding of our predicament and especially of the relative scope and proper relation of what I have called political choice and market choice—notably, in the persistent belief that there exists a definable area, perhaps less wide than it seemed to Fox or Priestley yet nonetheless defined, in which economic forces, mediated through the market, optimize the satisfaction of individual choice and into which political choice need not and should not intrude.

What account should we give to Mr. Fox or Dr. Priestley or the Prince Consort of the national and international scene today if they could revisit it under our guidance?

At first sight, they would see little reason to question that we still share the view so simply stated by the French economist, Mercier de la Riviere, two hundred years ago: "Humanly speaking, the greatest happiness possible for us consists in the greatest possible abundance of objects suitable for our enjoyment and in the greatest liberty to profit by them."

The abundance of objects "suitable for our enjoyment" would seem to have increased to an extent that might satisfy their wildest dreams; and so perhaps might that "liberty to profit by them" that comes from higher and more widely diffused money incomes. Far more people make far more market choices. To Priestley, most of our situation would seem much more "easy and comfortable" and he would note that we have indeed prolonged our existences.

This, however, has not freed men from subjection to political choice or from the need to make such choices more responsive and responsible. On the contrary, political choice has multiplied; even the apparent area of market choice increasingly depends on it. The effective distribution of incomes derives in an important part from the political choice that redistributes them through differential taxation and state benefits of a kind and on a scale that would shock the contemporaries of the Prince Consort. A large and growing proportion of these individual "choosers" draw their incomes by working for government and public agencies in the provision of common services. The market, immensely developed as a distributor of goods, employment, and incomes, has vastly diminished in importance in those of its functions that depend on competition and elasticity—that is, as an arbiter of value and a criterion of efficiency.[2] The distinction between the public and the private sector has faded to an extent that would surprise not only our ghostly visitors but also many of us, as we realized it in the course of answering their questions. The system that seemed to Mr. Fox to mirror the stable harmony of the heavens would be described as demanding far more regulation than even our vastly improved techniques know how to supply; and even that aspect of it that the economists claimed to have isolated would be seen not merely to have failed to assimilate the "irrational" elements, social and political, around it but to be slipping back into inseparable relation with them, becoming again "political economy," if not "social economy." How many of us, as we unfolded this picture, would feel nearer to our visitors, in our sense of a vision inexplicably lost, than to our own age and to its dawning sense of a vision being reborn?

*   *   *   *   *

A survey of British institutions about the middle of the last century would disclose a sharp distinction between the private and the public sector, a distinction largely corresponding with the distinction between the economic and the political field. Wealth was generated in the private sector by economic activities, carried out with resources privately owned. These activities were regulated and their proceeds distributed through the market, which was believed to contain, through freedom of competition, a built-in safeguard against the abuse of economic power. From the resources thus generated part was diverted, under rigorous safeguards, to support the public sector in functions almost wholly regulative. The political system generated and enforced the rules under which social, including economic, life should be carried on and controlled the exercise of power in regulating relations with the outside world. Such executive agencies as were under the control of political authority, notably the armed forces and the police, were adjuncts of their regulative function and were strictly "nonproductive." The public provision of economic services at common expense—highways for example—was minimal.

The central government in 1850 consisted of eight departments, of which four were concerned with external relations: the Foreign Office, the Colonial Office, the Admiralty, the War Office (India was still the province of a chartered company). The Home Office regulated order at home. The Treasury watched over the balancing function, then largely confined to the raising of public revenue and the control of public expenditure. The functions of local govern- ment were almost entirely regulative and were largely performed by the justices of the peace. No functional public corporations had yet been created. The postmaster had indeed begun to develop the postal service on a scale commensurate with the railway age, but this was an innovation only in scale. For several centuries, the postmaster, an ancient officer of the Crown, whose primary duty was to provide posthorses for the king's messengers, had earned revenue by carrying mail for private persons and governments in the past had often successfully resisted attempts by private enter- prise to break this monopoly, which was valued as a means of political espionage, no less than as a source of revenue. So the spectacle of a government exploiting a profitable monopoly was in this case too familiar to shock an age in the heyday of private enterprise and laissez-faire. It is hard to suppose that a minister of the Crown would have been allowed to develop a function so grossly out of keeping with the spirit of the age had not history already provided him with a role capable of being expanded practically and ideologically, without threat to the system. None would have dreamed of developing the railways by similar means, though they involved a greater invocation of public power and a higher degree of natural monopoly; though the manifest need to impose some public control of them was met by establishing the Railway Rates Tribunal.

The following hundred years saw a vast expansion in the provision of largely monopolistic common services, some at users' expense, some at common expense, by central government, local government, and private enterprise. By the end of that time, a fairly clear pattern had emerged. Most of such services at users' expense, however they had originated, had been transferred to a framework of public corporation intermediate in the degree of its political control between the methods exemplified in the 1850s by the railways on the one hand and the Post Office on the other. Rail and most air transport, coal, gas, and electricity were conspicuous examples. This type of corporation has found its most advanced application so far in the development of new towns under the New Towns Act of 1946. Services at common expense, on the other hand, were still being largely administered by central and local government, both of which had reorganized themselves in the process, by slow and painful stages, to meet the enormous challenge. In one major instance, the Regional Hospital Boards, the public corporation had been invoked in this field also to bridge the gap in scale between national and local areas of authority. The difference between these methods of management, still more between these methods of reimbursement are important in their impact on the policymaker, and I return to them later. For the moment, I am concerned with their similarities.

The provision of common services at users' expense, like common services at common expense, marks a further stage in the enlargement of political choice and the curtailment of market choice. The decision whether the education service or the hospital service shall expand and, if so, how much and at the cost of what contraction elsewhere is a political decision, to be influenced not at all by school children, parents, patients in their capacity as users of the service but solely as voters and participants in the political dialogue that helps to form the policies of central and local government. Yet in fact, market regulation, absent in these, is so slight even in the control of user-supported common services that the distinction is in reality small. The extension of the telephone service, no less than of the hospital service is a political decision. The distinction, however small in "reality," remains large in the equally "real" domain of our appreciative setting. For this still ensures that, so long as users collectively pay for their service, the presumption that they get what they want—or at least as much as they ought to have—remains to be displaced, even in minds open enough to recognize it as a presumption to be explored, rather than a self-evident fact of economics or even of nature. No such presumption operates in regard to the only slightly more political choices that govern the development of common services at common expense.

By 1956, ministerial departments of state had increased by fifteen, to total twenty three; and twelve of the fifteen had heavy executive responsibility. Local government had expanded correspondingly. More than one in five of the working population (even excluding the armed forces) were employed by central and local government or by public corporations (see Mackenzie & Grove, 1957). In addition, an important part of private industry was working on government contracts and in some critical areas had become dependent on government support. In the correspondingly shrinking area still nominally regulated by the market, changes equally great have taken place. The same need for more comprehensive regulation has produced even larger industrial complexes, hierarchically organized, sometimes with de facto monopoly of their chosen fields; and it has produced also some new, though often very inadequate, regulating mechanisms for coordinating the policies of agencies still not formally integrated. Developments in the organization of trade unions and employers' federations are conspicuous examples. This increasingly organized private sector is constantly required to cooperate in implementing public policy essential to its own survival but still far beyond both its institutional power and its appreciative reach, notably the combination of full employment, economic growth, and stable money values.

So there emerges the familiar picture of the "mixed economy"—familiar, that is to say, to us who live in it. To some in other cultures, it may already seem like one of those evolutionary monstrosities that have exhausted all their possibilities of piecemeal adjustment and must now mutate or disappear. The only justification for rejecting this prediction is to be able to envisage realistic ways of meeting in the future changes that will certainly be no less radical than in the past, whether in the world of event or in the world of ideas.

One constant trend runs through all these changes—the restriction of individual choice, expressed through the market and the corresponding enlargement of political choice as an arbiter of values and priorities. Some will regret this trend, as a shift from the firm ground of individual preference, mediated through a market to the shifting sands of sectional interest, mediated by warring pressure groups. Others will welcome it as a means to secure closer attention to the manifold aspects of the public interest, as distinct from those of the well- or ill-matched parties to a reciprocal transaction. Both views are valid, and anyone able to apprehend the change with all its associated losses and gains will share both.

Welcome *and* unwelcome, the trend is inevitable for obvious reasons. As interrelations multiply, the effects of every interaction ramify. Reciprocal transactions affecting only the parties to them become increasingly rare; and the public interest becomes correspondingly more pervasive. The political controversy that these changes generate is wholly irrelevant to the argument of this book. The market never did or could supply or express all the needs of men or arbitrate between all their priorities. It has always been necessary and desirable that the needs that it could not express or supply should be expressed and supplied politically. The proportion of these was bound to grow in volume and importance. There is room for debate whether this or that need can best be met by this or that combination of free market, executive agency, and regulative power, still more on the kind and degree of regulation needed to control any set of relations, most of all on the upper limits of *any* kind of regulation within our reach and on the relative costs in every sense of attempting to regulate it or, alternatively, of leaving it unregulated. But all these debates only accentuate the need to devise a regulative system for our basically political choices more sensitive and more powerful than we now have and in the meantime to understand the nature and limitations of our present regulators.

Notes

1. The utterance is by W. J. Fox, a notable speaker on behalf of the Anti-Corn Laws League. This quotation is taken from a sampler, beautifully worked, which hangs in William Cobden's old home at Dunford, Sussex, with other of the original furniture. The house is now a conference center.

2. The development of independent measures of efficiency in business and public administration, so conspicuous over the past decades, is due in part to the realization that success or failure in a competitive market is in itself neither sufficiently accurate nor sufficiently quick acting as an instrument of control except in a competitive market where the competing units are both very numerous and very small.

11

Growth

◆ ORGANIZATIONS VARY WIDELY in the ways in which they generate the resources needed for their survival and growth; and these differences in turn affect the standards of success and failure that are applied to them both by those who control them and by others. The most marked differences may be distinguished by the following propositions:

1. Some institutions (Type A) recover their costs from those who use their services; others (Type B) from public funds.

2. Of institutions of Type A, some (Type A1) must by their constitutions, or can and do, retain for their own purposes all surplus of revenue over expenditure, while in others (Type A2), some other party, commonly a body of shareholders, has some interest in it. (This, I shall suggest, is the real meaning of the distinction commonly drawn between "profit-making" and "non-profit-making" institutions.)

3. Of institutions of Type A, some operate in a competitive, some in a monopolist market. Those operating in a competitive market are

commonly but not always those that operate for profit; those operating in a monopolist market are commonly but not always non-profit-making.

These distinctions can be schematically shown thus:

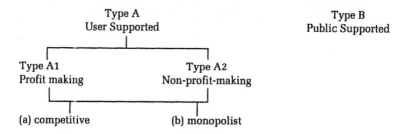

These distinctions do not correspond closely with legal distinctions. Most public corporations (gas, electricity, coal) are user supported, but regional hospital boards, which are equally public corporations, distribute free, with small exceptions, the best services they can provide from a money allocation derived from the exchequer and are thus public supported. The difference that this imports into their policy is in my experience far greater than that which divides user-supported corporations, whether public or private, whether competitive or monopolist and whether operating for profit or not. Some public corporations (such as air transport) are fiercely competitive; others (such as coal) have an extensive monopoly, though subject to competition with other fuels. Private undertakings range equally widely between the extremes of free competition and virtual monopoly. Most commercial undertakings operate for profit in that they have shareholders to satisfy; but some—for example, newspapers vested in a trust—operate, as public corporations do, not for profit, though in a highly competitive market. They may nonetheless seek to accumulate a surplus, as may the user-supported public corporations, but these surpluses can be used only to further the *function* that the undertaking exists to serve. This distinction has an important influence on what their policymakers adopt as criteria of success.

The types I have distinguished are not exhaustive. To make them more so, I must add three other types. Some undertakings maintain themselves by the gifts or subscriptions of those who support their objects. These may be for the benefit of their supporters, as with a trade union or a professional institution or a club; or they may, as with a charity, attract support for less obvious reasons. (A political party partakes of both.) I will call such undertakings "member supported" when they exist for the benefit of their supporters and "donor supported" when they exist for some other purpose. Finally, I need to distinguish those that are supported by what may be called *endowment,* the legal right to enjoy the current revenues derived from past accumulations of wealth. Charitable foundations, the colleges of the older universities, the established church are familiar examples; but some element of endowment is present in every institution whose current revenues benefit from past accumulations.

Hybrid types abound and multiply. Universities substantially endowed, are publicly supported through the University Grants Committee and are also user supported by the fees of students, most of whom are themselves state subsidized. Some of their research is user supported, being done under contract for public and private agencies; some is donor supported, often by grants from foundations that are themselves endowed. Public funds subsidize user-supported undertakings, sometimes through market operations—for example, through produce marketing boards and price maintenance schemes—sometimes by direct grant. (Beef production and opera production have this at least in common.) These supporting operations are arranged sometimes to secure government influence on policy (e.g., the Milk Marketing Board) and sometimes to minimize it in order to protect the autonomy of the recipient, the second objective being usually achieved by interposing as distributor some relatively independent body (e.g., the University Grants Committee, the research committees, the Arts Council).

These differences in the ways in which institutions secure their own survival and growth are important to their policy making in three ways. They imply, first, different degrees of dependence by those in control of an institution on those on whom its resources depend. We can rank these quantitatively, from the endowed foundation, wholly autonomous in its control of its own resources, to the Regional Hospital Board, subsisting on an annual allocation from government funds and subject to far-reaching control by its direct and indirect paymasters, the Ministry of Health and the Treasury. We can rank them also qualitatively, according to the fields in which they are thus subjected to control. Local authorities supported by central funds through block grants are subject to closer control of financial policy but less close control in other fields of policy than when they are supported by percentage grants—less close, indeed, in these, than are some endowed foundations, wholly in command of their resources but controlled in their activities by a limiting trust deed.

Even as a means of quantitative control, the categories that I have distinguished would need for some purposes more detailed analysis than I have given them. User-supported public corporations, securing their current revenues from their users, are subject to varying degrees of control over their power to raise capital. The National Coal Board borrows only from the government but at government rates; local authorities borrow partly on the market but with government consent. In the private sector, undertakings vary no less widely in the degree of their dependence on the capital market inasmuch as the nature of their business, no less than their success, determines how much of the resources required for growth they can accumulate from undistributed trading profits.

Viewed as means for subjecting institutions to varying degrees of quantitative and qualitative restraint and stimulus, the differences that I have described in this chapter, with others to be considered in the next, constitute a repertory of great flexibility and power; and they are constantly so used, both in the public and in the private sector, to meet the increasing and changing needs of regulation. They operate both quantitatively, by increasing or reducing the resources available to the institution controlled and qualitatively, by setting standards of success that those in charge of the controlled institution must at least accept as what is in fact expected of them by those on whom their resources depend and that may also affect the standards that those controlled expect of themselves.

These differences of type, however, are important not only for the kind and degree of external control that they imply. They are important also because the value that tour culture currently attaches to the growth of an institution varies greatly with the type of institution concerned. Broadly, it regards growth as itself a criterion of success in user-supported institutions but as needing justification by some other criterion when it occurs in public-supported institutions. Public corporations created to supply a service at users' expense, which are user supported but do not operate "for profit," are liable to induce the same kind of neurotic reaction as is produced in laboratory animals, conditioned to respond to different stimuli in different ways when they are presented with these inconsistent stimuli in combination.[1] These cultural attitudes toward growth are of great importance in determining the standards of success that are applied to institutions both by their own regulative bodies and by those outside. The two must always be distinguished.

*   *   *   *   *

Considering these criteria first from within, it is well to accept some plain facts about the internal, institutional urge to grow. Every individual in an organization, including every member of all its regulative bodies, is not merely a role holder in that organization. He is also a regulator of his personal life, in which those particular role-playing activities are only one among many constituents but an important one. If he feels his capacities to be underemployed, he is likely to try either to get another job or to make his own job bigger. The more difficult the first alternative, the more attractive will be the second. The growth of any institution, a prison or a hospital, no less than a brewery or a bank, is materially and psychologically good for all who depend on it for a living but especially for all who take an important part in its regulation. Furthermore, their organizational role, no less than their personal interest, impels them to strive for growth if they are competent. For every policymaker constantly finds his optimizing function curtailed by his balancing function. Nearly everything, however well done, can be done better, given more money, more staff, better conditions and equipment, and so on. The ideal norm must and should always surpass the operative norm. Our culture strongly encourages both these tendencies by its high valuation and graduated rewards for personal progress in the occupational pecking order. We must therefore accept, at least in our society as it now is, an inherent drive toward unlimited institutional growth; and we must accept it not as an aberration or a peculiar disease of bureaucracy but as an essential element in the dynamics of the system. Empires are built only by empire builders, and successful empire builders are much rarer animals than those who, after their passing, successfully tidy up their chaotic creations.

Across this general trend run the two currents that I have distinguished; the factual limitations on growth that are imposed by the organization's type and situation; and the appreciative limitations imposed by the way in which growth in its field is currently regarded. Institutions that cannot achieve growth as the result of anything they can do are likely to give up trying, and doubly likely if growth would bring not glory but odium. The result of these limitations is not always happy. For an institution that cannot grow must keep its workload from growing also, and it can usually do so only by averting its eyes from every new need and opportunity and meeting any unavoidable increase by dropping its qualitative standards. It has often seemed to me that "Treasury control" includes a dangerously efficient—though perhaps not consciously designed—device for inhibiting the emergence, even as matter for debate, of any policy proposal that, if it found favor, would seriously alter current priorities. Such refinements of control are likely to develop spontaneously in an organization in which an important proportion of the holders of policy-making roles are Treasury trained or dependent for their personal success as much on Treasury approval as on approval in their own ministries. Throughout most of its domain, the civil service has, for good and ill, developed a climate that might prove dangerously chilling even to empire builders.

In the private sector, growth is differently distinguished and differently valued. The difference is cultural: It springs from applying to our contemporary situation schemata for reality and value judgment that were developed in earlier days and are no longer adequate to classify or to value the mixed types of institution that our current needs are producing—inadequate even to distinguish between undertakings trying to make more money from the services they render and undertakings trying to give better service with the money they can make, inadequate and also unwilling, since they are the product of an appreciative system that does not admit the distinction, and even more inadequate to draw the more refined distinctions that we need.

For as I have already noticed, even the simplest organizations, those operating for profit in a competitive market, should and do measure their success in more than one dimension. They have many relations, internal and external, to maintain; and each of these can win attention in its own right when the basic relations that determine survival and growth are generating no strident mismatch signals. Conversely, organizations that have most complex standards of success may be forced, like their simpler fellows, to ignore all but one; a public corporation struggling to make ends meet becomes just as preoccupied with its profit and loss account as an insolvent shopkeeper.

Yet the basic differences in classification and valuation remain important. How culturally given they are is easier to notice in a foreign culture than in one's own. In the United States of America, the field of private enterprise is more sharply differentiated and more jealously guarded than in Britain. How else could so large a proportion of that remarkable people contrive neither to notice nor to be proud of an achievement so stupendous as the Tennessee Valley Authority? Similarly, at the time of writing, it is clear that a high proportion of them attach strong negative value to the provision of medical treatment for all at common expense, though in Britain this is probably the most highly valued of the common services so maintained. Yet in the United States, the art of *increasing* public expenditure on objects favored by particular interests is so much more developed than in the United Kingdom that I find it impossible to believe that the growth of public service, at least in many favored fields, is so negatively valued as in Britain. I know of no description of British practice comparable with Wildavsky's (1964) *Politics of the Budgetary Process*, but some of the underlying differences stand out clearly enough from Lord Bridges's (1964) account of the working of the British Treasury.

The concept of growth plays a critically important part in current policy making. Our oversimplified valuations of good and bad attach to oversimplified dichotomies between economic and political, public and private, competitive and noncompetitive; and this in turn reflects the lack of concepts sufficiently refined to deal with the variety of our institutions and the processes by which they grow. In default of more adequate concepts, we are bound to carry over implications that attach to concepts drawn from other fields. It is useful to examine four that play, I think, some part for good and ill in our thinking.

Biology gives us two models of growth. The process by which an organic structure as complex as a mammal is elaborated from the subdivision of a single cell appears to be guided by a program coded in every cell but interpreted by each with some reference to its position in the whole; hence the astonishing flexibility of response shown in repairing injury, regenerating organs, and changing form and function on transplantation. This model of disciplined cooperation contrasts strangely with the formless proliferation of the cell grown in isolation or subject to the strange indiscipline we know as cancer. The individual organism's life history shows these extremes alone—a combination of inner and outer regulation producing the phased development of a closely predetermined form of limited size and the formless proliferation limited only by the resultant destruction of the organism whose rule it ignores but on which it still depends.

On a larger scale of space and time, using populations and species, rather than cells and organisms as our units, we are familiar with two other models of growth and development, one supplied by ecology, the other by the theory of evolution. These differ in their time scale. The ecologist as he disentangles the mutual relations within and between populations that account for their distribution, growth and decay, depicts the milieu within which evolution works; the student of evolution explores the selective effect of this milieu on the species and populations that inhabit and largely compose it and presents a picture increasingly unlike that ceaseless struggle of each against all that seemed to our grandfathers to give cosmic justification to the marketplace.

None of these models is directly applicable to the growth and interaction of human organizations. The methods by which culture mediates continuity and growth are different from those of biology;

the parallel development and mutual interaction of "events" and "ideas" introduces a new order of complexity. Nonetheless, each of the four models answers a set of questions that have their counterpart in the field that is the subject of this book. Organizations emerge, endure, and grow only through a combination of inner and outer regulation inherent in their individual constituents. They sometimes lose these coordinating bonds and dissolve in chaos. They have limits of size, sometimes faintly discernible, beyond which their powers of coordination fail. Their institutional similarities and diversities are in some degree a function of their interaction in a limited field and change with time. Each statement marks out a field of inquiry parallel with those of the biologist, the ecologist, and the geneticist, though technically remote in some essential parts. The schemata developed in these more developed sciences are not without relevance in the social field. They should at least suffice to convince us that linear, unregulated growth in *any* dimension is neither desirable nor indefinitely possible.

No one today should suppose that *any* institution is a docile servant, created to serve some need and limited by the need it serves. All in varying degree help to create the needs they serve and often other supporting needs as well. All of them, therefore, need regulating; and all are capable of escaping from regulation. A crude example is the racket. The racketeer sells security against a risk that he himself creates. Since he creates the need, provides the antidote, and fixes the price, no inbuilt control prevents the extension of the system to the point at which all the consumers within his reach are paying the highest levy that can be squeezed from them. He cannot stop, even if he wants to stop; for he is a prisoner of his own organization, which requires him to go on. Such self-exciting systems can be curbed only by the exercise of external, political power.

Self-exciting systems commonly arise without criminal intent. Nearly all suppliers today seek to generate the demand that they aim to supply; few, as Professor Galbraith (1958) has pointed out, succeed unless they do so. Such systems also may easily get out of hand. In several branches of engineering, where technology is for the moment moving slowly, competition requires old models to be replaced by new at a rate higher than either producers or consumers would choose. Consumers must be conditioned to pay more, more frequently, to replace the serviceable by the no better. Producers must innovate, even when they cannot improve, in order to replace good products on which they have barely recovered their tooling costs. No one benefits but no one can stop.

The classic contemporary example is, of course, the self-exciting system that has been called the politico-military complex. Defense policy, product of a specific, historical crisis, initiates defense spending on a scale large enough to create great industrial plants and great research programs. These create not merely powerful vested interests in their continuance and growth but threaten new, intractable problems if they be discontinued. Defense spending thus becomes an instrument not only of defense policy but also of economic policy, of employment policy, of policy regarding the location of industry and population. This is accentuated by the fact that in these new connections it has few alternatives; for it is one of the few culturally acceptable fields in which government spending can vastly stimulate the private sector as producer, without competing with it as a distributor. (Its products are stockpiled and then scrapped in peace time and in wartime are given away on a scale not yet approached in any constructive field.) This activity calls into being a mass of ancillary civil activity; new posts are filled; new careers multiply. By the time the policy that created it is obsolescent, the machinery created to serve it has become part of the structure of society, part of its institutions, and equally part of its ideology.

This process has been analyzed at length and often in recent years, especially in the United States. It is abnormal in the size of the threat that it connotes but in no other way. Such things happen constantly. No human wickedness or stupidity, no ill turn of historical fortune need be postulated to explain it. It merely exemplifies in a striking way the size and ubiquity of the need for regulation more intensive, more deliberate, and more political than we have thought we needed.

It heralds also something more novel and more welcome, the emergence of concepts more nearly adequate to represent and to evaluate growth and development in our contemporary world, growth and development not only in the world of event but also in the world of ideas; and hence the hope of formulating more adequately our contemporary problems of regulation. It does not necessarily herald success. The successful regulation of human affairs is in any case exceptional. Given the scale of our operations, the changeability of our self-disturbed fortunes, and the limitations of our minds, it may well already have become impossible. But we seem at least to be approaching the point when we shall understand what it is that we must try to do.

Note

1. It is, I think, not unfair to detect some traces of this distress in what, at the time of writing this note, is the latest expression of government policy on the subject, *The Financial and Economic Obligations of the Nationalized Industries* (1961), in which the return on equity capital at risk in the private sector is assumed to be a datum of the market and hence a relevant yardstick in estimating the return to be expected by the state on capital loaned to the nationalized industries that it establishes. But an adequate critique of this statement would exceed the limits of a footnote.

12

Accountability[1]

◈ POWER IN OUR SOCIETY is now largely vested in institutions and hence is largely exercised by the occupants of
those roles that give control of institutions. The routes to power
are the routes by which men reach these seats; and the control of
power has been largely won by getting control either of the flow of
resources to institutions or of the power to appoint and dismiss
their controllers.

In politics, this is an old story. In a long constitutional struggle,
the executive was first made dependent on resources voted annually and later made, in effect, dismissible by the effect of Parliamentary elections, though only by the drastic and limited means
of preferring a single alternative. However imperfect the machine,
we have long accepted the principle that political power is *accountable* in this sense; and the debate through which political
power holders render their account and seek to generate enough
support to maintain themselves in office is an essential part of the
process whereby policy is formed.

It is useful to ask, in regard to the controllers of every institution, political or otherwise, to whom and for what they are accountable. I shall regard formal accountability as subsisting between holders of power and those who have the formal power to displace them. It follows that the content of accountability includes everything that those who hold them to account find relevant to their decision whether to continue or withdraw their confidence. Parliamentary elections show how varied are the issues that may thus become relevant.

Informally, it is convenient to give accountability a wider meaning. The controllers of a business enterprise, for example, need to retain the confidence of their customers and their employees, no less than of their shareholders; and if they fail to do so, they may be "called to account" by methods no less effective than those that are open to shareholders—for example, by customers withdrawing their custom or employees withdrawing their labor. In this informal sense, accountability is a section of the field of interaction and dialogue by which reciprocal relations are regulated, but the limited and formal sense that I am giving it is important enough to be distinguished.

In the economic field, the idea of accountability is more recent and less familiar than in politics. Even a few decades ago, the rich man, carrying on his business with his own wealth, was common enough; and the fact that he was "independent" and "accountable to no man" was not only a source of pride to himself but was acceptable and even admirable to his society. Like the landed gentleman whose long predominance he was usurping, he embodied a status that was felt to be desirable not only as a personal satisfaction but as an element of political security. The citizen rich enough and independent enough to stand up to the power of the state had always been a bulwark of liberty, and in defending his individual rights, he had often protected also the rights of individuals less powerful than he. To this ancient claim to respect was added the aura of the entrepreneur, who, according to a theory still widely accepted can get rich only by enriching others. His increasing wealth was regarded as an index of the wealth that he was creating; his increasing power was deemed to be preserved from abuse by the automatic, regulative power of the competitive market.

Accountability spread through the economic field primarily as the growth of the limited company increasingly separated those who controlled its institutions from those who provided its capital. The board, in its capacity as manager of an investment, reports annually to its shareholders, in their capacity as investors and as holders of the legal power to replace the board by another; and its primary purpose is to secure the renewal of their confidence for another year.

In fact, the board's report forms part of a much wider dialogue. It is a message to potential investors, whose reactions, expressed through the stock market and the business and financial press, inform the board often more fully and expertly than their own shareholders of the appreciation that their stewardship has evoked. It is also a message to their employees, to their competitors, to their suppliers, to their customers, and in each of these fields, it will carry a different meaning, perhaps more than one, will take its place in a different context of action and communication, and will affect a different set of relationships. It is carefully prepared with all these not wholly consistent functions in mind.

Primarily, however, it is addressed to the shareholders, who alone have the right to demand it, and it is designed to reveal what they primarily want to know, which is information simple and quantitative. As providers of the capital, the shareholders expect the board to preserve it, to augment it by employing it profitably in the business for which it was subscribed, and to distribute a reasonable proportion of the profit in dividends. The answer to these expectations appears in the accounts, which are well designed to show the results of a year's activity in terms of profitability, stability, and growth. The report provides whatever verbal commentary is necessary. Generally speaking, the more satisfying the figures, the fewer words are needed.

Strictly speaking, one satisfactory year's results give no positive assurance of the competence of management. The year may have been marked by disastrous errors of judgment, the results of which have not yet appeared. Nonetheless, repeated conformity with expectation justifies the confidence that it engenders, because of the presence of two conditions. The results expected are measurable, and they can be seen to be realistic by comparison, over a sufficient period of time, with the achievements of other broadly similar undertakings. In these circumstances, consistent achievement above or below the average for comparable undertakings raises a presumption for or against the competence of management, which is as reliable a guide as can reasonably be expected in an uncertain world.

Unhappily, these conditions are seldom present at the level of regulation that I am considering, and when even one of them is absent, judgment by results is displaced in favor of a much more refined and unverifiable process. Suppose, for example, that the results for a single year are disappointing. Questions are posed concerning management that the accounts cannot answer. Was the directors' judgment at fault? Or were they perhaps, if the facts were known, successful and deserving of increased confidence in averting worse disaster? Are they, in any case, likely to manage as ably in the future as any others who might replace them? On such questions the shareholders can only form a judgment, in the light of facts that are likely to appear not from the accounts but from the report.

"Success," in the limited and measurable sense that measures an investment, appears from the accounts, but failure can be explained only in the report. The directors will explain how the losses occurred, what they did to minimize them, and how they hope to recoup them; and the shareholders, in deciding whether to continue their confidence, will be influenced partly by the cogency of the argument, partly by their preexisting confidence in the directors, based on past experience. The auditors cannot help them here; it is no part of the auditor's task to express a view on the business acumen or administrative competence of the directors. The shareholders must make up their minds as best they can.

In deciding what to do, as distinct from what to think, they will also be guided by the bleakness of the alternative. For if in doubt, they can only appoint a committee or an expert or both to make an inquiry and give them advice, knowing that such a step, disturbing and expensive in itself, can, if it confirms their doubts, lead to nothing but another board, which may or may not be more successful. They cannot themselves manage the enterprise in which their money is embarked or even supervise its management. They must in any case depend entirely on the honesty and competence of the directors. Where their confidence is shaken, they can individually respond by selling their shares, cutting their losses, and reinvesting in some undertaking where the necessary confidence already exists, an alternative much less laborious and seldom more certainly expensive than the arduous process that might lead to reconstituting confidence where it has been broken.

Thus, even the relatively simple relations between the managers of an investment and those to whom they are accountable depend on regulation more refined than the mere comparison of results with expectations. This is even more true of the regulation of all those other relationships—with consumers, suppliers, employees, bankers, government, and many others—in regard to which the directors and the staffs of an undertaking recognize conditions and standards of success. Its extreme form is seen in the accountability of the central government, through its unending debate with parliament and the electorate, a relation that has shown a significant change. Even in this political field, there have been times in the not-so-distant past when the expectations that many of the governed entertained of their governors were relatively clear, realistic, and verifiable. Peace abroad, order at home, the maintenance and enforcement of an acceptable code of laws, a stable currency, and a stable level of taxation—these are standards that stable societies have sometimes been able both to agree in defining and to look with confidence to their governments to achieve. Such conditions are increasingly rare. We expect more from our governments yet with no certainty how far any government could fulfill our expectations. We know that the time span on which judgments of performance should be based is lengthening, and at the same time, we know that change, largely self-induced, has become so rapid that homogeneous time spans grow ever shorter, while the past becomes an ever less reliable guide to the future. Thus, the record of any administration becomes ever less conclusive, both because we are less certain what we might reasonably have expected of it and because we know that its most important achievements for good and ill have not yet had time to appear.

In such conditions, the confidence that accountability is supposed to engender depends—or should depend—ever less on the relation between some measurable course of past affairs and an agreed and realistic standard with which it can be compared and correspondingly more on those more difficult appreciative judgments that are only occasionally critical in the relations of directors and shareholders. It is a daunting prospect, made worse by the reflection that the issues involved are far more important to the citizen than to the shareholder; that the citizen, unlike the shareholder, cannot opt out of his dilemma by transferring his membership to another society; and that the issues must be discerned through the distorting medium of a struggle for power.

The accountability of a nationalized industry provides a convenient example, intermediary between the accountability of a political and an economic body, the more so at the moment of transition from private to public status. The act of Parliament that nationalized the coal industry transferred the assets, the current business, and the employees of more than six hundred private undertakings to a single newly constituted public board, which was made responsible to a minister and to Parliament for the duties imposed on it by the act. The day after the transfer became effective, the pits went on working as before, yet to the triple question, Who is now responsible to whom for what? three new answers were returnable. It was some time before any of the parties to the account fully realized what had happened to them.

The replacement of six hundred more or less competitive concerns by a single monopoly removed whatever *public* standard might have been derived for any of them by comparison with the remainder. (Privately, of course, that is to say within the new monopoly, such comparisons were more accessible, more detailed, and more valuable for regulative purposes than before.) Further, the replacement of these numerous predecessors by a monopoly that was, in the sense previously defined (see pp. 143-144), "non-profit-making," removed whatever public standard might have been derived from the return on capital invested.[2] The replacement of shareholders by the minister and Parliament as the parties to whom account was to be rendered, changed the location of the power and duty to hold to account, and the obligations imposed by the act vastly changed the content of the account. The last of these changes was by far the most important.

Broadly, the act requires the board to organize the industry, to get the coal, and to satisfy the consumer. These needs had not been absent from the thoughts of the predecessor companies and their federation, but none before had been formally accountable for achieving them. At the time when the board came into operation, each of these three responsibilities was known to be of urgent national importance; and none, as was equally well known, could be achieved in less than a space of years. The better organization of the industry had been a pressing need for decades. Its product, long superabundant, had become critically inadequate in the context of a national transition from war to peace, made under the shadow of an energy famine. Its consumers could find no satisfaction in the distorted price structure bequeathed by the war or in the uncertain correspondence between the coal they might want, the coal they might order, and the coal they might get. In each of these fields, the board had to find or establish standards of success shared with all those to whom it was formally and informally accountable. How best could they coordinate activities in nearly a thousand pits and more than twenty coal fields, differing from one another as much socially as physically? How quickly could they expect to increase production and productivity in an extractive industry that had been in decline for twenty years before the war? On what principles, having regard to their statutory duties, should their price structure take account of the manifold differentials, in extraction costs, transport costs, quality, and so on, that distinguish every pit from every other? The answers to these and many such questions were matters of judgment, admitting no finality but not beyond convergence, if not consensus, in the debate of informed and interested minds for which they called; and such answers were a precondition to regulation within and accountability without, for they alone could establish standards of success.

The early years of the Board's operations disclosed difficulties in establishing these standards within but far more outside the Board's organization; three features seem to me to be of special interest to this analysis. The first was the reaction of Parliament. So far from entering gladly on its new responsibilities, it was rent with doubt about its capacity to discharge them. Was Parliament a fit body for such a task? What new machinery was needed? A standing committee? A periodic inquiry?

The debate was useful, but its atmosphere seemed to me to demand some explanation. Parliament may not be an ideal body to hold to account a nationalized industry, but it is at least far more effective than a body of shareholders. The information made available to it by the board and the ministry was far greater than had ever before been available to anyone; and even when allowance is made for the greater difficulty involved in assessing performance of the new responsibilities imposed by the act, the resultant problems were surely less difficult than those more obviously political ones that Parliament so confidently debated every day. One cause of this initial malaise seemed to me to be the novelty—to some minds the impropriety—of even trying to assess the functional success of an economic enterprise without the aid of market criteria.

This impression was partly derived from the eerie power exercised by the ghostly simulacrum of a market criterion that haunted those early days. The board's price policy during that period was not subject to any market criterion. They were monopolists selling an essential commodity far below the price at which it could have been imported, even if important surpluses had been available for import from other sources. Some economists even advised the minister that this pricing policy was mistaken and counseled the raising of prices toward the world level—which would have given the board a vast annual surplus. The merits of the argument are not material here; it is sufficient to show that prices were fixed on *political* grounds, in pursuance, that is, of a policy derived from the duties imposed by the act. It was the board's policy, while energy was short, to maintain maximum production, even at the cost of keeping in operation some old and most expensive workings; and to sell the product at prices calculated to be sufficient only to cover costs.

The act requires the board, financially, only to make ends meet over an unspecified period of years; and though it does not preclude the accumulation of a surplus, it gives the minister unfettered discretion over the board's policy in accumulating and using a surplus—the only area in which the board's autonomy is so closely circumscribed. The minister's powers are formally wide enough to enable him to divert the board's surplus to the general purposes of the exchequer; but they have never been so used and it may be assumed that, in the absence of such a direction, the board will only accumulate a surplus to the extent that seems appropriate to the needs of the industry, having regard to their duties to present as well as future consumers. Rightly or wrongly, in the earliest years, when commercially it would have been most easy to accumulate a surplus, the political decision was not to do so. Indeed, even the price increases recommended by the board as necessary to balance the account received governmental approval only after varying periods of delay.

In the event, the board in its first five years of operation accumulated a deficit that by the end of that time amounted to £1.8 million, or about .4% of one year's turnover. The figure reflected almost exactly the result of the accumulated delays; it thus perhaps convicted the board of political naïveté. Apart from this, however, few figures in the entire report threw less light on the crucial question whether this untried body was succeeding or failing in any of the critically important tasks committed to it. Yet so strong was the tradition developed through the study of the accounts of profit-making enterprises that the board's profit or loss was the first variable seized on for comment, blame, or praise by every organ of public opinion, even the most responsible. Nothing, apparently, could eradicate the feeling that this magic figure, black or red, *must* somehow symbolize better than any other what the enterprise was really trying to do.

A further feature of the board's early years is relevant to this chapter. The members of the board carried a responsibility of far greater concern to the country than had been carried by its predecessors to their shareholders; but unlike most governing bodies, they did not inherit confidence with their office, for their office was new. No organization could have *grown* to a fraction of the size of the National Coal Board except by long continued success, which would have endowed its governing body with a vast capital of confidence. The newly created board, by contrast, had to earn the confidence it needed, both within and outside the industry;

and in the process, it illustrated dramatically how greatly account-ability, both formal and informal, depends on mutual trust.

Fifteen years later, the National Coal Board is a familiar feature of the institutional landscape, one among many public corpora-tions. Parliament no longer questions its own ability as a holder to account or the board's adequacy as an accounting party. Its com-plex of relationships, inner and outer, have been assimilated to our common appreciative system, which has itself developed in the process. Yet the signals that today generate confidence are not so very different from those that used to generate incomprehension or alarm.

*   *   *   *   *

I have used these examples to show, in the field of formal account-ability, a progression that I have already noticed in the field of internal regulation. The party that formally holds to account is a superior regulator, a regulator of regulators. Its function is to compare the performance of the regulator with some standard that it can regard as satisfactory and to react to present dissatisfaction in a way that is more likely than not to reduce it in the future. Like every regulator, it has three problems—to discern what the subor-dinate regulator is actually doing, to establish for comparison standards of what it might reasonably be expected to do, and to devise means to reduce the disparity. These means may include counsel, criticism, and support, but they find their ultimate ex-pression in the power to appoint and change the members of the subordinate regulative body. This power is to be conceived, I think, not primarily as a threat and hence as an indirect means of coercion but, rather, as the power of renewal, a power that is of critical importance in the history of every continuing body. For the adapt-ability of any group would be disastrously restricted by its mem-bers' always limited capacity for learning, were it not for the added possibility of constantly replacing them by well-chosen succes-sors. We not only grow old and die; we no longer learn fast enough.

As with internal regulation, however, the greatest problems are usually associated with the choice of standards by which to measure success. These may range from gross observable events, like the black or red figures in a profit and loss account (which might be discriminated even by a well-conditioned rat) to subtle judgments of what should be expected of an agent faced with a complex problem that the assessor can reconstruct only tentatively—problems often far more difficult than were illustrated in the earlier example of the manager and the buyer (see p. 42). The more refined the regulation required, the greater the dependence on such sophisticated techniques. The regulation of the coal board within and its assessment from outside were more difficult, precisely because it had been set more ambitious tasks than those for which its predecessors were accountable.

I have so far discussed accountability as a relationship between the governing body of some institution and those to whom it is accountable, but what I have written applies equally to the accountability of every employee in a hierarchy to those to whom he is responsible and especially to those who can promote or displace him. There is one significant difference. At lower levels of organization, it more often happens that those who hold to account share the knowledge, skill, and experience of those who are accountable to them; they may at some earlier time have themselves discharged the role that it is now their function to assess. Where this is so, the assessor is normally both better fitted to make reliable judgments of what should be regarded as success and also more likely to command confidence that he has done so. It is an unhappy but unavoidable fact that this shared experience is less extensive at higher levels of management, where none can have personally experienced all the roles beneath him, and least at the highest levels, where directors account to shareholders, or governments to electorate. It seems inevitable, therefore, that at these most important levels accountability should be most dependent, on the one hand on "match" and "mismatch" signals of the crudest and often most irrelevant kind and, on the other hand, on confidence not based on informed judgment.

Against the background of this analysis, it is interesting to note the correct form of the age-old struggle to make power "accountable." Viewed from without, the right to displace any power holder is the basic safeguard against irresponsible power. From the point of view of the power holder, however, this very power to displace him seems equally in need of some safeguard against irresponsible use, and industry is increasingly preoccupied with the problem of securing the employee against "irresponsible" dismissal. The issue becomes especially urgent in the increasingly wide field where one employer, be it a government or a national coal board, controls virtually all the opportunities of employment for whole professions and occupations. The risk to be guarded against is not merely or even primarily the risk of corruption but, rather, the risk of avoidable mistake; and this risk grows greater and less easy of remedy as the criteria involved become more refined.

The issue is not only between employers and employed. As trade unions acquire formal or factual power to deny employment in their fields to all but their own members, the expulsion of a member, for whatever grounds, involves dismissal of the employee and raises the same problem.

When we bear in mind the importance and ubiquity for nearly every individual and every institution of the problems thus involved in accountability and the inevitable conflict between the merits of crude but objective criteria on the one hand and refined but appealable criteria on the other, we may wonder that the ambitious structure of responsible power that Western societies have raised in recent times works as well as it does. We should certainly wonder still more how better to develop both the skills that refined regulation require and the discrimination that distinguishes when it deserves to be trusted and when it does not. For these are limiting factors in the higher levels of regulation and accountability that we need today and tomorrow.

Notes

1. This chapter draws on material first published in a paper "The Accountability of a Nationalized Industry" (Vickers, 1952).

2. The return to be expected is now set by a political decision (see *Financial and Economic Obligations*, 1961).

13

Internal Criteria of Success

IN PREVIOUS CHAPTERS, I have reviewed the influences *inherent in the structure of an institution* that affect, deliberately or otherwise, the working of its regulative body, either by setting what it must recognize as *conditions of success* or by affecting what it accepts as *standards of success*. These influences derive first from the means by which the institution has to win the resources needed for survival and growth; second, and more generally, from all the relations with its milieu that are implicit in its constitution and its ways of operating. Among these relations, which most comprehensively I call *interaction*, I distinguished a special class that I called *dialogue*; and among the means by which others, through these relations, can modify the powers and influence the policies of such institutions, I distinguished one power of special significance—the power to replace the members of the regulative body by others. I attached so much importance to this power that

I confined the concept of formal accountability to the relation between a regulative body and those who possess this power over it, while recognizing that in a less formal sense accountability may be said to exist between a regulative body and all who are in a position, through dialogue or even cruder forms of interaction, to react to and influence its policies.

In this chapter, I will describe the same process from the point of view of the regulative body. This is after all the viewpoint that matters. The levers of power can be handled only by those who sit in the appropriate seats; even those seated above them in the hierarchy are as impotent as outsiders or subordinates to displace the operator's hands by their own. Their only direct means of intervention, if they possess it, is to cut off power from the levers or to replace the operator by another. All else, however effective, is indirect. It is essential, therefore, to focus the differences that these institutional variables make to the mind of the operator and, in particular, the policymaker.

The differences inherent in this change of viewpoint are radical.

The manager of an undertaking is not only the centre of the regulative system which governs its internal and external relations. He is also an individual agent, to whom the undertaking is the means of support for himself and his family; one source, perhaps the greatest, of his status and success in the eyes of himself and others; the principal outlet for his energies; his principal social milieu; and the focus of his professional interests. Every individual agent, be he on an assembly belt, in a drawing office, behind the controls of a crane or in a manager's chair, is a separate, unique world, maintaining and depending upon an unique set of relations with his milieu, including the social milieu provided by his fellows in the institution and finding in it and in them his stresses and his supports. Only some of these relations are implicit in his role and even these have for him a significance different from their meaning for the undertaking. The social unit which the sociologist observes is never visible to any of the agents who compose it, except perhaps by an intellectual effort which none can maintain for long; nor is the vision of these agents accessible to the observer, except by an intuitive sharing of experience which is open to him not because he is a sociologist, still less because he is a scientist, but simply because he is human. (Vickers, 1965b)

This uniqueness of viewpoint is equally to be found, if we limit our attention to the highest policy-making echelon of an institution. If we postulate a regulative body, consisting of a small group of men who control some organization at present unknown, we can confidently assume that each of them looks out on the shared world from an inner world unique to himself, in which his role as a board member is only one element, which may vary widely both in character and degree. He may be paid or unpaid, wholly or only partly engaged on the work, dependent on it wholly or slightly or not at all, financially or psychologically or both. He may or may not have also some other role in the organization, as head of a department or with special responsibility for some function; and if he has, the two roles will certainly affect each other.

Having charted these confusing variables, I will ignore them so far as I can, to concentrate on the factors introduced by variations in institutional structure and function. I will illustrate these by five illustrations, drawn from different points along the spectrum drawn in Chapter 11.

The first example is a donor-supported body; it is in fact a voluntary organization that exists to further a branch of medical research. Its activities consist in raising funds, chiefly by gifts from those who share its concern or who it can persuade to do so, and in applying its funds first to maintain itself and then by making grants in furtherance of its aims. Four functions can be distinguished, which the governing body must regard as conditions of success or standards of success or both.

1. *Maintaining dynamic balance.* Somehow, the outflow of resources of all kinds must be kept in balance with the inflow. This applies not only to money but to all resources; staff vacancies must be filled, office stores replenished, an expiring lease renewed. This balance must not only be maintained overall; its temporary fluctuations must be kept within the limits that the flexibility of the system can accommodate. In money terms, these are the twin problems of solvency and liquidity. I will call this function *survival.*

2. *Optimizing self-maintenance.* This function of survival must be achieved as "efficiently" as possible. This is a dual objective; results must not only be achieved with the greatest economy; they must also be optimally chosen for the purpose in view. The lease

of the office must be "good value for money" *both* as a lease by the standards of the property market *and* as an office, when judged by the requirements of the organization. Everything, from the quality of the notepaper to the terms of service of the staff permits and requires some element of "policy making" (i.e., setting some standard to be aimed at) as well as of execution (i.e., finding how to attain it with the least expense of resources). I will call this double function *efficiency.* A charitable organization, such as I am describing is especially concerned with this dual function because it is expected to distinguish with special care between what it spends on self-maintenance and what it spends in furthering its objects. The distinction cannot be precisely drawn; it furthers its objects to some extent merely by existing. Nonetheless, it must draw the distinction as best it may; for its supporters, reading its accounts, are quick to note the ratio that "administrative expenses" bear to total revenue.

3. *Maximizing the flow of resources.* The greater the rate at which resources flow in, the higher the potentiality for action. Except in the rare cases where the field of potential use becomes saturated and is seen to be so, the nature of the organization requires its regulators constantly to seek to increase the intake of resources. I will call this function *growth.*

4. *Optimizing functional performance.* In addition to increasing, by growth and efficiency, the funds available for its purpose, the governing body has to apply them to that purpose; and this it can do with greater or less skill. (It might indeed act so unskillfully as to hinder the object that it exists to advance.) In judging what kinds of support to provide, which individuals, projects, institutions to support, it seeks to optimize its impact on its chosen field. I will call this function *functional success.* Though the most important, it is the least precise. Survival or nonsurvival is a manifest fact; growth is measurable; efficiency is not without its yardsticks; but functional success, in this instance, is a standard set by the not always unanimous judgment of the governing body.

These four dimensions of success and failure—the first three "metabolic," the fourth "functional"—are common to all institutions, and they impose on the regulators of all institutions what they must recognize as conditions of success. How dominant these respectively are and how far they are accepted by the governors themselves as standards of success depend in part on the nature of the institution. I will distinguish three aspects that seem to me of special importance.

As regards the getting of its funds, the charitable body I have described is as competitive as any commercial undertaking. It is in competition with every other charity for a share of that fraction of the national income that its owners can be persuaded to give away. It survives and grows solely by its own efforts; survival is not assured; growth has no obvious limitations. In such circumstances, to succeed competitively in growing will undoubtedly be found to be accepted by the governing body as one major dimension of success.

There is, however, no reciprocity between the process whereby revenue is gathered and that by which it is spent. Neither validates the other. Donors and recipients are different classes of people; and since the fruits of spending come slowly to maturity, donors have little opportunity, even where they have the qualifications, to assess the quality of functional success. Their giving is an act of faith, both in the goodness of the cause and in the competence of the organization, that experience can do little to confirm. The recipients of the society's bounty, on the other hand, are applicants and therefore unconvincing critics of their own applications. In such circumstances, functional success will undoubtedly be accepted by the governing body as another and separate standard of success, to be assessed as best they can—the more so because the individuals who form the governing body would not give it their time, their interest, and their support if they did not share its concern.

In the example I have in mind, the coexistence of growth and functional success as criteria accepted by those in control as separate and equally important led to the de facto division of authority between two committees with very slight common membership, one concerned with money raising, the other with grant giving.

The accountability of such a body is, formally, slight. It reports and accounts annually to its supporters, and machinery exists whereby these could replace the governing body; but this would require coordinated effort on a scale that only a major scandal would be likely to evoke. Its informal accountability, on the other hand, is much more rigorous than may appear. Those who raise its money operate in a closely integrated subculture with highly developed standards of what is proper and what is improper in charitable money raising. Those who distribute its money operate in a closely integrated subculture with highly developed standards of what is useful and what is harmful intervention in financing research. These two sets of individuals, who in fact manage the undertaking, are respectively members of the subcultures whose judgment they are invoking; they share the standards by which they expect to be judged, and they are personally concerned in the judgment passed on them in both capacities. They know that the body will be judged, both in money raising and in its grant-giving capacities, by the informed opinion of those to whom they are personally responsive.

Compare this with what may seem a very different type of undertaking—an engineering enterprise operating for profit in a competitive market. For it, as for the charitable body, survival is not assured nor is growth limited; both depend on the efforts of the regulator, and for both, growth is felt to be a standard, not merely a condition of success.

In the business enterprise, however, unlike the charity, there is a high degree of reciprocity between the process by which money is generated and the process by which it is spent. The proceeds derived from the recipients of the product must cover all the expenses of producing it, including the remuneration of capital and must leave a surplus for growth. Since the buyer is presumed to know what he wants, his choice of the product and acceptance of its price supplies, at least in a competitive market, some objective evidence of functional success. The governing body will devote anxious thought to the effort to predict what the customer will want, but its judgment is verified or disproved by event. It seldom has to decide which class of customer most deserves to be satisfied. Thus, "satisfying the customer," though dominant as a condition of success, emerges only slightly as an independent criterion; as such, it is subsumed under the criteria of profitability and growth.

Even that specific functional relation with shareholders that is the basis of formal accountability tends to appear as a condition rather than a standard of success. Profit distributed in dividends disappears from the assets of the company and the control of the directors no less than any other outgoing. It is the accumulated surplus that enhances their power, widens their discretion, reinforces their security, and opens the doors of further opportunity. The relation between a board of directors and its shareholders is ambivalent, both economically and psychologically. Their primary identification is with the undertaking that they regulate—an entity that depends for its separate existence not so much on a "legal fiction" as on a sociological reality, the unique and coherent body of internal and external relationships that make it an ongoing entity and that it is their function to preserve and direct.

For the same reason, the formal accountability of such an undertaking, so long as it is financially prosperous, is of relatively little importance, compared with the informal accountability that helps to regulate its other ongoing relationships with employees, consumers, suppliers, competitors, and others. The expectations of shareholders are not insatiable; in this, as in all other relationships, there is a culturally sanctioned though not static level of acceptable success. It remains nonetheless significant that the first concern of the board, as a condition, if not a standard of their own success, must be to satisfy an aggregate of individual investors, whose interests are purely financial and have no formal limitation.

The next move along the spectrum takes us to the user-supported public monopoly, operating "not-for-profit." Viewed from the boardroom, the prospect is different. Survival is not seriously in doubt; growth is not an unlimited prospect, for the field is largely defined and already occupied. Reciprocity exists, as with the private, competitive enterprise, between the processes of generating and spending resources; but the shareholder-claimant is removed; the financial requirements are defined, attainable (at least in the longer term), and clearly identified as conditions rather than standards of success. The content of formal accountability is correspondingly widened. In such circumstances, there is clearly a greater tendency for the governing body to identify its standards of success with those that for the time being are uppermost in the minds of those who hold it to account.

This tendency is sometimes limiting rather than enlarging. The policymakers may have—indeed, they should have—a concept of what success should mean, more comprehensive, more realistic, and perhaps even more ambitious than that of the opinion to which they are accountable. Something is lost if they are not free to show what *should be* expected of them. Public bodies seldom have the experience of feeling rich and irresponsible; their designers are at pains to protect them from so dangerous a stimulus. The problem of giving them scope for initiative on a scale that hitherto only the rich and irresponsible have enjoyed has not yet, I think, been fully solved, so it is well to note that it exists.

The member-supported body occupies a place intermediate between the user supported and the public supported; the governing body of a professional association may serve as an example. The body is maintained by members of the profession for their common benefit and supported, normally, by subscriptions from individuals at a common rate, though their interests in its various activities are sure to vary widely. Apart from any of its activities that happen to be user supported, it can only extend its activities by increasing its subscription, an act that needs a wide measure of common consent. Thus, though survival is assured, growth needs to be justified; it is, generally speaking, valued negatively by the members who support it and to whom it is accountable. Its governing body is drawn from those to whom it is accountable and is linked with them through the subculture of a profession; but the identity between those who find the money and those who benefit from the product exists in a formal and global way that covers much individual lack of reciprocity. There is, however, for the first time in these examples, complete identity between those who find the money and those to whom the formal account is made. These are already the lineaments of a political society.

I turn to the local authority, providing its services at the common expense. Its main features are the same as those of the member-supported body, but in nearly every instance bonds and relations are weaker. The body of citizens is less homogeneous than the members of a profession; the members of its governing body less closely related to it or to each other. The concern of individual members with the individual services for which they collectively pay is more varied and even less related to the contributions that they make. (Some, indeed, make none.) The process of accountability is less sensitive, both for these reasons and for another that deserves mention. The electorate, who are the ultimate holders-to-account, however seriously motivated, are much less well qualified to judge the performance of its governors in some fields than in others; much less, in some, than are the shareholders or the professionals in the areas where they exercise the same power. The citizen is probably a better judge of a road surface than of a police force; he knows whether his refuse is being acceptably collected, but how is he to know whether it is being acceptably disposed of? Such issues, in any case, unless they become symbolic, are not of the order that distributes political power at the level of local, still less of central, government.

In an adequate analysis of local government organization, we should need to distinguish the separate services (and their respective committees) for all of which the council is responsible but that, within it, compete for power and resources. Instead, I will notice, as a last example, one such service that is more detached. Regional hospital boards fulfill a function usually performed by departments of central and local government—the function of providing free (with small exceptions) as good a service as they can achieve within the limits of a revenue allocation fixed annually by the machinery of government. Although they and their staffs are not civil servants, the means whereby they secure the resources with which to continue are substantially the same as those available to subdepartments of some department of state. (They are significantly different from those of a department of a local authority, since every such department is controlled by a committee that, unlike a hospital board, has extensive common membership with the revenue raising authority.)

The annual needs of a hospital board must be met from an allocation made annually by the Ministry of Health. The allocation is based on a budget submitted by the board several months before, but is usually less than that budget required. In the interval since it was submitted, it has been aggregated with other hospital service budgets and again with all other services dependent on the ministry for support, to produce a ministry budget, which in turn has fought out its priorities with all the other departments of state within an aggregate limitation ultimately fixed by the cabinet in a dialogue in which the chancellor's voice is the most conclusive. The hospital board has, properly, had no part in this debate, and the allocation that emerges is the end result of battles far beyond its purview.

Once the allocation has emerged, the prime responsibility of the board is to spend neither more nor less than that amount in the next twelve months. To spend even a little less is still further to increase the difficulties of the undertaking in that and perhaps future years also; to spend even a little more is a breach of that discipline by which alone governments keep the annual spending of their department within the limits of their own plans and of Parliamentary authority and is correspondingly discouraged. Yet it is impossible, without unremitting and absorbed attention, to regulate expenditure in a single twelve-month period with anything like the precision required, having regard to the long-term commitments and short-term emergencies of which it is largely composed. The difficulty is, of course, inherent in all budgetary control, but in this instance a combination of circumstances makes it so acute as to give to small and transient disparities a significance usually reserved for crises of survival. To spend *neither more nor less* than its allocation may easily become, for a hospital board, a primary criterion of success *so* absorbing as to force into the periphery the functional standards that it exists to attain. This hypertrophy of the balancing function is a by-product of the particular institutional setup; it could not exist for a user-supported institution. Yet the decision to provide hospital service at common expense is an administrative decision. Such a service might, like coal, be provided, largely at least, at users' cost, the users being state subsidized, rather than the institution.[1]

The peculiar detachment of a hospital board has a further significant result on its accountability. Formally, it is accountable to the Ministry of Health, but that ministry is itself accountable to the Treasury, and Treasury officials have direct contact with the board for some purposes. The cases that the board argues with the ministry must often be reargued, usually in its absence, between the ministry and the Treasury. It is almost inevitable that such boards should feel that they are accountable to two bodies and are virtually out of contact with the one that matters most. At the best, the problem of maintaining sensitive mutual rapport between a governing body and those to whom it is accountable is made more difficult than in any of the other instances I have given.

I am not concerned here to discuss the question whether the form of organization adopted for the hospital service is on balance the least inconvenient that could be devised. I state some of its oddities merely to complete this summary survey of the main differences that may be imported into the attitudes of governing bodies in identifying the conditions and the standards of their own success by differences in the character of their institutions and the arrangements for their accountability. I would summarize these as follows:

1. Viewed from within, as from without, the conditions and the standards of success for an organization may be classified as metabolic or functional. These are not necessarily opposed or mutually exclusive, except that concentration on either, as a standard, tends to weaken concentration on the other. Along both the functional and the metabolic dimensions, there are many possible positions, some of which have been illustrated.

2. Where growth is dependent on and attainable by an organization by its own efforts and is further endorsed, as a standard of success, by those to whom the governing body is formally and informally accountable, it will certainly be accepted as the dominant standard of success. (A typical example is a competitive industrial undertaking in prosperity; the grant-giving body is in almost the same position.) Where growth is no less dependent on and attainable by the organization's efforts but is regarded by the holders-to-account as needing justification, its dominance in the minds of the governors will be muted but not extinguished. (The professional association is an example.) Where, on the contrary, the efforts of an organization are likely to add to the demands on it and hence to its workload, without attracting a corresponding increase of resources (as is often the case with public-supported

services), the prospect of growth may become not a promise but a threat to be avoided by all but the most ambitious and the most devoted. Where not growth but survival is in question and is even partly dependent on the efforts of the organization, survival—that is, the balancing, as distinct from the optimizing function—will be dominant; a situation that at some time or other, comes the way of most competitive industrial undertakings and some other voluntary organizations. This situation may be simulated, even when the organization is not in danger of dissolution, if the governors are held to account for a balancing achievement that in the circumstances can be achieved only by ignoring all other standards, a position sometimes approached by hospital boards and other public-supported bodies.

3. Whether or not growth is dependent on and attainable by the efforts of the organization, functional success will count for something among the governors' standards of success, so long as it is to some extent measurable or recognizable by them by criteria other than mere growth. For how much it will count will depend, among other factors, on the attitude of the holders-to-account. Where these endorse it, its weight will be increased, so long as the holders-to-account assess it by the same criteria as the governors. If the holders-to-account apply functional criteria different from those of the governors, the governors will distinguish the need to satisfy the holders-to-account as a *condition* of success but will preserve their own criteria, unless the pressure to attain the conditions absorbs all their energies. A double standard will thus emerge, as it frequently does in the regulation of political parties, when the governors take the view that the aspects of their policy that they believe to be the most important are not those most likely to win the support needed to keep them in power.

This analysis does not of itself tell us which institutional pattern will best serve any particular need; whether, for example, a particular need will best be met as a by-product of an undertaking that regards growth as its primary criterion of success or by one so organized as to attach importance to its function as such. It does, however, when read with the analysis in Chapter 11, provide some of the materials needed to answer such questions; and it throws useful doubt on the simplicities of some traditional answers, in particular on the crude differentials by which our culture at present attaches positive or negative valuations to growth. It is frequently said and even believed that every industrial undertaking that is not growing must necessarily be decaying; and the same valuation attaches in some degree to every user-supported undertaking—for example, to railways, when they lose traffic to the competition of road-borne motor traffic, which did not exist when they were built. Growth is thus depicted as a condition of success. No one draws the same conclusion regarding public-supported services. If they do not grow, the credit or blame attaches to the policymakers whose judgments of priority they thus express. The distinction reflects that sharp discrimination between the market and the political regulator—and the correspondingly distinct valuations—that I distinguished in Chapter 10 as corresponding neither to the facts nor to the valuation of today, still less of tomorrow.

The effect of institutional form on the criteria and hence on the performance of governors, is, I suggest, less simple and less critical than has sometimes been supposed. It is nonetheless important enough to merit the most careful attention from those who plan and modify the shape of institutions. It is much less important at levels below the top. The reason is obvious. The prime job of every regulator is to hold together internal and external relations, the distinction between internal and external being given by the position of the regulator. At levels below the top, the external relations of every regulator are still, for the most part, internal to the organization; and one organization is very much like another. This is an overstatement; if space permitted an analysis of the affect of nationalization on the coal industry, I should trace subtle differences in relationship all the way from the national boardroom to the coal face. It would remain true that if at each level one asked what change there had been either in the parties to account or in the matters to be accounted for, the major changes would be found in the upper echelons and especially at the top.

Institutional form, however, is a variable that can never be studied in isolation. Even in these examples, I have been led to distinguish between enterprises in conditions of prosperity and the same enterprises when in danger of insolvency, a distinction not of form but of circumstance. Decisions are taken, judgments are elicited in *situations,* collocations of circumstances that give to every appreciation an immediacy and a particularity essential to its character. It has been said that academic minds argue to a conclusion, business minds to a decision; in fact, both types of mind, if they are competent, argue to both and know the difference, but even conclusions, if they are meaningful, have a context and are only fully meaningful in their context. It is time to move the viewpoint much nearer to the subject matter, both in space and time, to examine in greater detail a few examples of judgments made and decisions taken in their actual circumstances and to notice their dual product—on the one hand, the decision itself, on the other hand, the change in appreciative system that the process of decision involved. Viewed thus, policy making may be regarded as the by-product of a *situational* process—a process, that is, by which the conjunction of a particular situation in the world of events and the world of ideas produces a new situation in both worlds, which in turn gives rise to new acts of judgment and decision.

Note

1. The methods by which developed countries provide or assist the provision of medical and hospital services vary widely not only in the extent of the assistance but also in their reliance on one or the other method or some combination of the two.

PART III

Policy Making in the Context of the Decision Situation

14

The Decision Situation[1]

◈ CASE HISTORIES ARE A LABORIOUS APPROACH to understanding. For situations are so varied that even a large number of cases may be a misleading sample, while each is so complex that even a detailed description may be too summary; and none is comprehensible outside the historical sequence in which it grew. I will take as my main example four episodes in the history of an imaginary small industrial concern. The policy making that they illustrate is abnormally simple in character and I shall oversimplify it, but it will suffice to show more complexities and obscurities than my analysis will resolve.

The first situation in which I will present the directors of this company is in an emergency meeting one Thursday. The bank had refused to extend the overdraft sufficiently to provide the wages payable next day, except upon onerous and unwelcome terms. This crisis, precipitated by the accident of a large and unexpected bad debt, was the outcome of a chain of events that I need not detail—a chain that I can more aptly describe, in a metaphor already used, as a two-stranded rope. One strand of this rope was the sequence of events that for many months had been eroding the company's solvency and liquidity; the other was the sequence of changes in the bank's estimate of its client's creditworthiness, changes equally factual but taking place in what I earlier called the world of ideas—more precisely, in the appreciative judgment of the bank manager, which produced, in the world of event, the ultimatum on this particular Thursday.

After some debate, the directors accepted the bank's terms, telling each other that they had no choice. Strictly, they had a choice; for they might have said "no" or failed to say "yes," which on this occasion would have had the same effect. This, however, would have been to choose the dissolution of the undertaking and of their own authority in a most untidy fashion. The conditions in which this would have been a serious alternative were not present, so no real choice arose. The effect of their debate was merely to satisfy them that there was only one thing to do.

The next situation arose six months later. It was provoked not by an external event but by an "appreciation," made partly to provide answers to some questions posed by the bank about the company's future prospects and partly in response to anxieties that the crisis had crystallized. This study convinced most of the board that, going on as they were, they had no real grounds for hope that they could replace their present obsolescent product with others from which they could hope to make a profit or conserve their capital. Should they try to sell the business with a view to liquidation—a course that would at best provide a poor return of capital to the shareholders to whom they would have to recommend it? Or drift on, almost certainly from bad to worse? Or reorganize—and if so, how? The third possibility elicited one positive proposal, simple but radical. The chairman, Mr. A, proposed that they should relieve from his executive duties their colleague, Mr. Deadletter, who had long been managing director and should appoint as general manager the young Mr. Redletter.

The six directors, other than Mr. Deadletter, after a long and embarrassed discussion, found themselves equally divided on this proposal. Each of the six reached his conclusion on different grounds, though each heard the arguments of the other five. Of those in favor, Mr. A thought there was a fair chance that competent management could make the enterprise pay. He believed in Mr. Redletter and was more closely aware than his colleagues that Mr. Deadletter was losing his grip. Mr. B found the choice too difficult for him, so he followed Mr. A, whose judgment he (rightly) believed to be better than his own. Mr. C could not bear to see the old firm founder, if there was any chance to keep it going, so he supported the only formulated course.that seemed to offer a chance, however slight, of its continuance. Of the dissentients, Mr. D agreed with Mr. A that the concern could be saved in time but thought it too late to try. Mr. E felt it unfair to displace a colleague on the basis of an estimate that, even if it proved correct, did not (he thought) necessarily reflect on his competence. Mr. F thought it unfair to shareholders to put their money further at risk. These at least were the dominant grounds for these men's respective decisions.

Despite their equal division, Mr. A's view finally prevailed. Neither view was certain; his was as well supported as the other. The alternative to acquiescence in his proposal was to insist on a negative course, which events could never validate. In any case, the board, even if they negatived his proposal, could never return to the mutual relations that existed before it was made.

Events, insofar as they prove anything, confirmed the judgment of Mr. A. Mr. Redletter was a success. The most important situation from which his success stemmed I will discuss in the next chapter. People began to look ahead with confidence, rather than dread to the critical year for which the estimate had predicted disaster; and this, when it came proved to be an upward turning point in the company's fortunes.

The fourth situation in this series occurred some ten years later. The position had been transformed. Output was maximal; orders and cash were alike embarrassing in their abundance. The only troubles were troubles of growth, and the worst of these was that the undertaking had no longer any physical room to grow. Mr. Redletter, now managing director, made a proposal. He wanted to build a new factory on a new site in a new town twenty miles away; and in it he wanted to devote a substantial slice of space to the development of a new business in molded plastics, which, with the reluctant consent of his colleagues, he had set up in some precious space in the existing works a year or two before.

The making of this proposal, like the making of Mr. A's proposal ten years before, "created" the situation that now required solution. The circumstances permitted a great variety of responses, any of which, had it been proposed, would have precipitated discussion in its own context. Mr. Redletter's proposal defined the context in which discussion should take place.

None of his colleagues supported Mr. Redletter. The arguments against his plan were impressive. The firm would lose most of its existing employees and would face others with hard choices. It would break its connection with its home town and its familiar source of labor. It would suffer expensive, immediate upheaval. The economies claimed in the long run were offset, in the minds of the dissentients, by an X, representing the unknown variables that would undoubtedly be set loose by so radical a change. And why molded plastics, when the traditional business was doing so well?

Mr. Redletter convinced his colleagues that they ought to do *something*. They had a duty to employ the available capital more fully: To do otherwise would be to invite a takeover bid. To him, these negative arguments were irrelevant; he knew what he *wanted* to do, so for him the mere opportunity was an effective signal. The others, however, had as yet no such personal urge to satisfy; but they accepted the fact that a commitment required them to act.

They were, indeed, ready to expand. They would have been glad to do so by buying control of some undertaking in their traditional line of business; but they had at the moment no concrete proposal of this kind, and meantime they must deal with the one they had. Among the difficulties of formulating an alternative was the fact that the managing director, on whom would fall the main burden of making it a success, favored and had advanced a detailed plan of his own. They experienced the force of the initiative that attaches to the role of the planner.

The final decision was not in the mind of anyone when the debate began, but it was unanimously adopted and pleased everyone. The undertaking would stay where it was, make better use of its existing site and swallow the coveted space begrudged to plastics. It would also buy a large site in the new place favored by Mr. Redletter and would build there a small factory for the molded plastic business only. Mr. Redletter was well content. His pet venture could develop all the better in this relative isolation; and the rest, maybe, could move out later on. His colleagues were well content also. They kept what they wanted, escaped all threats of which they were aware and kept Mr. Redletter "happy." It will be noted that Mr. Redletter, though he was in a minority of one and used no improper pressures, got his way in what most mattered to him, because all his colleagues regarded the relation between him and them and between him and his work as among the most important of the internal relations that they had to regulate.

*   *   *   *   *

This sequence of relatively simple situations will serve to illustrate some of the characteristics of what I will call the *decision situation*.

1. Although each of the three situations showed some valued relation deviating from a norm or approaching a threshold, the disparity noticed was differently generated in each case. In the first situation, it arose from an external event directly communicated—the bank's ultimatum. In the second, it arose from a forecast of the probable future course of events on various hypotheses, a forecast that created a change not in the actual state of affairs but in the board's appreciation of them. In the last situation, the disparity arose not so much through a change in the course of events, as through a change in the standard by which they were judged. The recognition of unused resources as a danger signal implied the recognition of a new standard of what should be regarded as acceptable performance by the company. The progression from the first situation to the third would seem to involve in different degrees the different mental skills involved in judgment.

2. These situations required increasing complexity both of appreciative and of instrumental judgment. In the first situation, both were precise. The situation extended only twenty-four hours into the future, and its course could be predicted with near certainty.

The most important thing to do in that period was undoubtedly to pay the wages, and there was one and only one way to do so. Inaction was not open as an alternative, for it would be equivalent to a negative decision.

The second situation extended much more deeply into the future, about two years. The course of events over this period, though its essentials seemed reasonably predictable, was subject to the vicissitudes of life; and the alternative course, if Mr. Redletter was appointed, was even more speculative. Thus, the reality judgment involved was more complicated; there was room for difference both in the substance of the forecast and in the more subtle difference that clearly distinguishes one mind from another in the way in which it responds to an event, however probable, which is remote in time. There was room also for different and conflicting value judgments. Relations to which important values attached (with a colleague, with shareholders) would be affected in ways that would be justified only on the assumption that the course proposed had a sufficiently high chance of succeeding. Instrumentally, there were alternatives, including inaction; for though the situation was in fact nearly as urgent as its predecessor, in that action needed to be taken at once if the company was to be saved, this urgency was *latent*, in that if the board had done nothing, things would have gone on as before probably for several months. (The refined abilities needed to respond to latent urgencies have already been noted; see p. 78.)

0In the last situation, the relevant reality judgment was as wide as the directors' interests and as deep as the range of their imaginations. The relations that might be newly set as governors for the future were in theory as varied as are allowable to a board of directors—and that is very varied indeed—and though in practice the scope for variation was much more limited, it was limited by the state of the directors' heads, rather than by the state of the company's bank account and was thus, at least in theory, more open to the subtle changes I have included in learning.

Thus, the appreciation of these situations and of the instrumental judgments to which they gave rise was a task of increasing complexity, making greater demands on the relevant mental skills. Differences in the relevant judgments were no doubt due in part to differences in the abilities of the agents concerned to focus numerous related variables.

3. Again, these situations varied both in the scope and in the stimulus they gave to innovation. An observer who could assess a decision situation in relation to the deciding mind, with full knowledge both of the possibilities of the situation and of the state of the mind, would see a range of possible decisions beyond the scope of the mind as set when it entered on the situation; and the observer might watch, with the fascination with which Koehler (1939) watched his apes, to see whether the mind, in the time available to it, could make the changes needed.

In other words, the decision situation is in varying degrees a learning situation. The state of the deciding mind, when it reaches its decision, is not the state at which it started, and the change is not merely the result of the decision; it might equally rightly or wrongly be called the cause of the decision. For we are describing a process of interaction that cannot usefully be analyzed into a chain of sequential events. I will examine this learning process a little further in the next chapter, when I return to the third situation in which Mr. Redletter first made his mark.

In considering the powers of various situations to generate innovation, it is useful to compare the second situation with the third. The second situation appears at first sight as hedged about with limitations, the third to abound in opportunities. Yet it was precisely the limitations of the second that enabled the chairman to win support for the radical innovation that he proposed; and it was equally the physical limitations of the third situation that enabled Mr. Redletter to win his colleagues' support for the innovation of building on a second site. In each case, the limitation provided the opportunity. And rightly so, for the unwillingness of the mind to innovate more than it need is well-founded. Every innovation disturbs the appreciative system, usually to a greater extent than can be foreseen. It always needs to be justified.

In both the second and the third situation, the innovation was greatest in the minds that did not propose it, and it was their capacity to "learn" that set boundaries to the rate and the depth of its penetration. (It always is, as I have already stressed in the

example of the Buchanan report, 1963.) Mr. A had long wanted to
see Mr. Redletter in a position of greater scope; the only innovating
achievement of his mind was to recognize that a moment had come
when the dramatic promotion of the man was not only necessary
but possible. Mr. Redletter had hoped for years for the chance to
develop his interest in molded plastics, and he had dreamed of
planning a factory from the bare site, as a young architect might
dream of being commissioned to plan a new town. He had only to
recognize that he now had at his disposal not only the resources
but also a reason sufficiently cogent to persuade those who did not
share his dream. The challenge to innovate came to those who had
not taken these preliminary steps, who had not merely to decide
but to realize and revalue the alternatives before them.

4. One further feature of the second situation deserves special
attention, though I can offer no adequate explanation of it. The
critical fact in this situation was that Mr. A "believed in" Mr.
Redletter and that his colleagues in varying degrees believed in
Mr. A. From his knowledge of Mr. Redletter, Mr. A confidently
postulated that he would successfully discharge the duties of a
position in which he had never been. The prediction was based on
experience of Mr. Redletter in other regulative positions but much
less exacting ones, and it was made of a future Mr. Redletter not
identical with the one previously experienced but older and
changed by experiences, of which the proposed promotion would
certainly be one of the most important. The other directors, in their
turn, having less experience of Mr. Redletter or having drawn less
positive inferences from the experience they had had, extended
increased confidence to him, because of the confidence they felt
in Mr. A's judgment. And the confidence they thus extended was
no mere sense of assurance that Mr. Redletter would do what he
was told or that he would not make off with the company's cash.
It was an assurance that he would solve competently and responsibly in his own way the problems known and unknown that would
come his way as the company's chief executive, a task that, once
it was assigned to him, no one could do for him or even effectively
supervise until after the event. This capacity of human beings to

build up, from what seems the flimsiest evidence, comprehensive expectations about each other, that prove on the whole sufficiently reliable to provide a basis for vital and irreversible commitments is a psychological and social fact of the greatest importance, which I think is too easily taken for granted.

*   *   *   *   *

Before leaving these examples, I would comment on one characteristic that they share with every situation—their extreme *particularity*. Each was conditioned by a vast number of unique facts—by the past experience and present health of the individuals involved, by the other matters that were competing for their attention at the time, and by a host of other particularities too numerous and diverse even to illustrate. This gives to actual decisions a character that hypothetical decisions can never truly simulate; for hypothetical decisions are never particular *enough*. To the question, "How would you vote, if there were an election today?" the serious uncommitted voter should reply, "In what circumstances am I to assume that an election has been brought about? I can't assume an election in a vacuum; they don't happen that way." There are of course those who would know the answer, irrespective of circumstances; just as there are those who would express a preference for celibacy, as against matrimony, irrespective of any particular partner. But for most people, the decision for or against matrimony is a by-product of a series of situations, each involving a possible mate.

Note

1. This chapter draws on material first published in the sixth Elborne Memorial Lecture "Judgment" (Vickers, 1961).

15

Decision as Learning

◆ I HAVE ALREADY STATED THE PROBLEM that Mr. Redletter inherited when he became general manager. All the undertaking's products would be obsolescent or obsolete in two years, and the plan for replacing them, which the former managing director had put forward, carried conviction to no one but himself. Mr. Redletter soon found that they also carried no real conviction to the heads of the three departments that would be concerned to carry them out. The head of the marketing department felt no assurance that he could sell the proposed product, except at prices below those at which the head of the production department thought it could be made, unless they incorporated some novel features, which the head of the research and development department had not yet suggested. In the absence of a policy that they could all accept, the three departments had fallen somewhat apart under the strain, and each tended to insist on his departmental viewpoint. The first reminded his colleagues that ultimately the public would decide the success of the product, and it was he who must sell it to the public. The second added that nothing could be sold until he had made it, and it was he who knew the possibilities and limitations of the plant. The third observed that nothing could be made until he had drawn it. He would integrate as much as he could of his colleagues' inconsistent requirements, but he would not ignore his own view of what the public would like when they saw it or what his colleagues could make and sell when they really tried.

At a meeting with his three department heads, Mr. Redletter led them first to reach agreed assumptions about the most probable course of the variables not under the company's control; the potentialities of the market, the trend of design, the nature of the competition, and the levels of prices two to three years hence—speculative estimates with a large margin of error but nonetheless necessary in building their common picture of the realities of the situation in which they would be acting and to which they must respond. Next, he had to settle those variables that depended on company policy and resources. The marketing manager's attitude depended to some extent on the amount of his sales promotion budget; the production head's on the provision for tooling and new equipment; the designer's on the staff available for the project and the pressure of other work; all of them on the amount of time allowed them for their respective tasks. Yet each of these factors affected those two crucial variables, the price at which the product could be sold and the date by which it could be ready.

Each of these departmental variables was a matter not of calculation alone but of judgment. What each of these men could achieve in his own field with a given amount of time and resources could not be known with certainty in advance. None could be forced to accept responsibility for what he believed to be beyond his powers; yet each was liable to systematic error, cautious or optimistic, in estimating his own capacity; and each would be affected by the systematic errors of the others.

There was of course nothing unusual in this situation; such subtle partnership is always involved in acts of collective creation. Each participant, but especially the planner, has to be aware of the limitations and possibilities of the other functions involved, not only as they are but as they might be. Mr. Redletter, in remaking this partnership, was both helped and hindered by the company's situation, which restricted the resources he could provide but sharpened the common sense of urgency to reach an agreed solution.

This sense of urgency was different, even at the level of Mr. Redletter's meeting, than it had been in the boardroom. Like the departments of a local authority, the departments of a company, even though more closely integrated, have their own criteria of success. For the marketing department, this includes beating their sales target, keeping good relations with their customers, and the respect of their rivals. For the production department, it includes the transformation of a design into a product in a way that yields professional satisfaction both in the process and in the end result, a transformation not so easy as to be uninteresting yet not unduly bedeviled by last-minute alterations, impossible datelines, "teething troubles," faults that elude inspection, or processes that make excessive scrap. For the designers, success means primarily the integration of stubborn, disparate requirements into a design aesthetically and functionally satisfying, a credit to the minds that produce it. These departments exist to make sales, to make products, to make designs, not to make money; and all of them will succeed more easily the lower the profit margin required. For each of them, the company's growth and prosperity is only a *condition* of their own success—a condition in which the engineer is more likely to get the new equipment that he covets, the marketeer the increased advertising allocation, the designer the extra staff.

Mr. Redletter's exercise with his department heads confirmed the forebodings of the board. Within the limitations of the three departments as they then were, it appeared impossible to produce, by the required date, in any price range, any product that had a reasonable chance of competing successfully with what was likely to be in competition with it at the date of its appearance. He displayed starkly to his department heads the implications of this finding. If they could not produce a brighter prospect, the undertaking would have to go out of business. He pressed and beguiled them for innovation.

To Mr. Redletter the failure of the exercise was neither a surprise nor a disappointment. He had long reached in his own mind the conclusion that the board had only now attained. The company was coming to the end of the road it had followed so long. He saw only one way, given its size and resources, in which it could put itself in a sufficiently commanding position in part of its market. This was not a part that had previously been its chief target, and the change would involve radical alteration in manufacturing technique, which would also restrict the designers in their customary line of development and would involve abandoning a feature that was strongly associated with their past success. Thus, the change would involve difficulties and unaccustomed limitations for all three departments yet would depend for its success on a high degree of commitment and resolution on the part of all of them. To achieve this with his already somewhat demoralized team so soon after taking his new office would, he rightly judged, be more difficult than to persuade the bank to finance the new plant that would be needed. So he deferred making the suggestion until he was satisfied that each of his subordinates had accepted both the need for innovation and his own responsibility for contributing to it. He would have been glad if any part of his plan could have been elicited from one of them.

At the end of the meeting, Mr. Redletter put forward his plan clearly and persuasively, making clear his own confidence in it and in their capacity to make it a success. He gave his colleagues long enough to ensure that they fully understood it and then adjourned the meeting for three days, pointing out that they must then work out the details of his proposal or of some workable alternative. When the meeting reassembled, he sensed that a new spirit was abroad. The department heads were still concerned to discuss the difficulties and limitations of the new plan, but he could sense that while they did so their minds (with one possible exception) were already intrigued with its possibilities. Within the new technological assumptions, it was possible to plan the general features of a product on which they could all embark with hope and confidence, and this they did. They had passed what I will call the stage of initial acceptance.

Many more meetings were to follow, as the product passed from sketch to model, from model to prototype, becoming at each stage more precisely defined; and at each stage the weight of decisions already taken would narrow ever more rigorously the scope for further change. I will not follow the sequence further; it will be sufficient for the purposes of this chapter to analyze the changes that took place up to the stage of initial acceptance. These changes took place in the minds of the four participants and can all be described as learning, partly also as teaching.

The first step was to achieve in the minds of all concerned an appreciation of the situation; an appreciation common to all in its essential features and vivid enough to elicit a commanding mismatch signal, although the picture that it threw on the screen of today was of a situation that would arise two years later. This signal could be regarded as a threat or as an opportunity, a threat to the continuance of the organization and an opportunity for creative innovation; and it was so regarded by each of the four characters in the story, according to his temperament, in one way or the other or both.

All four men responded to the signal by a series of instrumental judgments, beginning with the most familiar and extending as far as the range of their imaginations permitted. If we could follow their mental operations, we should see, for example, the production manager reviewing all the possible changes in technique with which he was familiar, then debating with himself the possible usefulness of new techniques that he had read of but not used. We might see each attempting to see the problem as a whole, to envisage changes in the practices of other departments as well as his own. Probably some possibilities escaped the attention of each of them. That the general manager produced a solution that had not occurred to his colleagues may have been due to his greater skill in instrumental judgment, but it certainly owed something to his position.

The impact of the proposed change on the company considered as a whole was notably less than its impact on each of the departmental subsystems, especially the production department. Yet each of these had to assimilate it if it was to be successfully produced, and each had to assume its assimilation by the others. Only when the general manager pressed them to suppose themselves possessed of plant not yet acquired, committed to the use of a technique not yet practiced, and divorced from a class of product with which they were identified did they seriously apply their judgment to this aspect of hypothetical reality; and even so, it would not have had a fair examination if the general manager had not been in a position—partly because of his authority, partly because of the external situation—to keep it on the agenda until his colleagues had made painful adjustments to their appreciative systems.

All this was easier for the general manager. He had, in fact, a wider knowledge of engineering practices throughout the world and a livelier consciousness of how they were developing. He took a longer view of the development of the market. But apart from these advantages, his role freed him from departmental limitations and emphases, which made the proposed change seem more radical for each department than for the undertaking as a whole; and it involved a smaller change in his personal standards of success. The "setting" of his system of readinesses—to see, to value, and to respond—was more apt to produce the instrumental judgment that was adopted and to appreciate its possibilities. Similarly, the slowness of his colleagues to think of this solution or to appreciate it when they first saw it argues no abnormal dimness on their part. An appreciative system is necessarily selective; its distrust of experiment performed solely with hypotheses and hypothetical situations on the mind's machinery is well-founded; and its preference for the less radical, rather than the more radical is based on a true judgment of the cost of unlearning and relearning, however necessary.

Nonetheless, this slowness was a fact of the situation of which Mr. Redletter needed to take full account. His appreciation of the situation included the possibility that it would make demands on his department heads greater than one of them at least—the "possible exception" to whom I referred earlier—would be able to compass; and it soon became apparent to him that this man, though intellectually satisfied with the need for the change and loyally doing his best to play his part in it, was unable to identify himself with it sufficiently to do what it required of him. The new dispensation did not fully succeed until this man had been replaced. Two other valued men, at other levels, whose satisfaction in their work had been reduced by the change, were also lost in the next twelve months; so the change was not affected without cost, though this was minimized by the way in which it was introduced.

The changes that I have described altered the mental organization of all the parties to the debate in ways more subtle than we can yet describe. In the terms that I am using, it altered both the ways in which they were ready to see and value their situation (their appreciative setting) and the ways in which they were ready to respond to it (their instrumental system). These terms are inadequate to describe, still more to explain these complex changes, but they serve to keep in view the principal dimensions of change. One change deserves special attention, because it is both specially important and specially obscure. This is the change that occurred at the point that I described as the point of acceptance. From this time on, all the protagonists except one accepted the plan not merely as something that was going to happen but as something that they were going to do. One man's inability to take that step made him, from that moment on, a drag on the wheel and a danger to the enterprise. We have a number of expressions in common speech to describe this change. We may say that they "identified themselves with" the plan; perhaps we should do better to say that they identified the plan with themselves, assimilating its achievement into their personal standards of success. I do not mean merely that they came to like what they had previously disliked; the change was of a far more radical kind. By accepting what they had at first rejected, they became committed to what would otherwise have been merely something that was going to happen. *A potential fact had become a potential act.* I will not pursue further here the nature of this obscure change, but it seems to me important to stress it, both as a psychological change that is theoretically obscure and as one of the most familiar facts of experience. Mr. Redletter knew that for the success of his plan it was essential not merely that his team should understand it or that they should dutifully obey his orders in attempting it but that they should *accept* it in the sense that I have just described; and he knew this not because he was a psychologist (which he was not) but because he was a competent and experienced business man.

16

The Elusive Issue

◆ THE SITUATIONS THAT I HAVE DESCRIBED in the last two chapters are abnormally simple. The policy-making discretion of the directors and chief executives of small commercial undertakings, though much wider than is commonly supposed, is narrow by comparison with that of many other policy-makers. The number of persons involved in the dialogues that each situation involved was manageably—but unusually—small. The examples were chosen with this in view; and they were chosen as a sequence, because no situation is understandable unless it is seen in its place in the unfolding, dual sequence of events and ideas that condition it—the two-stranded rope of which it is a tiny section. A representative set of case studies would be far beyond the scope of this, perhaps of any, book. Yet I would not wish to leave the study of situations, in all their particularity, without adding some further examples, also on a small scale but taken from different milieus. For the first, I will revert to the local authority, which, as

I have already suggested, illustrates in its policy making, more clearly than the profit-making undertaking, the obscure though familiar process of optimizing disparates.

This authority, I will suppose, is approached for permission to develop an area of land within its borders by building an important industrial plant and an associated housing estate. The proposal, if it were accepted, would involve altering the order and hastening the speed of the authority's proposed development and making one substantial change; but the authority is not so far committed as to make such changes impossible. A policy issue is thus posed for decision. In Britain, such questions are now decided within so complex a net of national policy, organization, and precedent that it would be hard to state the problem both simply and realistically in a British context, so I will suppose that it arises in one of the many places, for instance in North America, where such matters are still decided substantially as a matter of local policy. Even so, it is complex enough.

As in previous examples, the proposal not merely constitutes a new fact in the situation; it creates a situation. Before it was received, the future development of this area was outlined tentatively and in general. The authority must now choose whether to commit it irrevocably and in detail or to refuse a particular commitment, which will itself involve a decision carrying commitment to the principles on which the refusal was based. The mere proposal has irrevocably changed the status quo.

The development, though it is to be financed by private capital, will, if it is permitted, affect every relation that the authority is concerned to maintain. It will increase in different degrees and at different rates the demand on all services, roads, sewerage, education, public transport, and the rest and hence their cost and also the burden and responsibility—and perhaps the importance and rates of pay—of the staff concerned. It will also increase the ratable value of the area and hence the authority's potential revenue but in a different proportion and at a different tempo. Those primarily concerned with "metabolic relations," be they officials or members of the council, will be concerned first to see whether the development will jeopardize or aid the balancing of revenue and expenditure. Those primarily concerned with functional relations will think first of its impact, quantitative and qualitative, on those relations. It will overwhelm the present sewage disposal facilities and upset the assumptions underlying the present plans for expanding the educational service. At a lower level but one nonetheless important to those who are responsible at that level, it will increase the peak load on an already crowded road, provide a welcome addition to the demand on an underloaded branch of the public transport service, and so on. To each individual concerned with any aspect of the regulative process, the proposal will appear as an impact on a different current problem, which it will affect for good or ill.

It will also have more general effects. It will increase the number of available houses, increase employment, and change the character of the town; and these, too, are of concern to some or all of those who have some influence on the decision. These are only a selection from among many other changes that the development will make to the internal or external relations regulated by the council; and they are noticed (if they are noticed) because they affect appreciations on which current policies are based. Their effect on relations that are not of concern to the council or to anybody of opinion who can influence the council will remain unrecognized, however important they may seem to outsiders or to a later generation.

We can regard the proposal as posing one or both of two questions to everyone concerned with any of these relevant relations, and inviting the reappreciation needed for an answer. Can the proposal be accepted? Should it be accepted? The answer to the first depends on a reality judgment, to the second on a value judgment. The answers to the first question amounted in total to "Yes, if—." The thing could be done, if its factual implications were accepted and dealt with, as they could be. Two of these were of particular importance. The first was its impact on the town's sewage disposal system. This was already near the limits of its capacity and was giving unsatisfactory service in some outlying areas, including the one to be developed. To accept the proposal would precipitate the time when a new, centralized disposal plant would have to be installed and the whole system reorganized.

A scheme for this development had existed for some time, but it was expensive and had never yet won the necessary priority. Meantime, the increasing disparity between the system as it was and as many of those concerned thought it ought to be was generating pressure in its favor. Councillors representing the ill-served area were sensitive to their constituents' complaints and so, to a lesser degree, were some of their colleagues. Owners of property in the area looked forward to the enhancement of values that the new scheme would bring. The chief engineer, who had invested much professional thought in the new scheme, was increasingly frustrated by its delay, for the existing, piecemeal arrangements hurt his professional pride and made endless trouble, and he infused his committee with some of his discontent. All those who for whatever reason were sufficiently concerned with this issue to make their views felt I will call the sewerage interest; they included what I will call a sewerage lobby, consisting of those outside the council who were uniting to bring pressure on the council to expedite the scheme. The sewerage interest was disposed to welcome the development scheme, apart from any other merits or demerits it might have because it would carry with it the desired priority for the new sewerage scheme.

The proposal, however, ran foul of another powerful interest. It involved restricting or redrawing an area that had been reserved, in the authority's long-term planning, for purposes of amenity. Any proposal to modify this part of their plans reawakened a dispute on principles that had deeply divided the council when the question first arose—a dispute reflecting differences not only in their rating of the value of open spaces as such but also in their conception of the proper scope of planning. Any threat to this tentatively protected area awakened intense resistance in those who saw it as a threat to the principles of long-term commitment, which they believed to be essential to planning, while this very resistance seemed to others no less a threat to the flexibility that they prized and that they felt to be threatened in an increasingly planned society. Many of these would never have consented to its original, tentative protection, if they had not thought that technical difficulties would in any case restrict the development of this particular site. The advance of technology had, as usual, upset their appreciation. So here too the development proposal raised issues other than its own.

Thus, to the second question, "Should the proposal be accepted?" there were those who answered yes or no without reference to the merits of the proposal but solely by reference to the effect that acceptance or rejection would have on other issues that they judged to be more important. I will leave these aside (though they might have been decisive) and ask, "What were the answers of those who considered the merits of the proposal *in itself?*"

The proposal *in itself* had no merits—or demerits. There was indeed a "development lobby" of interested persons who were trying to get the proposal accepted. Some saw it in the context of their personal, material interests; they wanted to sell their land at an enhanced price. Others saw it in a wider context and welcomed it as "growth" or as promising more employment. There was also an "antidevelopment lobby," ranging equally widely from those who wanted to protect their adjacent property from depreciation to those who resisted what they thought would be a change for the worse in the character of the town. The proposal had no merits, except in relation to one or more of several configurations of current relationships that it would affect in ways judged good or bad by the appreciative judgments of those concerned.

Yet these were not of equal relevance. The primary purpose of the control that the council was exercising was to influence the physical development of the town in a way that would "optimize" the values that development would bring, while conserving the dynamic balance of the resources on which that development depended; and those responsible for exercising the power had a duty to take into account *all* the changes in what they regarded as the relevant variables that were likely to flow from assent or refusal. Which values mattered most or at all was a matter for judgment; only another judgment could decide between those who, trying to answer the right question, produced different answers. It was, on the contrary, a matter of fact (though of fact seldom possible to ascertain) whether a deciding mind had applied itself to the right question.

The "settlement" of such an issue involves two different processes and has two different meanings. It involves deciding both what to think and what to do; both revising appreciative settings and agreeing on an executive decision. The two are distinct. Among the directors of the previous example, those who agreed on action differed widely in the appreciative judgments that led them to do so. Similarly, in the present instance, the prodevelopment party and the antidevelopment party differed equally widely both in the nature and in the propriety of the appreciations that made them advocates of assent or negation.

The result in terms of action was that the sewerage scheme got its priority; another area was scheduled for "amenity"; and the development was sanctioned, though with aesthetic requirements that would not have been imposed but for the historical accident that made it necessary to placate the "amenity interest." The limitations that this imposed on the architect of the development appeared at first as a barely tolerable limitation, but as it happened, they produced a solution that was twenty years ahead of its time.

The other result was expressed in changes in the appreciative systems of influential minds within and without the council and in the general culture that they influenced. The idea of the town as it was and as it might be and of the relative importance of the various elements of this idea was changed as a result of the debate; and the future policy of the council was affected both by these inner changes and by the physical changes that accompanied them.

This example helps to make a point that has been growing clearer from earlier examples. Considering how many different relations are affected by a change in any of them, it might be thought that "the issue" that creates a decision situation has no necessary connection with the "issues" on which it is decided. What starts as a proposal for industrial development may be decided as an issue about the priority of a sewerage scheme or as a battle for power between parties divided on the merits of long-term planning or on any of a number of still more remote issues, none of which has any a priori right to be regarded as the issue. This is in one sense true; yet in another sense, the decision situation is deeply conditioned by the nature of the question that has to be answered. In the example just given, an application was made, which had to be granted or refused. However varied the reasons, these were the forms that the possible answers must take. However wide the debate on "optimizing" that the question released, the restriction of possible answers gave it a limitation and a direction that would have been different if the debate had been released by a different question. The choice to be made is not in general how to optimize but which of usually only two alternatives is on balance to be preferred. More often, it is further narrowed; for the two alternatives may be so related as to cast the burden of proof on the exponents of one answer or the other. In the instance just given, it is probable that refusal would have been politically more difficult than assent. In all such cases, a binary choice is involved, which falls one way, unless it engenders enough resistance to reverse it. These facts are well-known to those who wish to arrange the business at policy-making meetings so as to favor an optimal debate or alternatively to secure the result they desire. They also help to explain how something so difficult as policy making is ever done at all.

17

The Budgetary Decision

◆ THE POLICYMAKER'S FUNCTION, as I have described it, is to "balance" and to "optimize." He must maintain those relations between inflow and outflow of resources on which every dynamic system depends; and he must also adjust all the controllable variables, internal and external, so as to optimize the values of the resulting relations, as valued by him or by those to whom he is accountable. The two elements are present and inseparable in every decision, but in different situations one or the other may be dominant. Thus, in the first and second of the situations described in Chapter 14 the board's problem was primarily to balance—how to keep the concern solvent—while in the fourth it was primarily to optimize—how to make the best of surplus resources.

The balancing judgment is a judgment of reality; the optimizing judgment a judgment of value. They are interconnected, as judgments of reality and value always are. In the second situation, the alternatives open for balancing the budget were limited, for two minds, by judgments of value inconsistent with the value of survival. In the fourth situation, the optimizing problem was set by the managing director's appreciation of the fact that the limitations of balancing at last permitted the development of which he had long dreamed.

When appreciative judgment, having set a problem, sits in judgment on the proposed solutions that instrumental judgment offers, it applies both balancing and optimizing criteria—first, Can this solution be contained within the resources available? and second, Will it provide as good a solution as is available to the problem set when judged by the manifold and inconsistent standards of value that are applicable? Both types of criteria are always applicable, though one or the other may attract attention as the limiting or difficult one; and each may have to be applied to several aspects of the problem, perhaps with different results, as the local authority found in the illustration in the last chapter.

The balancing judgment is wider than its name implies, for it includes two kindred judgments concerning the return to be expected from any expenditure of resources; first, What surplus (i.e., profit) will it show in terms of any of the resources involved? and second, Is this as large a return as can be secured from each unit of resources spent? I will replace the term *balancing* by *budgetary* to include more naturally these three types of judgment. Thus, budgetary judgment covers what I have described as the three metabolic criteria of success; survival, growth, and efficiency. I shall be chiefly concerned in this chapter with budgetary judgments and the situations in which they dominate.

Budgets cannot be balanced, any more than values can be optimized, once for all; the process is continuous. It is nonetheless divided for the policymaker into particular spans of time, partly by his own decisions or habits,[1] which may require annual accounts, five-year plans, and so on, but also by the accidents of history that punctuate its course with moments of opportunity and threat. The policymaker may be concerned at the same moment with both short-term and long-term problems; the way in which he divides his attention between the two is one of the measures of the quality of a policymaker. The long-term problems with which the directors dealt successfully in their second situation (see p. 184) were already with them even before the first situation arose. One of the most important results of the first situation, apart from evoking its own solution, was to adjust their appreciative systems sufficiently to enable them to face and deal with the second situation.

In money terms, short-term and long-term problems may be distinguished, as in the two instances just given, as problems of liquidity and solvency; but budgetary decisions are not concerned only with money. All resources have to be budgeted—materials, energy, skill, time, and attention. None can be spent at a greater rate than that at which it can be generated, except by some form of borrowing, which must some time be repaid, and few of them admit such credit operations. Mr. Redletter in his third situation dealt skillfully with budgetary limits of another resource—morale. The steps needed to regenerate the morale of his staff involved an initial strain upon it, and he was at pains to minimize this strain, knowing that the resource was nearly exhausted.

A famous Antarctic journey gives a good example of a problem of "liquidity" set in terms of energy over a period defined by accident (see Mawson, 1915). On December 12, 1912, a disaster that destroyed half his party left Sir Douglas Mawson with one companion and ten days' rations at what seemed the extreme range of their possible return to base. His budgetary problem was to restrict their food intake to what would maximize their traveling powers, having regard to the energy reserves in their bodies; a subsidiary problem was to decide whether, as their six weak dogs successively died, to eat them or to feed them to the surviving dogs.

Mawson reached his base fifty-eight days later. From the twenty-third day, when his companion died, he was alone. His budgetary problem was largely solved on the forty-seventh day when, in the dimness of an Antarctic summer night, he spotted a cairn, hopefully raised by his anxious base party to mark a cache of food. At that time, he had still thirty ounces of his original rations and twenty-three miles to go.

The example is abnormally simple. The total supplies of energy available to Mawson were the food on his sledge and the physical reserves of his body and these he could by no means increase; he could only adjust their input so as to maximize their output in terms of distance covered. This standard was set and maintained to the last by his inflexible resolve to return to base if he could, a resolve that remained unshaken, even when he no longer had any serious hope that it could be achieved. Given these inexpansible resources and this unchanging norm, his problem was purely the budgetary one that I have called *efficiency* or how to maximize the value gained per unit of resources spent. The measure of value, however, was not a budgetary decision and remains the most interesting aspect of the illustration; for no one reading his story can doubt that his will to return to base derived from something stronger as well as subtler than the biological will to survive. (Few men can have gone on so long in circumstances in which it was both so hard to live and so easy to die.) It derived from a commitment, required by the mutual expectations that bind together the members of such an expedition and govern their mutual behavior with a firmness seldom felt in societies less threatened and less mutually dependent. Had Mawson admitted, among the norms to be integrated on that occasion any mitigation of his physical suffering, his budget would have been different—and so would the outcome.

The budgetary decision is usually more complex than Mawson's in at least two ways. Both the intake and the spending of resources are usually controllable to a greater extent. The local authority can raise more money; and it can defer work or even discharge staff. More important, solutions that do not pass the budgetary test can usually be excluded. Mawson's achievement is an example of a special kind of decision-making situation, calling for what I will call a *desperate decision*. It deserves a special name, for it has provoked nearly all the greatest glories and the greatest crimes of history. It arises when one governing norm or "goal" (as defined on p. 32) is set above all others, held constant, and pursued without regard for the claims of any rival "value" or of any budgetary criterion except efficiency—efficiency being reckoned, of course, by the unit of value defined by the governing norm. Such is the situation created when a mind irreversibly committed to a single norm meets a situation that denies its passage.

Such a situation may arise either, as with Mawson, because a change in the external situation gives this desperate quality to a preexisting commitment or because a change in the setting of a mind or a whole culture sets up a new commitment inconsistent with and intolerant of its situation. In either case, the policymaker, becoming the unquestioning executant of his own policy, ceases to "count the cost," except in terms of efficiency—and usually becomes in consequence possessed of superhuman or inhuman potency. The Third Reich is the largest and most sinister example likely to occur to contemporary minds, but nearly every movement of liberation or conquest, political or otherwise began in the same way. Like Luther, the hero, inspired or demonic, if he troubles to explain himself at all, says, "I can do no other"; and the cost-counting world, watching the massacres and the martyrdoms, the destructions and the creations, is silenced by a deep ambivalence. Is it wise or cowardly, farsighted or blind not to share these liberating simplifications?

The situation that calls for desperate decisions is indeed an oversimplified situation. One intolerable relation must be broken, or one irreplaceable relation must be preserved from an imminent threat. The simplification results not only from commitment to a single norm but also from a shortening of the time span over which the course of action is to be evaluated. It deserves attention, for the policymaker must often act in more or less desperate situations. Yet the desperate decision is not the paradigm of human decision making, for it is a major goal of policy to ensure that the situation that demands desperate decisions does not arise. The policymaker, seeking to optimize competing values within the limits of available resources, is seldom entitled to simplify his problem by ignoring all but one; and when he is so placed, he has lost, often through his own prior incompetence, the scope that makes policy making possible.

The cost-counting voice of budgetary judgment should never be silenced; yet it should never be mistaken for the voice of policy making, for it is concerned only with the conditions, not the criteria of success. Among the psychological strengths needed by the policymaker, none is more important than the ability always to listen to this voice yet never to be unnerved by its forecasts, however intoxicating or intimidating. In industrial organizations, it is common to keep the budgetary function in its place by putting responsibility for budgetary judgment on an official who is not responsible either for the making of policy or for its execution. This is essentially the function of the "controller." Independent and uninvolved, the controller watches the estimated future course of those variables on which the dynamic balance of the system depends. It is for him to say, "These are the limits within which your plans should fall"; or later,

> What you plan to do will probably require an incoming flow of resources greater than you can at present expect—greater by about so much at such a time or indefinitely. To that extent, your plans are or will probably prove to be self-defeating.

It is not for him to say how these imbalances should be redressed; and it is on that account easier for him to point them out.

The policymaker himself must of course see the future with a balancing as well as an optimizing eye, but the two views are not only hard to combine but require psychological skills and attitudes that are seldom combined at their highest power in one man. Many of the great industrial empires were built by a series of outrageous risk takings, each committed by its visionary creator and consolidated, after a period of crisis, by the efforts of alarmed "controllers." It is a wise and convenient practice to vest the watchdog function of budgetary judgment in a separate official, to whom it is increasingly common to attach, as a separate function, the measurement of efficiency. The extent to which the Treasury intervenes in the optimizing decisions of British government departments in the interests of budgetary control is in striking contrast to business practice, and the extent to which this is necessary or desirable is a matter of current controversy. The differences may perhaps be justified by the greater difficulty of the balancing function.

The functions that I have attributed to a "controller" are appreciative. His concern is with the first part of the regulative cycle. He generates signals, "match" or "mismatch." It is for others to respond to them (see p. 42). In the French and German languages, this is the primary meaning of the verb corresponding to *control*. It is curious that in English there should be no word with this specific meaning, since control has appropriated most of the meaning that attaches to *direct*. The "controls" of an automobile suggest the wheel, the accelerator, and the brake rather than the informative indices on the instrument panel, such as the thermometer, the speedometer, and the oil pressure gauge; and a skidding car is said to be out of control, although the driver is painfully aware that the "actual" is deviating unacceptably from the "norm." Such semantic untidiness should not be accepted in an age conscious at last of the significance of information, for it masks the important distinction between knowing what is the matter and knowing what to do.

The controller is a watchdog on a chain; he can bark and alert the householder, but he cannot bite. Both his freedom to bark and his lack of freedom to bite are appropriate to his role. The budgetary judgment is unpopular and too easily silenced; hence the need for a watchdog free to bark. On the other hand, it provides no adequate criterion of success and hence no adequate basis for policy making, except when survival has *properly* become an end in itself; and in consequence, instrumental judgments directed to solving purely budgetary problems are bound to be inadequate contributions to policy making, even at the most trivial level. How most cheaply to buy stationery of a given quality is a problem that budgetary judgment can precisely answer, but to specify the quality to be bought requires a small but authentic exercise in policy making—an optimizing of the subtle contributions that such details make to the way the institution is viewed by those who receive its communications and those who prepare them, made within the limits of what is deemed to be worth spending on them, to the exclusion of other spending or saving.

The tiny illustration exemplifies the chief factor that tends to exaggerate the influence of budgetary judgment; it appeals more cogently to factors that are measurable—or even that, being quantifiable and expressed in figures, look as if they had been measured or calculated, even though they have not. Budgetary judgments are not alone in relying on quantifiable data, but they can appeal to such data as proof of their correctness in a way in which optimizing judgments never can. As an illustration, I will compare two decision-making situations in a field of familiar controversy. I will suppose two large industrial enterprises, each with several divisions operating from a number of centers throughout the country. In Corporation A, each division organized its own transport. In Corporation B, transport was centrally organized. Each corporation had become concerned with the question how "best"—or at least "better"—to organize its transport.

The concern in Corporation A had been turned into a decision situation by an appreciation produced by a controller at headquarters, which claimed to show that transportation centrally organized for the whole group would provide all divisions (with one possible exception) with a much cheaper service than they were providing for themselves. This study in comparative economy, if accepted, threw the burden of proof on those who contended that in terms of real efficiency the additional cost of the current arrangement brought a more than commensurate return.

The study was not wholly accepted. Its critics pointed out that some of its figures were based (as in such a study they must always be based) on judgments rather than data. For example, the real cost to the group of the net increase in the commitment of its land and immediately available capital that the new scheme would involve could be computed only on the basis of assumptions. Moreover, the estimate made no attempt to quantify the indirect effects of the change, such as the increase in high administrative load at headquarters and its reduction at divisional level and thus valued both these variables (and many others) at zero, although this was the only value they could not possibly have. When all allowances had been made, however, the economies forecast remained so large that the burden of proof remained with the objectors.

The main (overt) reason why divisions were reluctant to part with the control of their transport was that they felt they needed it to ensure a sufficiently flexible service for their customers. The business involved distributing a brittle product to customers who expected to be able to call for small quantities at short notice; divisions felt they must keep the means to do this under their own immediate control. The argument was weakened by the fact that, with the one exception, none of the divisions was judged by headquarters or even by itself to be giving a satisfactory performance. The amount of damage in transit, as well as the transport costs were judged to be higher than they should be, and this caused endemic stress within divisions and between divisions and head-quarters. Something had to be done, and the only alternatives to centralization that were proposed had already been tried without success.

So in the end, the controller's report prevailed. A new division was formed, solely concerned to provide transport in the service of the group. The objections of the one division that was agreed to be operating satisfactorily were met by appointing its transport manager to control the new division. Two years later, the change was judged a success, both by headquarters and by divisions. The expected economies were realized. Damage in transit was being reduced. Against these two measurable gains, no serious loss of goodwill was reported; the service was judged to be on balance better than before. A budgetary decision had, it seemed, been validated by results.

In fact, the change had had far more extensive results than appeared. The debate that preceded its adoption had focused attention on several questions that underlay the general concern about transportation. First, was it really necessary to give such prompt, individual service to every call? The discussion showed that divisional practices differed; some divisions retained traditional practices that were no longer required, at a cost that in individual cases was indefensible. These standards were changed to some extent by the mere process of examination that led to the decision.

Next, given the standards to be maintained and the pattern of distribution that would result, was the existing arrangement of depots and distribution points as good as could be devised for economic distribution? This was recognized as a problem that could be put on a computer. The answer showed that it was far from optimal; it was changed.

Further, need transportation involve so much damage? The mere focusing of attention on this problem increased the general unwillingness to accept the customary level and thus raised what I have earlier called the *operating norm,* and its solution was speeded not so much by centralization as by putting in charge of the new division the man best fitted and most strongly motivated to solve it, the divisional transport manager who was already successfully engaged with it.

Finally, need the product be so brittle? This question was raised by the debate to a level at which it sent a signal to the research and development department loud enough to claim more than marginal attention. Five years later, a new design eliminated the brittle element that had previously been regarded as irreplaceable and that had caused half the trouble.

Thus, the changes that the reorganization caused were far wider than those of which the budgetary appreciation took account. As it happened, the major ones, which I have mentioned, increased its success, as measured by the two measurable criteria from which it started. In theory, each of these changes could have been effected without centralizing transport, and if the decision situation had arisen in a different context—for example, in a proposal to make a computer analysis of the distribution system most suited to current demands—it would certainly have deferred centralization, perhaps indefinitely. In practice, it may well be that the decision to centralize transport *at that moment* and *under that man* was the best way to achieve all these changes, but the financial measure of success in reduced transport charges and reduced damage in transit measured the result of far more changes than were apparent and got the credit for far more success than it was designed to achieve.

Corporation B faced a problem of the opposite kind. Its transport was already centralized in the manner finally chosen by Corporation A, but in Corporation B, this had long been the occasion of bitter complaint from all the other divisions. The transport division, they asserted, was alien to them, concerned only with its own criteria of success, which it measured in its own costs per ton-mile; and it was indifferent to the wider and more important standards of success governing the divisions that it was supposed to serve. Not being free to go elsewhere, they were in the grip of a monopoly, and even its costs, as charged to them, were excessive as the price of so bad a service.

This issue was crystallized into a decision situation by a formal request made by one division to be allowed to organize its own transport. The board of the corporation, alerted to the intensity of the general dissatisfaction by examining this division's request, narrowed the alternatives before them to two. They must either say "no" and appoint a new manager of the transport division, or they must say "yes" and allow all divisions to do the same. The controller prepared an appreciation that showed that the second course would be the more costly and cast the burden of proof on those who favored it, but the appreciation was both more vulnerable in itself, because of the greater importance attached to its assumptions and unquantified omissions, and also less cogent, because of the greater importance attached to the imponderables on the other side. Eventually the second course prevailed. The corporation disbanded its transport division and gave divisions a free hand to run their transport in their own way.

Two years later, this also was judged to have been a success. Divisions rejoiced in their independence; group headquarters also enjoyed their change of role. Instead of mediating disputes between the transport division (which was identified with the central organization) and the operating divisions, they were now free to hold the operating divisions accountable for the discharge of a function devolved on them at their request. Divisional costs for transport reflected more directly the divisions' own decisions and were thus more effective as controls at divisional level, while comparison of the performance of each against the others was an invaluable control at headquarters. Better service to customers and better control of divisions were judged to be worth some addition to the cost of transport.

In fact, however, transport costs had dropped. The controller prepared a further appreciation to show that the results were not comparable, and indeed they were not. Faced with the need to plan their own transport, divisions had made major alterations in their practice of distribution, and these had produced startling economies. As in the previous example, these too might in theory have been made without decentralizing transport, but in fact they arose as a by-product of that shift of responsibility, and though they were its most important product, they were not and perhaps could not have been foreseen.

The examples may seem perverse, but I do not think they are more so than life usually is. They are intended to show the curiously indirect and partial dependence of the policymaker on measurable data. The scientist in his laboratory can repeatedly test the effect of changing one variable, all others being held constant. The social scientist cannot; still less can the policymaker, caught in the net of his own unfolding situation. He needs all the relevant factual information he can get. Even speculative forecasts, so long as their assumptions and margins of error are not forgotten, are better than guesses even wilder than they need be. We can be thankful that at this moment of time policymakers at every level are being provided with data and with means of processing data far beyond all previous hopes and dreams; and since many of them are not yet fully aware of these enhanced opportunities and hence of their increased responsibilities, it is timely to stress their importance. Nonetheless, at a time when these new illuminations may tend to blind, it is equally timely to recall that even the simplest of the policymaker's problems is not to be resolved by even the most complicated of his calculations.

Our outstanding respect for figures, and especially the extent to which this is enjoyed even by estimates containing the widest margins of error and based on wholly incalculable assumptions, seems to me to derive from something more subtle than their manifest value and convenience, something more even than the solace that their seeming precision brings to an uncertain world. They possess in our current appreciative system a prestige and a mystique derived from the happily obsolescent belief that science deals only with the measurable and hence that only those who cling to the measurable can be accounted scientific. "The cleavage between the scientific and the extra-scientific domain of experience," wrote the late Sir Arthur Eddington (1928), is ". . . between the metrical and non-metrical" (p. 275). What then, asked Professor Dingle (1952), of the theory of evolution?

It is concerned with qualitative changes and it treats them qualitatively. True, its subject matter might be measurable. . . . The bones of fossils could be weighed but Darwin did not weigh them. Refraining from establishing his scientific credentials by measuring the properties of the water in the Pacific ocean, he brought all his attention to bear on the non-metrical characteristics of the creatures in it. And the result was a scientific theory which changed the course of the world's thought without introducing or relying on a single measurement. (pp. 5, 6)

Note

1. The tradition of annual budgeting has no doubt a long history, rooted in the agricultural cycle; the use of much longer periods for some purposes is increasing both in government and in industry. The length of the period is too important to be left to tradition.

18

Allocative and Integrative Decisions

■ THE CLAIMS THAT THE POLICYMAKER has to optimize
may be incompatible in either or both of two ways. They
may be mutually inconsistent in themselves, and whether consistent or not, they may compete for resources too scarce to satisfy
them all. The optimal allocation of scarce resources between
competing claims requires what I will call *allocative judgment*. The
reconciliation of inconsistent claims sometimes admits of a more
elegant solution that I will call *integrative judgment*. I include both
allocative and integrative judgment in the concept of optimizing.

The relation between optimizing and budgetary judgment is
perfectly illustrated by the Buchanan (1963) report. Maximum
accessibility to buildings cannot by any means be fully combined
with the maximum enjoyment of all the other values that buildings
can derive from their environment. Nonetheless, the extent to
which these incompatible values can be integrated in a single
solution depends, up to a point, on the amount of resources that

we are prepared to devote to that purpose—and, of course, to deny to all the other purposes that compete for the same resources. There is thus an inescapable mutual relationship between the balancing (or budgetary) function and the optimizing function of the policymaker. It is an essential part of his task to keep the budgetary function constantly in view as a condition of his optimizing function without allowing it to become in itself a criterion of success.

The policymaker can solve his optimizing problem in ways that may be deemed more or less successful, even though none would transgress its budgetary limitations. This gradient of success may be observed at three points along what is in fact a continuous scale. At the first point, the solution is by conflict. Such conflicts may be made explicit when incompatible views are held round a board table, but they are equally common and familiar when they take place within a single head. The effect of solution by conflict is that the view that for whatever reason is better placed for survival survives with the least possible change to itself. Some element of this is present in most decisions. The directors (Chapter 14) in their second situation must either continue in business with increased energy and resolution or address themselves with equal energy to their own dissolution. Any intermediate course can only combine the demerits of both. These clear-cut choices, it should be noted, negative all but the approved course of *action*. They do not necessarily weaken the appreciative judgment that supported the rejected course; they may even strengthen it and ensure its later success. I examine this situation in the next chapter on "the decision under protest."

At a further point along the gradient, solution may be reached by what I will call *compromise*. At its most conflictual, solution by compromise apportions satisfaction between the exponents of incompatible solutions by a bargain, which takes account of their relative strength, their relative willingness to fight, and the common interest in avoiding a struggle. The more dominant and comprehensive is the sense of common interest, the less conflictual is the solution. It remains a compromise so long as each participant regards it as less satisfactory than the one he advocates, though better than any other obtainable.

Still further along the gradient of success lie the solutions that I have called *integrative*. The characteristic of an integrative solution is that it commands the assent of all the contestants as doing full justice to all their different claims; and it is attained only by changing the way in which the situation is regarded or valued (or both) by some or all the contestants, a change that enlarges the possibilities of solution beyond those that existed when the debate began. The conflicting priorities of the directors in their fourth situation, which were irreconcilable within the conceptual frame of a single multipurpose factory, were readily integrated within the concept of two single-purpose factories in different locations. The integration of the far more intractable problems of the Buchanan committee depend equally, for the *possibility* of their integration, on envisaging the possibility of replacing the multipurpose street. These are simple examples of changes in the ways in which the minds concerned are predisposed to see the realities of the situation.

Changes are equally possible in the ways in which they are predisposed to value it. Sometimes, these changes in valuation are achieved merely by reclassifying the situation in a way to which a different value attaches (see p. 69); sometimes by assimilating it to a different value schema. Sometimes it occurs in more subtle ways—for example, by the process that I called *acceptance* and illustrated in Chapter 15 (see p. 187)—or by more subtle forms of acceptance, as when a partisan in one role, such as road user, identifies himself also with some other role, such as town dweller or even fellow human. We are here in a field where we have not yet attained even a coherent system of description. It is nonetheless a field in which there already exists much practical knowledge and expertise. The most highly developed example known to me of the integrative process is the time-consuming but effective method by which the Society of Friends deals with its common business.[1] Their procedure depends for its success not only on the belief that, given time and properly conducted dialogue, an integrative solution will emerge but also on acceptance of the fact that time is indispensable to the process of restructuring reality systems and value systems, on which integrative solutions depends. The same insight led Mr. Redletter, in the situation analyzed in Chapter 15, to interrupt his meeting for three days after his new idea had been clearly presented but before those concerned had had time to commit themselves publicly to their first reactions. He was unusual in treating human reactions with as much respect as he would have accorded to chemical reactions.

The integrative judgment depends on innovation, and innovation is limited not only by the natural resistance to change of all appreciative systems but also by the inertia and momentum of past allocative judgments. In any political or economic system, the current distribution of resources is the result of a historical process and can be changed only within limits set by its own commitments and its own momentum. In any large undertaking, these are substantial, far-reaching, and interlocked. Policies are being implemented, departments are in action, buildings are in occupation, men are in midcareer. These dynamic configurations are resistant to sudden change.[2] At each review, the possibilities of change are limited, but they vary with the situation. I will distinguish five such situations.

Optimizing is easiest in conditions of regular, vigorous but not runaway expansion. At each review, the several, conflicting claims for more can be met to some extent. Changes in valuation can be expressed by differing degrees of favor; A's gain is not made possible only by B's manifest loss. In such conditions, budgetary pressure is minimal—unless, of course, it is created by the intrusion into the value structure of strikingly new or more ambitious norms demanding achievement.[3] Successive reviews serve not only to mediate growth; they also create confidence that further growth will be mediated later. They are *communications* from the policymakers to all who are affected by their policies, and this may be their most important aspect.

Where policy making proceeds, even for a limited period, within the limitation of resources that are held constant, different problems arise, and a different message is transmitted. Changes in valuation favorable to one of the factors to be optimized must be unfavorable to others; A's gain is necessarily someone's loss. In such circumstances, not only is competition keener, but the message implicit in every change of priorities is more eagerly scanned and carries a more powerful overtone of promise or threat. In such conditions, the policymaker is more actively driven to review his priorities but can make changes only at greater cost. Optimizing grows ever more urgent and ever more difficult.

A more acute situation is reached when sudden and severe retrenchment has to be accepted. Where there is reason to think that this is only a temporary oscillation of the system, as, for example, the alternating expansion and retrenchment that characterized the British economy during the 1950s, the policy problem is to ensure that the long-term effect of the check is minimized. This, however, would require a review of priorities and a distribution of the burden in a highly disproportionate way. If it is judged (as it usually is) that such a change would almost certainly fail to secure sufficient agreement to be implemented or even framed, such crises are usually met by applying a pro rata cut to all spending, irrespective of its relative importance and of the long-term effect to be expected of such a cut on particular activities. Such a decision is at first sight the negation of policy making, but it has some justification when it is regarded as a message addressed by the policymaker to all the constituents of the organization, who may read it as an assurance of intention to keep priorities unchanged and to distribute present burdens in the way regarded most equitable by the culture. It has to be judged by comparison with the response to be expected of any other course, which must equally be regarded not only as a possible act but also as a message to be read in the mental climate prevailing at such a time.

Businesses undergoing a sudden recession have the same experience and are often driven to the same solution. Faced with a sharp reduction in demand so serious as to make necessary a cut in staff, management would naturally wish to preserve from interference and even to strengthen that part of the staff that is engaged not with the current unsuccessful production but with the development of the new products that alone can reverse the trend, but the effect on the rest of the staff of exercising such a discrimination is sometimes judged too dangerous to permit it.

There exists, however, one type of restrictive situation that liberates rather than inhibits major revaluation. This is a situation perceived by all concerned as carrying so acute a threat as to produce an appreciative judgment widespread, dominant, and new. In politics, the classical example is the outbreak of war, when energies and attention, focused on meeting the new threat, are unconsciously withdrawn from a host of familiar norms that would otherwise have competed fiercely for attention. An outstanding peacetime example is the reaction of all classes of the British people in 1931 to the suspension of the convertibility of sterling. It is hard to conceive, only thirty years later, that the right of every holder to turn banknotes into gold at a fixed rate could have been so potent a symbol of national strength and safety that its suspension should have been enough to secure the acceptance of general cuts in wages and salaries, massive repatriation of funds, and the establishment of a coalition government. So potent and apparently irreplaceable are external threats as a solvent of entrenched valuations that all who are concerned to promote change are constantly tempted to exaggerate their sharpness and their nearness in order to secure the acceptance of appropriate policies before it is too late.

The fifth situation that I will examine is the revolutionary situation. This is a specific situation, which can be defined with some precision in the terms that I am using. It arises when there develops within a society rival appreciative systems, each fiercely exclusive of the other. In this situation, the transfer of power from the representatives of one system to their rivals not only makes possible but precipitates an abrupt revision of previous priorities—not merely because the party newly come to power is anxious to realize values that it regards as too long neglected but also because the visible overturning of preexisting priorities is both a symbolic act and a potent communication. Thus, the revolutionary situation not only admits but favors solution by conflict. On the other hand, within the dominant system, it admits and favors solutions by integration.

The revolutionary situation demands to be understood—its logic clear and inescapable. "Peaceful change," whether in politics, business, science, or art, proceeds by progressive changes in the appreciative system of all concerned, innovations being assimilated at a rate gradual enough to preserve the basis of communication within the changing culture or subculture; and it is recognized as a primary responsibility of all concerned to see that it is preserved.

Appreciative systems, however, are limited not only in the rate at which they can assimilate change but also in the kinds of change they can assimilate at all. While some changes can be made slowly, others cannot be made so, because the self-preserving forces of the system are organized too strongly to admit their gradual entrance. Such changes can come, if at all, only by the sudden displacement of one set of dominant values by another. Such changes are seen in the individual only in the phenomenon of "conversion"; in the social scene, they appear in the more common form of revolution. It is the judgment of the revolutionary that the changes that he wants to see cannot be introduced into his culture by peaceful means and that they are worth introducing even at the cost of revolution. Thereafter, all his procedures are shaped by this decision. Whereas the process of peaceful change depends on continually exposing the appreciative systems of each of its members to the influence of his fellows through a process of dialogue, the revolutionary method is to build up new schemata of fact and value, insulated by every means from those they are designed to replace, to accentuate their difference and to reject every invitation to compromise.

Thus, revolutionary ideologies always aspire to be comprehensive. The mystified observer may ask, "What has politics to do with art or social ethics with biological science? How can one interpret an income tax regulation according to a 'national-sozialistsiche Weltanshauung'?" The revolutionary is not impressed; knowing consciously or unconsciously how closely interlocked are people's ways of seeing and valuing throughout every part of their appreciative system, he will not assume that any of the old can be assimilated into the new without contamination.

Given his premises, the revolutionary is right. There will be time later, when the new faith is established, for it to absorb on its own terms, some of the tenets and some of the votaries of the old. While the war is on, there is no place for compromise or negotiation. The methods and attitudes and objects of those who seek revolutionary change are fundamentally different from those of peaceful change.

Every revolutionary solution is hideously expensive. As biological life on the planet is wholly supported by a patchy film of humus inches thick, a seed bed compounded of the detritus of its own past, to which each generation, dying, adds its quota, so social life is dependent on the culture in which it grows and to which it contributes. Postrevolutionary life, like vegetation on an island denuded by an eruption, begins again, however vigorously, in a soil thinned and impoverished by the holocaust. Part of the heritage of mutual expectation and understanding has been washed away and will be replaced by others as strong only after centuries. Nonetheless, revolutions happen when revolutionary situations emerge. The revolutionary premises are not always escapable, and they are not always wrong. We are all heirs of many revolutions.

Revolutionary situations, in the sense in which I am using the term, arise increasingly in these days and are likely to arise even more often. They threaten whenever, in any field, a society's inherent powers of peaceful change seem unlikely to be able to change the values implicit in its entrenched allocations of resources sufficiently quickly to admit new valuations for which life will not wait. They are not to be mistaken for peaceful change merely because no blood flows in the gutters, because the barriers are raised and shattered only in the mind. They have all the characteristics of revolution—the violence, the efficacy, and the waste.

How powerful these entrenched allocations may be is eloquently conveyed by the comment (even though it be ironic) of the Robbins (1963) committee, debating whether the processes of peaceful change might raise the claims of higher education in the British budget from .8% to 1.9% in twenty years. "It is quite conceivable that there are items in the present composition of the (national) budget that on calm consideration may be deemed less urgent than a better educated population." A reader turning from this cautious estimate to the views of the Buchanan (1963) Steering Committee on what peaceful change may be expected to do to the appreciative system of a car-owning democracy (see p. 54) may reflect that, if this is the measure of peaceful change, revolutionary solutions may not be far away.

*   *   *   *   *

In describing the limitations imposed on the optimizing role of the policymaker by the inertia and momentum of his past allocative decisions, I referred several times to the importance of policies implemented or even announced, not merely as actual or potential acts but as communications. I will pursue this a little further with the aid of an example already used. The rate at which the processes of higher education in Britain will produce graduates and post-graduates during the current year is virtually fixed by historical developments up to the present moment; and so is the distribution of this stream between different branches of art, science, and technology and the character, quality, and content of the educative experience that they provide. Even the rate and direction of change of all these variables over the next few years is largely given by decisions of policy already taken—primarily, by commitments to capital expenditure and revenue provision and subsidiary alloca-tive decisions about the subdivision of these resources. All these decisions are or should be mutually related and complementary, amounting to a balanced program.

This program is effective both as a commitment and as a communication. It involves on the one hand an advancing network of commitments to contractors, staff, and others; and it constitutes also a communication of intention to all concerned with providing and with using higher education, be they university authorities, teaching staff, career advisers, or even students still some years from graduation, contributing to their appreciation of what will be and what should be, and influencing, among other things, their choices of career.

It is possible to check such a program fairly quickly but ex-tremely difficult to do so without incurring self-magnifying costs and consequences; partly because any change within such a pro-gram is likely to throw the whole out of balance but chiefly because the effect of any such change, *regarded as a communication of change of intent*, will spread faster and further than its effect as a curtailment of future commitments and will be far harder to reverse. On the other hand, it is impossible to speed or expand such a program except within much more extended limits of time. Decisions taken now cannot be translated into commitments, still less into action for some years; and though their effect as a communication is no less immediate than in the opposite case, it is less informative, since it confirms and extends existing expectations rather than revoking them. Expectations, like walls, are improbable structures, intimately self-supporting and much more easily leveled than raised, and policies depend on expectations.

Notes

1. Some account of these and their relation to other forms of conference procedure will be found in Pollard, Pollard, and Pollard (1949), *Democracy and the Quaker Method*.

2. I have drawn here on an analysis of the historical process that I used in a paper, "What Sets the Goals of Public Health?" (Vickers, 1958b).

3. For reasons already given (see pp. 189-190), these are, unhappily, conditions in which strikingly new or more ambitious norms are least likely to appear.

19

The Decision Under Protest

IN CONCLUDING THIS PART, I will notice a type of decision situation that exemplifies especially clearly the dual role of the appreciative process. It produces what I will call *decision under protest*. What has to be done is inescapable—but it is also unacceptable. The process of decision produces not only the decision but also the protest, and the protest is potent to reset the system. This resetting may consist merely in lowering the norms that raise the strident protest, in revising them so as to reduce their inherent incompatibility, or in altering the future course of affairs so as to avoid a repetition of the situation that evoked the protest.

On June 24, 1859, the Italian town of Castiglione was flooded with casualties from the battle of Solferino. These casualties far exceeded the capacities of the contestants' medical services, and the citizens of Castiglione did their best, through several crowded days and nights, to alleviate a flood of human suffering that in its character and volume was beyond their previous experience and expectations. Among them worked a Swiss stranger, Charles Dunant, whom chance had brought to the town a few days before. Like the others, he did his best with such skill as he had and such resources as were available, but the experience raised in his mind a protest that such things should be. Several months later, he described his experiences in a short book and made the suggestions from which stemmed two of the largest organizations of voluntary effort ever achieved by man. One is the International Red Cross Committee, a nongovernmental committee of Swiss citizens that, with no organized force whatever, has proved powerful enough not merely to secure the adherence of governments to the conventions that it has framed but to secure for itself access to the prison camps of unwilling sovereign powers, to see whether its conventions were being observed. The other is the League of Red Cross Societies, which now associates 180 million people in many countries in learning and practicing the skills that the citizens of Castiglione needed and could not mobilize in 1859.

The situation in which Mr. Dunant found himself at Castiglione moved him to action and to protest. In action, he was judged successful; he was conspicuous among the volunteers who organized and worked in the improvised casualty wards. This did not mute his protest, born of the sense of disparity between the most he could do and the least the situation demanded; and his protest, in the fullness of time, set an effectively new threshold to what the culture of his day found tolerable and evolved new institutions to mediate the action called for by the new standard. Few individual protests have been so fruitful, and few are so well documented.

Yet the process is endemic and continuous. Suppose a social worker who must advise whether a child, neglected and ill-treated in its home, should be "taken into care" by the local authority and placed in a foster home or an institution. The judgment is formed within a complex set of culturally given norms concerning the proper limits of interference with parental rights, the effect on children at various ages of separation from the mother, the duty of society to secure to children opportunities and protections deemed to be important to them, and so on. Suppose that these call clearly on balance for a better provision than the defective home.

Action, however, has to be taken within a set of limitations that define the concrete alternatives to the status quo. Is acceptable foster care available? Is there a place in an institution? And if there is, does the institution in fact provide what it might and should provide? The institutions of today were mostly created decades ago, in response to felt needs that may then have been already obsolescent; today's needs cannot produce the facilities they call for until further years have passed. For the social worker, as for Mr. Dunant, the battle must be fought with the weapons available. Maybe the child had better stay where it is and be supported and protected as best it may against the dangers and the deprivations that threaten it.

This, however, is only one half of the appreciative judgment. The question has been answered, but the problem has not been solved. There remains the protest, born of the very process that determined that there was nothing better to be done. At present, it is simply a psychological disturbance within a single mind—as was Mr. Dunant's when he left Castiglione. What will the disturbed mind do? Still the protest by dropping its standards of what to expect, learning to "take the world as it is"? Forget the protest, by taking other work where it will not arise again? Or at the other extreme, leave the service and create an institution that will show its own society and others how to meet the needs of today and tomorrow? Any of these are possible; all of them happen; but the efflorescence of a seed of protest is seldom so dramatic as was that of Mr. Dunant. The most probable outcome is that the worker, living with her protest and expressing it whenever opportunity offers, will contribute her quota to the endless dialogue by which appreciative settings are changed and thus to the process of political choice. For the democratic process is not merely, perhaps not primarily a process by which opinions are expressed; it is essentially a process by which appreciations are formed and changed.

I will add one further imaginary example, in which a single mind debates a personal problem.

One February 1, Mr. A, a rising biologist in the British University of X received a letter that surprised, delighted, excited, and perplexed him. It was from an eminent scientist whom he had met but could not claim to know. The writer had been asked to suggest a man to become head of a new research department in a large industrial concern in Canada. There followed an account of what would be expected of the person appointed. Would Mr. A like his name to go forward?

Mr. A found himself at first without the means to appreciate this situation. He had received a compliment and he had been offered an opportunity; this much was clear and welcome. But he lacked the materials with which to picture and evaluate the prospect offered to him. He had not worked or thought of working in industry; his ambitions so far had been academic. The post offered was unusual in its requirements and its opportunities; he had no picture of it, ready made. He did not know Canada. But even while he was counting over these difficulties, his mind was already at work to overcome them.

He turned first to the major satisfactions and limitations of his own work and sought comparisons. Would he have more scope? Less freedom? More administration? These questions were answerable, with the help of others if not from his own knowledge, and the answers told him things he wanted to know. Whether they were the things he most needed to know he could not tell. He was building up the likeness of a new life in features drawn from his present one; he had no means of knowing whether he was missing its most important characteristics.

Even more baffling was the need to revise his idea of himself. The letter showed him that he was better known and more highly esteemed than he had supposed and credited him with powers of organization that he had not counted on. How far were these estimates of his potentialities right? If right, did he want to develop them? And in Canada? He had always had in mind the possibility that he might spend part of his life in some other English-speaking country; this was a common feature of an academic career. It was the least unfamiliar idea in the whole proposal and it appealed to him in principle. Yet as he included in his judgment of the still hypothetical reality all the implications of emigration, they proved as disturbing as any. He had always known that to leave X where his children were being educated and his wife's parents lived, infirm and aging, would set off a round of repercussions in the relations between them, his wife, and himself, but he had not needed to think out these implications. (Other people managed; no doubt he could also.) Now the possibility was present, they had to be faced.

Mr. A's problems of valuation were equally difficult. To some particular questions he could give definite replies. He would miss teaching but not prohibitively. He would like to take charge of the organization of a new project. He would be sorry not to bring up his children in England. These and a dozen other fragmentary responses obstinately failed to fuse into a coherent response, and in the effort to make them do so, he irrevocably changed them all, though the changes presented themselves to him as "discoveries" that he valued this more, that less, than he realized.

For three weeks, Mr. A, as he went about his daily work, was preoccupied. At moments opportune and inopportune he would slip away mentally to share the hypothetical experiences of two hypothetical selves. One self had said "yes" and was creating a new set of relationships from a base in Montreal. The other self had said "no" and was pursuing his accustomed course. Neither brought him any peace of mind.

Nonetheless, after three weeks of mental work, they brought him the answer to his immediate question. He was powerfully attracted by the job, but the difficulties inherent in emigration at that moment were more than he could accept; so he must say "no." By what mental process Mr. A reached this conclusion I will not speculate. The forces favoring acceptance, whatever they were, did not build up to a level sufficient to overcome the resistance that they met, so he opted for the status quo. He sadly wrote to his would-be sponsor accordingly.

The status quo, however, had been irrevocably changed. Mr. A's awakened ambitions were not put to sleep by being frustrated. His decision was as disturbing as was the offer to which it was a reply. On February 1, he had been in a state of relative equilibrium. The offer had disturbed this equilibrium; the negative decision did not restore it. To follow the disturbance to its conclusion, insofar as such cycles can be separately distinguished, we should have to look far beyond the date of his refusal.

Mr. A's month of mental activity had left his appreciative system substantially changed. He had learned something—something much more than a new possibility of instrumental action. He had learned to want and welcome the prospect of a specific new relation with his milieu, the whole complex of relations offered by the Canadian post; and with it, he had learned to envisage and welcome the prospect of a change. (The offer had *unsettled* him.) He had also discovered a limitation in the complex of relations, family and professional, that he had already undertaken, and he had learned something of their value to him. The first lesson altered the setting of his system; the second prevented him from responding to the change. The results of this disturbance were important in the short term and in the long.

The immediate result was to confront him with the need to deal with imperious mismatch signals that he had no obvious means of stilling. The life that had contented him before did so no longer because of a change in his aspirations, yet he saw no certainty or immediate prospect of bringing the two into line. He dealt with this situation successfully in the course of the next few months. He found some outlet for his newly awakened ambitions by studying the industrial application of part of his work. He took a new interest in teaching, as an activity that might not be his for life. He returned to the writing of a neglected book. He put more of himself into the family relationships that had brought their importance so sharply to his notice. In these and other ways, he redistributed his energies between the relationships immediately available to him, and without wholly giving up his new dreams, he managed in time to confine them to that curious limbo to which I have already referred (the status of the "ideal norm," p. 102) where they remained an influence without disturbing his current regulative cycle, even though he found himself noticing advertisements for biologists in industry, which would not have caught his eye before.

In the long run, these changes in his setting proved important. When, some years later, he had the choice of academic preferment in England or nonacademic employment abroad, he chose the second, as he was then free to do. It may well be that he would not have made this choice or even that it would not have been offered to him but for the changes in his "setting," resulting from the weeks of distressful and apparently negative mental work that I have just described and from all that flowed from it.

Mr. A might have responded in many other ways to the problem set by the original invitation (some less consistent with the development of a "mature personality") than the one I have described. Whatever the response, the system known as Mr. A would have been reset, as the result of largely unconscious adjustment extending over several months, to the offer received on that February 1st. In this transformation, his decision would in any case have played a decisive part, not so much by settling his problems as by deciding what problems he should face.

PART IV

Policy Making Within the Human-Ecological System

20

The Human-Ecological System

◆ I HAVE DISCUSSED THE POLICYMAKER as an exerciser of skills; as the player of an institutional role; and as at once the captive, the product, and the creator of an endless series of situations. In doing so, I have overstressed his isolation and his importance. Before I leave him, I will try to put him in perspective, by extending the focus, in space and time, to comprehend the system that he seeks to regulate and of which he is part. For the policymaker is neither so identifiable nor so powerful as these examples might suggest.

In a world in which political choice becomes more ubiquitous and more responsible, more people become involved *as agents*, concerned directly or indirectly in forming or frustrating policy, as well as in their capacity as beneficiaries or sufferers from its results. I have already mentioned four capacities in which they may be involved. Policy making, I pointed out, depends on all who help to formulate the concrete alternatives between which the policymaker must choose; on all who must help to carry it out; on all whose concurrence is needed, legally or in practice, to put it into effect; and, by no means least, on all those who, by giving or withholding their trust, can nurse or kill its chances of success. Everyone in our society is constantly involved in one or more of these ways and carries, however carelessly or unknowingly, the corresponding responsibility. So, incidentally, is nearly everyone in other societies, whatever their political shape; we should do well, in comparing the merits of different types of polity, to look behind the forms and ask how far they in fact restrict or encourage the playing of these essential roles.

These roles not only limit the policymaker; they also contribute to policy making through the dialogue in which all are involved. In both respects, they place responsibility on those who play them. Our political system is devised to curb the exercise of irresponsible power over the citizen rather than to ensure the exercise of responsible power by the citizen; and though we regard it as a school of political democracy, we must admit that it is still a very elementary one. So I want in this chapter to consider the *social* responsibility for policy making. And since all policy making is an attempt to impose on the flux of affairs some pattern different from that which it would otherwise take, I will begin by drawing a summary picture of the system within which this peculiarly human function is exercised.

In a well-defined habitat, like a rain forest or a pond, the densities distribution and mutual relations of the creatures that inhabit it tend to assume a stable form; and if disturbed by some change in the environment, they soon assume some other form, equally stable. This is basically due to the constancy of three underlying factors—the amount of energy that the system generates, the volume of information on which it relies, and the needs that its members have to satisfy remain relatively unchanged. Until recent times, the addition of humans to the other animal species in such a field made no substantial difference to the picture. Humans have long shared the Amazonian jungle with its other fauna without disturbing its ecological balance.

In Western and "Westernized" countries, all these constancies have disappeared and with them the stability of the system. As an earlier example showed, the inhabitants of Britain, twenty years hence, will be unable to use the streets in their towns for any of the essential purposes that these have always served, unless they can produce, several years in advance, an anticipatory response that is new in character. The institutions that produce the disturbance will not produce the solution. We have the institutions to make more and more motor cars; we have not the institutions to build new and different towns.

The example, serious enough to Britons capable of attaching reality to it, will seem trivial to inhabitants of Asia, which in the same period at current rates, will double its population. Here again, the kind of change needed to equate population and food supply in Asia, and soon, elsewhere, are different from the kinds of change that produced the imbalance. To change the procreative habits of a people, even to expand a primitive agriculture, involves interventions different from those that reduce infant mortality.

Such systems, of course, can be relied on to regulate themselves, after their own fashion. War, famine, and disease have adjusted populations to their living space many times before, and they can be relied on to do so again.[1] If war, raised to a new power by another developing source of instability, the proliferation of nuclear arms, were to make the planet uninhabitable by man, other species more tolerant of radiation would expand and colonize the vacant space; and the earth, relieved of its most destabilizing element, would soon assume a new ecological balance. To our successors—cockroaches, I understand, are favored for the succession—this might seem a dramatic example of the power of a dynamic system to regulate itself.

This, however, is precisely not what we mean by policy making. As policymakers, we aspire, as T. H. Huxley put it in a famous lecture, "to maintain and improve, in opposition to the state of nature, the state of Art of an organized polity."[2] And when we are not wholly absorbed in averting the perils that we have generated (the "balancing function"), this is the dream that absorbs us (the "optimizing function"). It is a dream born of *human* values, a dream born of the fact that the planet is still dominated by men, not cockroaches; and we deem it a noble dream, because we value it so with the best value judgment we can achieve.

It is, moreover, not just the dream of some policymaker. Policies issue from the seats of power that have the allotted function of framing them, but in their formation everyone plays some part in one or more of the roles I have distinguished.

> We have all some responsibility for action, some area, however small, in which each of us and he alone can play the part of agent. There is a second field, wider and not congruent with the first, in which each of us can contribute to the making of policy. There is a third, wider still, in which each of us has power to give or withhold assent to the policy decisions of others. There is a fourth, yet wider, in which the only responsibility of each of us is the neglected but important responsibility of giving or withholding the trust which supports or inhibits our fellows in the exercise of their inalienable responsibilities, as their trust or distrust supports or inhibits us. There is . . . a fifth field . . . the creative function which shapes the work thus and not otherwise, whether the work be a building or an institution, a nation's history or a human life. Here lies the possibility for the vision that is manifest, for good or ill, whenever a "state of art" is imposed on a "state of nature" . . . the authentic signature of the human mind. (Vickers, 1963b)

Individually, we may rate these responsibilities as slight. Positively, they may be slighter than they need be. Negatively, they are already great enough to be lethal—as the Buchanan (1963) Steering Committee so blandly acknowledged when they rated a "car-owning democracy" as incapable of learning, in twenty years, the new conditions on which alone it can continue to use its cars.

An observer from another planet,[3] endowed with power to watch in total and in detail all the changes of our observable world, would recognize the features of a self-maintaining and self-exciting system; but he would find it hard to infer the nature of its regulators, unless he also understood the appreciative system of its human denizens, the other strand of the two-stranded rope. Nonetheless, what he saw would not be without meaning. He would notice countless centers of activity to which people flocked daily and through which flowed, in varying volumes, streams of material. That part of the material (mostly paper) and activity that served the purposes of information, including nearly all the transfers of money, would escape his understanding; but even with this lacuna, he would be fascinated to watch, for example, Antarctic whale oil and tropical ground nuts converging and mingling to become margarine in European larders. When he had taken in the whole picture, he would realize that the greater part of the whole product was consumed, as food and fuel, in providing the energy needed to keep the whole process going, while the rest replaced and on balance enlarged, the stock of human artifacts on the planet.

If he focused his attention on a single factory, he would see the same process in miniature. He would notice material of many kinds flowing toward the center, where part would be consumed, part absorbed by the productive plant, and part would pass through the fabricating process and flow out again as finished products or scrap. He would notice that the constituents in this stream flowed at different rates. Materials might be processed in a few weeks, machines would last a few years, buildings for decades; but ultimately, even the channels through which the material flowed would be revealed as themselves transient, processes rather than structures, destined in time to be replaced by others. The entire assembly would appear as a process not unlike a candle flame, though more complex, for the "steady state" representing the balance between inflow and outflow may wax and wane without imbalance. Even the human beings whose activities kept all these tides flowing would be seen to obey the same law. Any individual watched for long would disappear from his accustomed place to reappear elsewhere or not at all, and his place would be taken by another. Viewed as an organization of people, the enterprise would appear as a stream of men and women, flowing into, through, and out of the undertaking through invisible but enduring channels.

If our visitor asked us how the plant was regulated, it would not be sufficient to take him into the manager's office. Regulation, we might explain, is diffused throughout the organization, and we would produce the organization chart. These people, we might say, are organized in a hierarchy of subsystems. Each department is responsible for maintaining some aspect of this dynamic balance—for processing, for marketing, for recruitment and promotion of staff, for financial control, and so on. Within each department, each place, from the manager to the cleaner, has its allotted role, consisting of duties and discretions that are expected from the holder and of rights that he is entitled to expect from the holders of other roles. This pattern of complementary roles distributes responsibility for action, establishes channels of communication, and makes it possible for large numbers of people to combine in complicated and enduring operations, even though few of them have even a summary notion of what is being done.

We should have given too rigid a picture of an organization, unless we expanded our description of a role. Each role has both a prescribed and a discretionary content. Here is an engineer whose prescribed role it is to make the undertaking's products with its existing plant. What he shall make is prescribed for him, but none can prescribe for him how best to make it; for this, he must consult his own skill and experience that won him the post. The same is true of every role, from the highest to the lowest. Every executive role has some creative element.

It has also an advisory element. The engineer has a contribution to make to the decisions how best to expand the plant so as better to make its products and even how best to modify its products so as to make them more apt for manufacture in the plant. These decisions are not his to take; they involve other considerations besides the ones with which he is familiar. Nonetheless, he can contribute to them, and this will or should involve him in dialogue, formal and informal, with colleagues, superiors, and subordinates. Every role carries some responsibility for contributing to a field of policy wider than its own.

The factory is an authoritarian structure to the extent that each role has its allotted field of authority within which it is entitled to have its judgments accepted by others and, equally, its allotted field of subordination, within which it is *required* to accept the judgment of others. It is nonetheless true, as Chester Barnard (1938) and others have observed, that authority must be conceded by those over whom it is exercised. Role structure can encourage these concessions, but it cannot enforce them; and it will not function unless it is supplemented by concessions that are not formally required.

These roles are not mere decisions of management, to be framed and changed at will. Management must get its rulings accepted by the role players concerned, and here it must reckon not only with the resistance of so self-supporting a system to change but also with other role-setting authorities. The expectations attached to industrial roles are part of the general culture of a society; no undertaking can readily attach to its roles expectations grossly different from those attaching to the same roles elsewhere. Again, subordinates have their own ideas of what to expect from their chiefs and their own ways of getting it and are thus potent contributors to the roles above them. Trade unions and professional societies are powerful guardians of roles. Not least, role bearers themselves develop and modify their roles according to their own abilities and expectations. The development of roles in business undertakings is a process different only in degree from that which develops social and political roles in the same society.

If we ask to whom the duties implicit in these roles is owed, we must give an equally complex answer. Although in an industrial undertaking these duties are owed formally to the employer alone, they are enforced by a much wider sense of obligation. They are owed to all who act in reliance on them and whose actions must in part miscarry if their expectations are disappointed, be they superiors, colleagues, or subordinates. Their power will depend largely on the extent to which the role holder has come to expect them of himself. Wide, unacknowledged differences may develop between the expectations attached to the same role by different people, by employer, immediate superior, subordinates, colleagues, outside contacts, society, and the role bearer himself no less than between the demands of different roles played by the same person.

Yet if this essentially dramatic business is to proceed, it is clearly necessary that the actors shall know and accept not only their own roles but all the other roles that affect their own; that they will not only inspire others with the confidence that they will play their roles but will act in the confidence that others will play theirs; and that they shall have sufficient information about the plot, at least insofar as it concerns the scene in which they are acting.

We should still be a long way from explaining how the regulator works even as well as it does. We should, however, have made it clear—clearer perhaps even to ourselves than it was before we undertook to explain it—how greatly it depends on, among other

things, an elaborate and closely woven structure of mutual expectations and self-expectations of human agents.

Thus, even in the simple authoritarian, role-structured world
of the factory, the five aspects of policy making are genuinely
diffused—more diffused than they were, still more diffused than
they were admitted to be a few decades ago. It has taken time to
assimilate the truth that an aggregate of people, assembled, like an
aggregate of capital or machinery, through the market, would insist
on becoming in some degree a social entity and indeed must
become a social entity, if it is to do what is required of it. Business
management is still busy exploring the implications of this truth
in theory and practice. Meantime, not only the social rights but
also the social responsibilities of these role players are coming
quietly to the fore.

In the wider society in which these individuals, free from their
self-chosen roles, participate as citizens, their rights are more
conspicuous than their responsibilities. As members of a free and
egalitarian society, each is potentially as free as his fellows to act,
to utter, and to organize and, equally, to doubt, to question, and to
criticize. No authoritarian structure *requires* him to take anything
on trust from anyone, merely on the strength of the role he plays.
Authority and trust play no less a part in the political society, and
they are no less needed for its successful functioning; but they have
to be won and kept—and usually competed for—in the field of
political debate.

In this political society, the channels of dialogue differ strikingly from those within an organization. Instead of these trunk
lines, with their junctions and branches, which carry information
up and down such an organization, a net of communication links
each with all in a way both piecemeal and comprehensive and
mediates mutual influence. This network—it is tempting to call it
a reticular system[4]—is indeed undergoing change. The mass media
are controlled by organizations and the volume, importance, and
influence of the communications that we receive through these
sources is rising rapidly, by comparison with interpersonal dialogue. (We should be amazed, I expect, if we could step back two
centuries and experience for ourselves how large a proportion of
the communication of those days took place between persons

known to each other on subjects familiar to them both.) Moreover, the substitution of radio and television for so much of the written word may be having a qualitative effect of which we have not yet taken account.[5] Nonetheless, we assume that "freedom of speech" is accompanied by such a degree of willingness and ability not merely to speak but also to read and to listen that we may assume the members of our society to be effectively engaged in continuous dialogue. This, many would claim, is what chiefly distinguishes it from a society of insects or of slaves.

Political dialogue is indeed essential among the mediators of change, but if we compare our political society as it is with what even this book's analysis suggests to be the demands on it, it is hard to believe that it is up to its job. Like so much else in our institutions and our appreciations, it opposes massive defenses to the threats of yesterday and, in doing so, ignores and even hampers itself in meeting or even noticing the new and greater threats that are knocking at its door. The responsibilities for policy making— and policy blocking—must be more clearly identified by our culture and our institutions, if our policy making is to ensure our "balancing," let alone the most modest "optimizing."

For if my analysis is remotely right, the future of our society depends on the speed with which it can *learn*—learn not primarily new ways of responding, though these are needed, but primarily new ways of appreciating a situation that is new and new through our own making—and thus of finding a basis to combine in securing, so far as we still may, what most belongs to our peace.

To "our" peace—but who are we? How wide are "our" frontiers? How remote are the unborn whom we already include among "us"? This is one of the things we have to learn.

Notes

1. In other species, overcrowding seems to develop subtler physiological controls of fertility, but it seems to me unlikely that humankind would tolerate such conditions long enough for similar controls to develop.

2. T. H. Huxley, Romanes Lecture (1893).

3. This and the next paragraph substantially reproduce a passage from my paper "Human Relations in Industry and Mental Health" (Vickers, 1965b).

4. This parallel with the neural reticular system is intended only as a broad analogy. Its relevance is suggested by a most suggestive paper by Professor le Gros Clark (1958):

> Just as anatomically the reticular system appears to provide a generalized sort of diffuse matrix or background against which the more specific tracts and nuclei stand out as circumscribed and discrete formations, so it provides the medium for a sort of background of generalized and diffuse sensory activity upon which, so to speak, the main (and immediately relevant) elements of sensory perception are high-lighted as discrete items of conscious experience.

An observer, viewing the articulated and the generalized channels of human communication would be struck by a similar contrast and might be led to a similar speculation.

5. Professor McLuhan (1962) has suggested that the significance of printing was not primarily to bring within the reach of many a form of communication reading—which had hitherto been the prerogative of the few, but rather to change for *all*, including scholars, the proportion in which communication was received through the visual, literal symbol and thus profoundly to change both the physiological organization of the sensorium and the character of human thought. According to this theory, even the scholar in the days before printing communicated by speaking and listening rather than by reading and writing to an extent so much greater than even the nonscholarly today that the expression "literate" should be reserved for the generations since Caxton. Loss, as well as gain, came from this change of emphasis, the loss inherent in the dominance of the objective, scientific attitude—"the single vision and Newton's sleep." History will soon show whether this view is valid, for with the advent of radio and television, the literate age has closed. Already by the middle of the twentieth century, the sensoriums of the young are being developed by a sensory input of markedly different makeup, and with them the "postliterate" age begins.

References

Abercrombie, M. L. J. (1960). *The anatomy of judgment*. London: Hutchinson.

Adams, G. B. (1994). Sir Geoffrey Vickers: An appreciation on the occasion of his centenary. *Administrative Theory and Praxis, 16*(2), 279-283.

Adams, G. B., Forester, J., & Catron, B. L. (Eds.). (1987). *Policymaking, communication and social change*. New Brunswick, NJ: Transaction.

Barnard, C. I. (1938). *The functions of the executive*. Cambridge, MA: Harvard University Press.

Bateson, G. (1972). *Steps to an ecology of mind*. New York: Ballantine.

Blunden, M. (1994). Vickers and postliberalism. *American Behavioral Scientist, 38*(1), 11-25.

Blunden, M., & Dando, M. (Eds.). (1994). Rethinking public policy-making: Questioning assumptions, challenging beliefs. *American Behavioral Scientist, 38*(1), 7-192.

Boulding, K. E. (1961). *The image*. Ann Arbor: University of Michigan Press.

Bridges, E. (1964). *The treasury*. London: Allen & Unwin.

Buchanan, C. J. (Chairman of working group). (1963). *Report on traffic in towns*. London: Her Majesty's Stationery Office.

Bury, J. B. (1932). *The idea of progress: An inquiry into its origin and growth*. Westport, CT: Greenwood. (Reprint of 1912 edition)

Cardozo, B. (1921). *Nature of the judicial process*. New Haven, CT: Yale University Press.

Catron, B. (1984). Letter to Geoffrey Vickers (January 1981). In Open Systems Group (Eds.), *The Vickers papers* (p. 38). London: Harper & Row.

Checkland, P. (1981). *Systems thinking, systems practice*. Chichester, England: Wiley.

Clark, W. le Gros. (1958, January). Sensory experience and brain structure. *Journal of Mental Science.*

Dicey, A. J. (1905). *Law and opinion in England.* London: Macmillan.

Dingle, H. (1952). *The scientific adventure.* London: Pitman.

Eddington, A. S. (1928). *The nature of the physical world.* Cambridge, England: Cambridge University Press.

The financial and economic obligations of the nationalized industries (Cmnd. 1337). (1961). London: Her Majesty's Stationery Office.

Galbraith, J. K. (1958). *The affluent society.* Boston: Houghton Mifflin.

Gowers, E. (Chairman of the Royal Commission on Capital Punishment, 1949-1953). (1953). *Report* (Cmnd. 8932). London: Her Majesty's Stationery Office.

Jaques, E. (1956). *Measurement of responsibility.* London: Tavistock.

Jaques, E. (1961). *Equitable payment.* London: Heinemann.

Jaffary, S. K. (1963). *The sentencing of adults in Canada.* Toronto: University of Toronto Press.

Koehler, W. (1939). *The place of values in a world of fact.* London: Kegan Paul.

Lowe, A. (1937). *The price of liberty: A German on contemporary Britain.* London: Hogarth.

MacKay, D. M. (1964). Communication and meaning. In H. Livingston (Ed.), *Cross-cultural understanding: Epistemology in anthropology.* London: Harper & Row.

Mackenzie, W. J. M., & Grove, J. W. (1957). *Central administration in Britain.* London: Longmans Green.

Mawson, D. (1915). *The home of the blizzard.* London: Heinemann.

McLuhan, M. (1962). *The Gutenberg galaxy.* London: Routledge & Kegan Paul.

Oakeshott, M. (1991). *Rationalism in politics and other essays.* Indianapolis: Liberty Press.

Open Systems Group. (Eds.). (1984). *The Vickers papers.* London: Harper & Row.

Parsons, T., & Shils, E. A. (Eds.). (1951). *Towards a general theory of action.* Cambridge, MA: Harvard University Press.

Peters, R. S. (1957). *The concept of motivation.* London: Routledge & Kegan Paul.

Polanyi, M. (1958). *Personal knowledge.* London: Routledge & Kegan Paul.

Pollard, F. E., Pollard, B. E., & Pollard, R. S. W. (1949). *Democracy and the Quaker method.* London: Bannisdale.

Robbins, Lord (Chairman of Committee on Higher Education 1961-1963). (1963). *Report* (Cmnd. 2154). London: Her Majesty's Stationery Office.

Robson, W. (1965). Book Reviews: *The art of judgment: A study in policymaking,* Sir Geoffrey Vickers. *Political Quarterly, 36,* 477.

Report of the Royal Commission on Population (Cmnd. 7695). (1949). London: Her Majesty's Stationery Office.

Seeley, J. S. (1963). Social science, some probative problems. In M. R. Stein & A. J. Vidich (Eds.), *Sociology on trial.* Englewood Cliffs, NJ: Prentice Hall.

Shackle, G. L. S. (1952). *Expectations in economics* (2nd ed.). Cambridge, England: Cambridge University Press.

Simon, H. A. (1947). *Administrative behavior.* New York: Macmillan.

Simon, H. A. (1960). *The new science of management decision.* Englewood Cliffs, NJ: Prentice Hall.

Sutton, S. (1983). Sir Geoffrey Vickers, an affectionate portrait. In G. Vickers, *Human systems are different* (pp. v-xvi). London: Harper & Row.

Thatcher, M. (1993). *The Downing Street years*. London: Harper Collins.

Tinbergen, N. (1951). *The study of instinct*. Oxford, England: Clarendon.

Vickers, G. (1919). Poetry and war. Paper read to the Bodley Club, Merton College. (See Open Systems Group, 1984, p. 8)

Vickers, G. (1940a, April). *A bill of duties for men in England*. Unpublished manuscript. (See Open Systems Group, 1984, p. 14)

Vickers, G. (1940b, May). *The end of the gentleman*. Unpublished manuscript. (See Open Systems Group, 1984, p. 5)

Vickers, G. (1952, Spring). The accountability of a nationalised industry. *Public Administration*.

Vickers, G. (1956a). Incentives of labour. *Political Quarterly, 27*(3).

Vickers, G. (1956b). *Stability, control and choice* (the ninth Wallberg Lecture). Toronto: University of Toronto Press.

Vickers, G. (1956c, November). *Values and decision-making*. Paper for circulation at the University of Toronto. (See Open Systems Group, 1984, p. 23)

Vickers, G. (1958a, June). Positive and negative controls in business. *Journal of Industrial Economics*.

Vickers, G. (1958b, June 20). What sets the goals of public health? *Lancet*.

Vickers, G. (1960). The concept of stress. In J. M. Tanner (Ed.), *Stress and psychiatric disorder*. Oxford, England: Blackwell Scientific Publications.

Vickers, G. (1961, January). Judgment (the sixth Elbourne Lecture). *The Manager*.

Vickers, G. (1963a). Appreciative behaviour. *Acta Psychologica, 21*(3).

Vickers, G. (1963b). Ecology, planning and the American dream. In L. J. Duhl (Ed.), *The urban condition*. New York: Basic Books.

Vickers, G. (1964a). *Industry, human relations and mental health*. Address to 17th Annual Meeting of the World Federation of Mental Health. (Published in 1965 as Tavistock Pamphlet No. 9, Tavistock Publications, London)

Vickers, G. (1964b, July). The psychology of policy making and social change (The 38th Maudsley Lecture). *British Journal of Psychiatry*, pp. 465-477.

Vickers, G. (1965a). *The art of judgment*. London: Chapman & Hall.

Vickers, G. (1965b). *Human relations in industry and mental health* (Tavistock Pamphlet No. 9). London: Tavistock.

Vickers, G. (1979, March 14). Letter to Guy Adams. (See Open Systems Group, 1984, pp. 20, 21, 26, 35, 36, 38)

Vickers, G. (1980). *Responsibility: Its sources and limits*. Seaside, CA: Intersystems Publications.

Vickers, G. (1981, January 19). Letter to Bayard Catron. (See Open Systems Group, 1984, p. 3, 20, 22, 38)

Vickers, G. (1982a). Autobiographical notes. (See Open Systems Group, 1984, pp. 3, 4, 5, 6, 9, 17, 34, 35, 36, 39)

Vickers, G. (1982b, February 23). Letter to Guy Adams. (See Open Systems Group, 1984, p. 29)

Vickers, G. (1982c, December). Taped interview by Margaret Blunden at Goring-on-Thames, Open University Media Library, Milton Keynes, UK.

Vickers, G. (1983). *Human systems are different*. London: Harper & Row.

Vickers, G. (1984). Ecology, planning and the American dream. In Open Systems Group (Eds.), *The Vickers papers*. London: Harper & Row. (Originally published in *The Urban Condition*, edited by L. J. Duhl, New York, Basic Books, 1963)

Vickers, G. (1987). Foreword. G. B. Adams, J. Forester, & B. Catron (Eds.), *Policy-making, communication and social learning* (p. vii). New Brunswick, NJ: Transaction.

Vickers, G. (n.d.). Undated letter (addressee not known, probably written after Ellen's death, 1972). (See Open Systems Group, 1984, p. 7)

Vickers, J. (Ed.). (1991). *Rethinking the future: The correspondence between Geoffrey Vickers and Adolph Lowe.* New Brunswick, NJ: Transaction.

Waddington, C. H. (1960). *The ethical animal.* London: Allen & Unwin.

Wiener, N. (1950). *The human use of human beings.* Boston: Houghton Mifflin.

Wildavsky, A. (1964). *The politics of the budgetary process.* Boston: Little, Brown.

Wootton, B. (1963). *Crime and the criminal law.* London: Stevens.

Books and Articles
by Sir Geoffrey Vickers

Books

Adams, G. B., Forester, J., & Catron, B. L. (Eds.). (1987). *Policymaking, communication and social change.* New Brunswick, NJ: Transaction.

Open Systems Group. (Eds.). (1984). *The Vickers papers.* London: Harper & Row.

Vickers, J. (Ed.). (1991). *Rethinking the future: The correspondence between Geoffrey Vickers and Adolph Lowe.* New Brunswick, NJ: Transaction.

Vickers, G. (1959). *The undirected society.* Toronto: University of Toronto Press.

Vickers, G. (1965). *The art of judgment.* London: Chapman and Hall.

Vickers, G. (1967). *Towards a sociology of management.* New York: Basic Books.

Vickers, G. (1968). *Value systems and social process.* New York: Basic Books.

Vickers, G. (1970). *Freedom in a rocking boat: Changing values in an unstable society.* New York: Basic Books.

Vickers, G. (1973). *Making institutions work.* New York: John Wiley.

Vickers, G. (1980). *Responsibility: Its sources and limits.* Seaside, CA: Intersystems Publications.

Vickers, G. (1983). *Human systems are different.* London: Harper & Row.

Articles

Vickers, G. (1954). Human communication. *British Management Review, 12.*

Vickers, G. (1955, December). Cybernetics and the management of men. *The Manager.*

Vickers, G. (1957). Stability, control and choice. *Yearbook of the Society for General Systems Research, 2.*

Vickers, G. (1958, January). Adaptation as a management concept. *Journal of the British Institute of Management.*

Vickers, G. (1958). Positive and negative controls in business. *Journal of Industrial Economics, 6.*

Vickers, G. (1958, July). The role of expectations in economic systems. *Occupational Psychology.*

Vickers, G. (1959). The concept of stress. *Yearbook of the Society for General Systems Research, 4.*

Vickers, G. (1959, July). Is adaptability enough? *Behavioral Science.*

Vickers, G. (1961). What do we owe the children? In B. W. Heise (Ed.), *New horizons for Canada's children.* Toronto: University of Toronto Press.

Vickers, G. (1962). Mental disorder in British culture. In D. Richter et al. (Eds.), *Aspects of psychiatric research.* London: Oxford University Press.

Vickers, G. (1963). Appreciative behaviour. *Acta Psychologica, 21.*

Vickers, G. (1963). Ecology, planning and the American dream. In J. L. Duhl (Ed.), *The urban condition.* New York: Basic Books.

Vickers, G. (1964, July). The psychology of policy making and social change. *British Journal of Psychiatry.*

Vickers, G. (1967, April). Community medicine. *The Lancet.*

Vickers, G. (1967). The multi-valued choice. In L. Thayer (Ed.), *Communication: Concepts and perspectives.* Washington, DC: Spartan.

Vickers, G. (1967, July-September). Planning and policy making. *The Political Quarterly.*

Vickers, G. (1967). The regulation of political systems. *Yearbook of the Society for General Systems Research, 12.*

Vickers, G. (1968). Individuals in a collective society. In W. R. Ewald, Jr. (Ed.), *Environment and change.* Bloomington: University of Indiana Press.

Vickers, G. (1968). The promotion of psychiatric research. *British Journal of Psychiatry, 114.*

Vickers, G. (1968, May). Science and the appreciative system. *Human Relations.*

Vickers, G. (1968, January). The uses of speculation. *Journal of the American Institute for Planners.*

Vickers, G. (1969). Two streams of medicine. *Public Health, 83.*

Vickers, G. (1970). A classification of systems. In *Yearbook of the Society for General Systems Research, 15.*

Vickers, G. (1971, June). Changing ethics for distribution. *Futures.*

Vickers, G. (1971). Institutional and personal roles. *Human Relations, 24.*

Vickers, G. (1972). Commonly ignored elements in policy-making. *Policy Sciences, 3.*

Vickers, G. (1972, September). The emerging policy sciences. *Futures.*

Vickers, G. (1972). Incomes and earnings—A steady state. In M. Schwab (Ed.), *Teach-in for survival.* London: Robinson & Watkins.

Vickers, G. (1972). Management and the new specialists. *Organizational Dynamics, 1.*

Vickers, G. (1972, June). The management of conflict. *Futures.*

Vickers, G. (1972, December). Towards a more stable state. *Futures.*

Vickers, G. (1973). Communication and ethical judgment. In L. Thayer (Ed.), *Communication: Ethical and moral issues.* London: Gordon & Breach Science Publishers.

Vickers, G. (1973, December). Education for planning. *The Planner.*

Vickers, G. (1973, May). Educational criteria for times of change. *Journal of Curriculum Studies.*

Vickers, G. (1973, July). Motivation theory: A cybernetic contribution. *Behavioral Science.*

Vickers, G. (1973, March). Values, norms and policies. *Policy Sciences.*

Vickers, G. (1974). The changing nature of the professions. *American Behavioral Scientist, 18*(2), 164-189.

Vickers, G. (1974). Levels of human communication. *Exploration in Communication, 1.*

Vickers, G. (1974, February). Policy-making in local government. *Local Government Studies.*

Vickers, G. (1974, October). Population policy: Its scope and limits. *Futures.*

Vickers, G. (1974, April). Projections, predictions, models and policies. *The Planner.*

Vickers, G. (1974, August). The uses and limits of policy analysis. *Futures.*

Vickers, G. (1976). Problems of distribution. In C. West Churchman & R. O. Mason (Eds.), *World modelling.* Amsterdam: North Holland.

Vickers, G. (1977). The future of culture. In H. A. Linstone & W. H. Cline Simmonds (Eds.), *Future research: New directions.* Reading, MA: Addison Wesley.

Vickers, G. (1977, December). The weakness of Western culture. *Futures.*

Vickers, G. (1978). Practice and research in managing human systems. *Policy Sciences, 9.*

Vickers, G. (1978). Rationality and intuition. In J. Wechsler (Ed.), *Aesthetics in science.* Cambridge, MA: MIT Press.

Vickers, G. (1979, February). The equality of responsibility. *Futures.*

Vickers, G. (1979). Setting social priorities. *Journal of Applied Systems Analysis, 6.*

Vickers, G. (1979, October). The future of morality. *Futures.*

Vickers, G. (1980). Education in systems thinking. *Journal of Applied Systems Analysis, 7.*

Vickers, G. (1980). The poverty of problem solving. In *Systems analysis in urban policy-making and planning.* London: Plenum.

Vickers, G. (1981). The assumptions of policy analysis. *Policy Studies Journal, 9.* Also in W. N. Dunn (Ed.), *Values, ethics and the practice of policy analysis.* Lexington, MA: Lexington Books.

Vickers, G. (1981). Systems analysis: A tool for problem-solving or judgment demystified. *Policy Sciences, 14.*

Vickers, G. (1981). Three needs, two buckets, one well. In A. White (Ed.), *New directions for teaching and learning: Interdisciplinary education.* San Francisco: Jossey-Bass.

Vickers, G. (1984). Violence, war and genocide. In Open Systems Group (Eds.), *The Vickers papers.* London: Harper & Row.

Vickers, G. (1984). Will and free will. In Open Systems Group (Eds.), *The Vickers papers.* London: Harper & Row.

Index

About the Editors

Guy B. Adams is Associate Professor of Public Administration and Director of Graduate Studies in the Department of Public Administration at the University of Missouri–Columbia. His doctorate in public administration is from George Washington University. His research has focused on organizational symbolism and culture and on public administration history and ethics. He is coauthor of *The Tacit Organization* (1992) and coeditor of *Policymaking, Communication, and Social Learning: Essays of Sir Geoffrey Vickers* (1987) and *Research in Public Administration* (Sage, 1994). He has published widely in scholarly journals.

Margaret Blunden is Dean of the Faculty of Business Management and Social Studies at the University of Westminster in London. She earned B.A. and M.A. degrees in history from the University of Exeter and a D.Phil. in history from Oxford University. Her current research is concerned with defense policy. She edited *Science and Mythology in the Making of Defense Policy* (with Owen Greene, 1988) and the special issue "Rethinking Public Policy-Making: Questioning Assumptions, Challenging Beliefs," *Ameri-*

can Behavioral Scientist, 38, September-October, 1994, a collection
of essays in honor of Sir Geoffrey Vickers on his centenary.

Bayard L. Catron is Professor of Public Administration in the
Department of Public Administration at George Washington University. He earned his doctorate in social policies from the University of California at Berkeley. He is well-known for his work in
public service ethics, having founded a national ethics network
and organized the first national conference on this topic in 1989.
He is coeditor of *Policy-Making, Communication, and Social Learning: Essays of Sir Geoffrey Vickers* (1987) and *Images and Identities
in Public Administration* (Sage, 1990). He has published a number
of journal articles on public administration theory and ethics.

Scott D. N. Cook is Associate Professor of Philosophy at San Jose
State University. He was trained in both philosophy and social
science, receiving his B.A. and M.A. degrees from San Francisco
State University and a Ph.D. from Massachusetts Institute of Technology. His research is in the area of technology studies and
applied ethics. His recent publications include *Cultures and Organizational Learning* (with Dvora Yanow, Sage, 1993). He is
currently doing research on ethics and learning within technological innovation at the Xerox Research Center in Palo Alto, California, under a grant from the National Science Foundation.

Printed in the United Kingdom
by Lightning Source UK Ltd.
116900UKS00001B/292